JOHN OF GAUNT S(
THE TROWBRIDGE HI
THE FIRST ONE HUN

With best regards from Keith.

Cover – Foreground: Crest of present John Of Gaunt School;
Background: Crests of Trowbridge Boys High School and
Trowbridge Girls High School.

K D Berry, Head of the John of Gaunt School, 1979-91.

JOHN OF GAUNT SCHOOL
and the
TROWBRIDGE HIGH SCHOOLS:
The First One Hundred Years

Keith Berry

First published in 1994 by
Keith Berry
14 Meadowfield
Bradford on Avon
Wiltshire

Typeset in 10 point Palatino

Design and typesetting by
Ex Libris Press
1 The Shambles
Bradford on Avon
Wiltshire

Printed and bound in Britain by
Cromwell Press Ltd., Broughton Gifford, Wiltshire

© Keith Berry 1994

ISBN 0 9524103 0 3

I have had playmates,
I have had companions,
In my days of childhood, in my joyful schooldays –
All, all are gone, the old familiar faces.

Charles Lamb

Contents

Acknowledgements	6
Introduction	7
A Private Venture: Trowbridge Grammar School: 1859-1867	9
Court Street: Trowbridge and District Secondary School: 1897-1902	11
At the Victoria Institute: County Day School: 1902-1912	15
A Methodist Boarding School: Trowbridge (Wesleyan) High School: 1884-1912	19
To Wingfield Road: Trowbridge and District Secondary School for Boys: 1912-1914	25
Arrival of Edel Moore: Trowbridge and District Secondary School for Girls: 1912-1915	29
Growth and Expansion: Trowbridge and District High School for Girls: 1915-1922	35
Mistresees and Masters: Trowbridge and District High School for Boys: 1914-1922	45
Common Concerns: The Two High Schools: 1921-1922	53
2.1875 Years: Trowbridge and District High School for Girls: 1923-1927	60
Towards a Change in Management: Trowbridge and District High School for Boys: 1923-1927	66
Contrasting Inspections: The Two Trowbridge High Schools: 1927-1932	70
A New Broom and a Fading Light: The Two Trowbridge High Schools: 1932-1937	85
The Pre-War Years: The Two Trowbridge High Schools: 1937-1939	99
Exigencies of Wartime: The Two Trowbridge High Schools: 1939-1947	105
New Blood and a New Impetus: The Two Trowbridge High Schools: 1947-1954	117
Reconstruction: Trowbridge High School for Boys: 1954-1969	129
A Golden Age: Trowbridge High School for Girls: 1954-1969	139
Together Again: Trowbridge High School: 1969-1974	150
Trauma: The John of Gaunt School: 1974-1979	164
A Brighter Future: The John of Gaunt School: 1979-1991	173
Postscript	185
Appendix A: Chairmen and Clerks	186
Appendix B: Head Teachers	187
Appendix C: John of Gaunt School staff to 1979	188
Appendix D: John of Gaunt School staff: 1979-1991	190

Acknowledgements

I should like to thank the Headmaster and Governors of the John of Gaunt School for the help they have afforded me and for the school facilities that I have been allowed to use in the writing of this history, and Mrs Jenny Barnes for her practical assistance in many ways.

I also wish to thank the staff of the Wiltshire Times, the staff of the Wiltshire Record Office in Trowbridge, the staff of the Public Record Office at Kew, and the staff of the Library of the Wiltshire Archaeological and Natural History Society in Devizes for their efforts on my behalf.

I am grateful, too, to Virago for their permitting me to use extracts from Maureen Duffy's *That's How It Was*, and to David Higham Associates for their similarly allowing me to use Bel Mooney's 'A Sweet Shambolic Man.'

Many individuals have shared their memories with me, both in writing and orally; to them I give my grateful thanks. They include: Gilbert Bealing, John Broome, Mrs Margaret Bruce-Mitford, Geoffrey Bucknall, Kenneth Culverhouse, Mrs E Curtis, Mrs B M Dunning, Miss J A Fletcher, Mrs Sylvia Garlick, Gerald Gibson, John Greenaway, H E Gunstone, Mrs Sue Keefe, Stan King, Michael Lansdown, Miss Dorothy Luckman, Miss Bronwen Morris, Jack Pafford, S R Pile, Bob Randall, Dr Marjorie Reeves, Mrs Bessie Rodway, Ken Rogers, Norman Rogers, Ivor Slocombe, Mrs Pam Slocombe, T W Snailum, Geoffrey Suggitt, Jack Trott, Miss Dorrie Urquhart, John Williams, and Tim Woodman.

Contributors to school magazines over a period of more than seventy years – some named, others anonymous – have contributed to this history, and to them, too, I acknowledge my indebtedness.

Introduction

As Head of the John of Gaunt School from 1979 to 1991 I was a busy man, for ever concerned about the school's present and mid-term future. Therefore, when echoes of the past occasionally reached me, I had little time or patience to spare in researching them or thinking about them. An old wooden chair, clearly commemorating someone or some thing, a faded postcard showing a picture of a school very different from the school I knew, a staff register, mention of a forgotten scandal, a teacher from half a century ago who had been locally famous in his time, a prize awarded in the name of a formidable former Head Mistress....These were things and people from the past that I came across but of which I had no real knowledge. Retirement gave me the opportunity, belatedly, to do something to rectify matters. However, there was litle to build on. J R Broome and Miss J A Fletcher did some work in the 1960's to celebrate the Jubilees of the two High Schools, but there is nothing else, and it is to try and fill that gap, and to give an over-view of where the present school has come from over a period of almost one hundred years, that I have put together this book.

A tracing of the history of the John of Gaunt School, Trowbridge, takes us back almost a century to modest beginnings in a mixed Secondary Day School which was established in the middle of the town in 1897. Within a very few years, this single institution split into separate boys' and girls' schools which became the Boys' High School and the Girls' High School at around the time of the first World War. As it was purely lack of suitable accommodation that initially led to, and later perpetuated, this division, it is no surprise to find the schools merging again in the late sixties as a mixed High School, and then, in line with government policy, becoming a mixed comprehensive school – The John of Gaunt School – in 1974. Such is the brief history of the present school, condensed, stripped of detail, saying nothing of the personal triumphs and disasters of the pupils and teachers in these schools, or of the political plannings and manoeuvrings that from time to time created and altered them. This survey attempts to put flesh on these rather bare bones, adding detail from archive records and, where it exists, from personal memory, though memory, of course, can no longer go back to 1897 as I discovered it could with one or two elderly inhabitants when I first came to Trowbridge in 1979.

Wiltshire was not well endowed with grammar schools before the nineteenth century, and there is no direct line of descent from the few foundations that we know existed in Trowbridge in the sixteenth and seventeenth centuries to the school of today. These establishments disappeared without trace, whereas one or two other local schools – St. John's School, Marlborough, for example – can point to a continuity of development over several centuries. Equally, a grammar school of the mid-nineteenth century cannot in any real sense be seen as the precursor to secondary education in Trowbridge today, but, as it is the closest in time to the founding school of 1897, perhaps the Trowbridge Grammar School of 1859-1867 deserves some mention, false dawn though it proved to be.

Keith Berry
August 1994

A Private Venture:
Trowbridge Grammar School: 1859-1867

For a month or two prior to the event, very prominent and challenging advertisements had announced the opening of Trowbridge Grammar School on 2 May 1859. It was to be in Ashton House, Polebarn Road, Trowbridge, and it was founded by the Rev F H Wilkinson, MA, incumbent of West Ashton. (Ashton House no longer exists. It was approximately on the site of the car wash that is now at the junction of West Ashton Road and County Way.) Its Board consisted of the President (the Rev F H Wilkinson), and four Vice-Presidents (the Rev J D Hastings, Rector of Trowbridge, Walter Long, MP, of Rood Ashton, William Stancomb, JP, of Springfield House, and Thomas Clark of Bellefield House). The Head Master was Mr J W Gawn, BA (of Trinity College, Dublin), "assisted by efficient masters".

"This school," we read in the advertisements, "is founded with the special object of affording to the middle classes a sound and liberal education based on religious principles....As the school has been established to meet a very general desire evinced in Trowbridge, as elsewhere, for an improved system of teaching in schools for the middle classes, and is not a private speculation, the quality of the education must not be estimated by the moderate scale of charges." These were £18 - £22 a year for boarders, depending on which courses they took, with lesser charges for day boys, again according to their programmes of work. The general education consisted of three courses – the ordinary English course, the mathematical, and the classical. Teachers from both Bath and Trowbridge were to be recruited to teach additional subjects: French, German, music, and drawing.

> "The Rev F H Wilkinson has selected Mr Gawn as Head Master, under the belief that, in him, are united qualifications for the post rarely found in one individual. Mr Gawn has been engaged in teaching since the age of 18....It is proposed to secure the aid of an assistant classical and mathematical master, educated at Cambridge or Oxford, at once....A respectable housekeeper will have charge of the house....The school room is placed on rising ground, and the school premises are situated in a meadow of nearly two acres.
> All boys are required to wear the square collegiate cap."

Thus, Trowbridge's new Grammar School for Boys announced itself to the town with pride and no undue modesty in 1859.

There was in existence at this time a corresponding girls' boarding school at

West Ashton, also under the propriatorship of Mr Wilkinson, the Principal being a Mrs Fishburn. In the advertisement for this school it is made clear that "each child must be supplied with a pair of galoshes and an umbrella" – a requirement which would be well understood by the pupils at the John of Gaunt School, with its widely dispersed buildings, some 130 years later!

Sadly, things went wrong. At its peak, the Boys' Grammar School attracted 75 pupils, but by the time of its closure, in October 1867, there remained only 15 and the school was clearly no longer financially viable. The situation was discussed at a public meeting in June of that year, but an attendance of 14, most of whom were not potential customers anyway, emphasised the problem of the lack of local support that led to the school's demise. Mr Wilkinson had not long survived the Grammar School's opening, there had been changes of Head Master, and "the school had lived a sort of fluctuating existence, sometimes giving hopes of prosperity, and sometimes giving rise to feelings of despair." When the last official Head Master left, in midsummer 1866, there had been 25 pupils – a number that made survival just about possible. With 30 it was felt that the school could flourish, but the lack of numbers in June 1867, together with the fact that a Mr Porter for the past year had been acting as Head Master without any salary, made closure inevitable. So local indifference, exacerbated by the unpopularity of the school's geographical location ("which was a dead weight against its interests, as parents shrank from sending their children to that particular spot") spelled failure. (Unfortunately, I have been quite unable to establish what it was that popular estimation held to be wrong with that part of Trowbridge in the mid-nineteenth century. Close to the Biss and the Paxcroft Brook, it may have been unhealthily damp. Or was it notorious for other reasons?) Bankruptcy ensued, and all the school's furniture and effects were disposed of at public auction on 4 November 1967. Another 30 years were to pass before more permanent foundations for the establishing of secondary education in Trowbridge could be laid.

Court Street:
Trowbridge and District Secondary School: 1897-1902

The school of which today's John of Gaunt School is the direct descendant was a little two-teacher establishment set up on the top two floors of an old hand-weaving mill in Court Street in 1897. Renovated and looking rather smart, though in outward appearance much as it was in 1897, the building is now called Court Mill House, and it stands on the corner of Court Street and Mill Street. George Lansdown had suggested to the Technical Education Committee a year earlier that there was a need for secondary education in Trowbridge, and that a school to bridge the gap between elementary education and higher schools, as had been created at Chippenham, was desirable. A committee was set up to look at the suggestion, and the little school in Court Street was the result. It came into being under the aegis of the Technical Instruction Acts of 1889 and 1891 as a Technical School, and continued as such until the Balfour Act of 1902 gave the Local Education Authority the right, and the duty, to maintain it as a County Secondary School. From the start, its premises were intended only to be temporary. In the same year that it opened, a decision had been taken to design and create a building in the centre of the town to celebrate Queen Victoria's Diamond Jubilee, but it was another five years before the fledgling secondary school was able to move into the Victoria Technical Institute which was seen as being its more permanent home. In the meantime, the new Trowbridge and District Secondary School advertised for pupils in the local press, and opened at 9.30 on 27 September 1897 with 21 pupils – 12 boys and 9 girls. These were children of 11 years or more, and their fees, payable in advance, were 10 shillings per term.

The curriculum of the school was to include the usual subjects – scripture, English, history, geography, French, mathematics, theoretical and practical chemistry, book-keeping, shorthand, drawing, and manual instruction. The girls were to have instruction in needlework and domestic economy, and arrangements could be made if required for the teaching of Latin, typewriting, and (for the girls) botany. Whether chemistry was eagerly looked forward to or not is unclear, but instruction in this subject took place at the Technical Institute in Bradford on Avon, to which establishment the pupils proceeded by train, returning to Trowbridge on foot.

The Head (or Resident) Master of the new school deserves early mention as he was to remain in post for the next 40 years and become a person of stature and eminence in the town of Trowbridge. Joseph Warner Henson was 25 when he was appointed Head of the Secondary Day School. A grammar school boy from the Midlands, he stayed on at Wellingborough for two years as Junior Master before going for professional qualification to Chester Training College. There he obtained a Board of Education Certificate, first class, in 1893. The following year he was appointed Senior Master at Bedford Harpur Trust Schools, and from Bedford he came to Trowbridge in 1897, to retire 40 years later, in August 1937. In 1910, he was awarded a BA (Hons) degree by examination from the University of London.

The mill in Court Street, home of the County Day School, 1897-1902.

"Jimmy" Henson's duties in Bedford kept him there for the first week of his new school's existence, and so Canon R Ewing, Rector of Holy Trinity Church, and a member of George Lansdown's committee in 1896, filled in for him. Acting as Head for the week was the other permanent appointee, Mr C G Watkins, whose subject was science, and it was he who, seeking to get to know his pupils and in difficulty over the non-arrival of his new Head, decided in that first week to establish some sort of base line from which to work. He, therefore,

"issued a general information paper, asking for answers to questions relative to everyday life. Some of the replies were quaint in their simplicity. The paper used for the purpose was about six inches or seven inches wide and slightly beyond that in length, yet one of the girls gave it as her opinion that it was one and a half inches wide, and put its area at thirteen inches. Several were entirely beaten by the query: 'About how many miles can you walk in an hour?' and others appeared to be unaware that the terminus of the Great Western Railway is at Paddington. One little damsel has not allowed her mind to dwell too much on politics, for in the innocence of her heart she put down Mr Gladstone as being the representative of West Wiltshire in Parliament....To the query: 'Who is the Prime Minister of England?' one student replied: 'The Bishop of Salisbury'."

What Mr Watkins made of these answers and to what use he put them, we no longer know. Nevertheless, work began at Trowbridge Secondary School, and it obviously flourished in the next few years as, by the time of its move to the Victoria Institute, the number of its pupils had increased from 21 to 51 and additional staff had been appointed. Its name was changed in 1901 from the Trowbridge and District Secondary School to the County Day School, but both – with other variants – were regularly used in official correspondence and papers.

In 1902 the school moved the two hundred yards or so from Court Street to its new premises in Castle Street, where the boys were to remain for 10 years and the girls for 30. As early as 1897, another committee of local people had been formed to decide what should be done to mark Queen Victoria's Diamond Jubilee. There was a feeling that some facility for higher education should be provided to meet a need in Trowbridge that other Wiltshire towns (Bradford on Avon and Swindon, for example) had already foreseen. A suitable site was not easy to find, however. Eventually, two local tradesmen offered the committee a block on the corner of Castle Street and Market Street that, at that time, was occupied by a number of small shops, for the building of a Technical School. This was accepted, and the foundation stone for the Victoria Technical Institute was laid in 1897. The work, undertaken by Linzey's of Trowbridge, took almost five years, but it was never fully completed; the building remained unfinished, and, indeed, it still looked incomplete at the time of its demolition some eighty years later.

In some ways the erection of the Victoria Institute seems to have been an ill-starred venture from the start. The intention had been that it should be financed by public subscription, but insufficient money was raised and the cost had to be made up by a grant from the Wiltshire County Council. The site, too, was unpropitious for a school – in the very centre of a busy market town – and complaints from inspectors about street noise and the obtrusive activity of the market soon led to tensions between the local Education Committee and the recently created Board of Education in London over the latter body's reluctance officially to "recognise" the school. The building had been designed by the London architect, T R Davison, after a public competition that attracted 50 entries and that was judged by E W Mountford, architect of the Old Bailey. He praised the practicality of the building; but, despite this distinguished pedigree, the Victoria Institute never seemed to gain public affection, and soon proved to be quite inadequate as accommodation for a mixed secondary school. It seems always to have suffered from a schizophrenic inability to decide whether it was a monument to a much revered monarch or a practical, working building. At its opening, it provoked a snide comment from the Wiltshire Chronicle: "The building bears no pretence to external elegance but it is thoroughly in keeping with the other buildings in the town", and some 7 years later the Trowbridge Ratepayers Association were voicing strong objections to any further money's being spent on it.

Nevertheless, the Victoria Institute was an imposing building with a central position on the corner of Castle and Market Streets. From educational use, it was eventually reduced to being pressed into service as council offices and magistrates courts, pending the internal re-designing of the Town Hall just across the road, before falling empty in the late 1970's. Thereafter it began to look increasingly forlorn and derelict, became the haunt of glue-sniffers and tramps, and was finally demolished in 1984. The site now has on it low brick buildings that house the Wiltshire Holloway Benefit Society and a number of retail outlets.

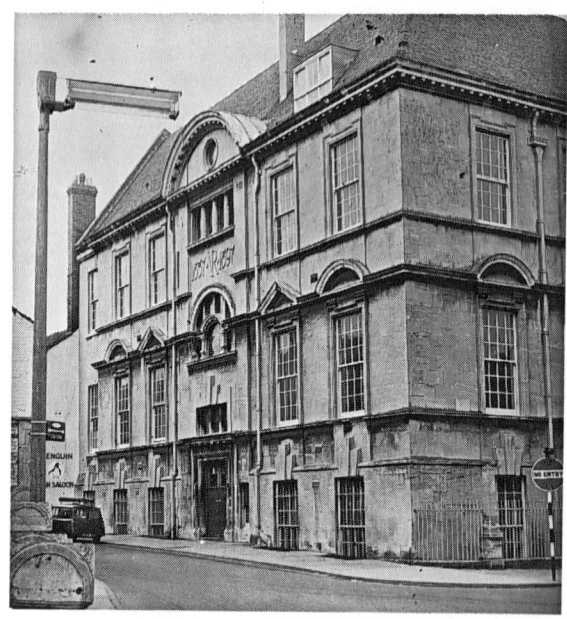

The Victoria Institute in Castle Street.

If its history as a building is gloomy, the Victoria Technical Institute was certainly opened in March 1902 with some pomp. Its principal function was to provide a home for the Secondary Day School, though it served other purposes too, and the opening ceremony was performed by Sir George Kekewich, Secretary of the Board of Education. This official ceremony was an event of great local interest, and it was followed by a concert in the evening. The Town Band gave a rendering of "Tannhauser", and there were songs, one of which was the "Bedouin Love Song", performed by the Head Master, Mr Henson.

The days of the hesitant start in the old Textile School premises in Court Street were now well in the past, and the County Day School's future, launched in new premises, on a tide of local enthusiasm and patriotic fervour, looked rosy.

At the Victoria Institute:
County Day School: 1902-1912

It is clear that, for the County Day School, the next 10 years were, in many ways, a successful and happy time. The number of pupils on roll increased significantly: from 51 in the final term in Court Street, they rose to 56 after the Victoria Institute was opened. In 1904 there were 98 pupils, 109 in 1905, and 133 in 1910, so, in 13 years, from 1897 to 1910, the school's roll increased more than six-fold – an indication of its popularity and success. New staff were engaged, too. By 1903, Mr Watkins had left, and Mr Henson had been joined by Mr Elliott, Mr Judd, Miss Jenkins, Miss Parsons, Miss Lewis, and Mr Hallett. Trowbridge had an expanding school. But the fact that its requirements could not be met as long as it remained at the Victoria Institute, combined with the unhappiness of the Board of Education about the general unsuitability of the premises for the accommodation of a mixed secondary school, were to lead, unfortunately quickly after the grand opening of the new building, to thoughts about the necessity of finding a new home yet again.

However, in 1902 the County Day School was well led and had a rising reputation with both parents and with the members of the newly formed Trowbridge Education Committee. The latter had powers very similar to those of the Governing Body of a secondary school today, and for the whole of this period (from the Committee's inception, in fact, in 1903, until 1915) the Chairman was J Poynton Haden JP. He and his Committee were charged by the Board of Education in London with responsibility for appointing teachers to the staff of the school, for determining salary levels, for all expenditure (including salaries and wages), for authorising repairs, for ensuring the maintenance of standards, and for the over-all supervisory functions that were to be exercised by Governors at a later date. Some of their tasks were necessarily routine and uncontroversial, but two topics came to dominate their deliberations during these 10 years. The first, as has been said, became evident very soon after the school's move from Court Street to the Victoria Institute and it was, even at this early date, that of the inadequacy of the new accommodation for a mixed secondary school that was rapidly growing in size. And the second was the difficulty posed by the determination locally of salary levels for the teaching staff.

The Victoria Institute was inspected in 1904, two years after it opened, and the subsequent report emphasised the need for better apparatus in science, a requirement for an improvement in the teaching of English, some curricular changes that would enable the girls to continue with needlework and cookery rather than take up Latin in forms 5 and 6, and a clear indication that the accommodation was inadequate for the purpose to which it was being put. Most of these suggestions were accepted and implemented. On the subject of the suitability of the accommodation, however, the Education Committee were very defensive. They claimed that it had long been understood that the Secondary Day School would move into the Institute from its temporary home in Court Street, that the plans for the new building had been drawn up in accordance with the suggestions of a former inspector of the Board, and that they had been passed and approved by both the Board of Education and the Wiltshire County Council. Nevertheless, correspondence between the Board in London and the Trowbridge Education Committee left little room for doubt about where power lay. The Board was only willing to "recognise" the secondary school on a year by year basis, and, finally, in 1909, solely on condition that definite proposals were forthcoming within that year about how the problem of the inadequacy of the building was to be overcome. The issue could no longer be ignored; the Trowbridge Education Committee had to do something quickly about the unsatisfactory state of its secondary school.

Options, therefore, were examined. The first formal suggestion that an approach should be made to the Trowbridge Wesleyan High School – which should not be confused with the later High Schools, the forerunners of today's John of Gaunt School – with a view either to the purchase or the lease of their building in Wingfield Road came as early as 1908. (The Wesleyan High School, to which I shall return later, had been founded in 1884 and had moved to new premises in Wingfield Road in 1890.) The following year, a small sub-committee of members of the Trowbridge Education Committee was formed to meet the Governors of the High School, and, armed with the Board of Education's view that one secondary school was sufficient for a town the size of Trowbridge, negotiations opened in earnest. Purchase, lease, and amalgamation were all possibilities. Very soon (in May 1909) a letter was received from the High School authorities in London indicating that they were not interested in leasing their Wingfield Road property, and that the purchase price of the building, together with its furniture and apparatus, would be £6,500, with a further £1,000 for the adjacent playing field. These prices were thought to be prohibitive, and, in the event, the property was eventually obtained at a much lower cost.

In 1910, plans for the reorganisation of secondary education in Trowbridge came to a head. The decision that the Secondary Day School (or a part of it) was to move had been made; suitable replacement premises had been found at the High School; negotiations about the cost of the venture were moving towards a conclusion. Accordingly, the Education Committee drafted a number of alternative proposals. One was that, although a mixed school was always the long-term goal, the Wesleyan High School building in Wingfield Road, once it had been bought, would be used to house either the boys or the girls from the Secondary Day School, pupils of the other sex remaining for the time being at the Victoria Institute. A second possibility was that the girls would remain where they were and that the boys would transfer to the Secondary School at Bradford on Avon, which could accommodate them comfortably. A third was for the boys to remain in Castle Street and for the girls to go to Bradford on Avon. And a fourth scenario was for the Education Committee to seek representation on the Governing Body of the Wesleyan High School and for capitation grants then to be paid, as already happened in Salisbury. In this case, boys would be admitted to the High School and the girls would either continue at the Victoria Institute or go to Bradford.

In December, the scheme that was eventually adopted (the first of the four detailed above) was formally proposed, and the final decision was taken a year later, in December 1911. The boys were to move to Wingfield Road and the girls, temporarily, were to stay where they were, in the Victoria Institute. This "temporary" state of affairs lasted, we now know, for twenty years until the Girls' High School opened in new premises, on a site adjacent to the Boys' High School, in 1932.

Alterations, of course, had to be made to the High School buildings which had been designed to house a boarding school, and not all of these were completed before the move was made. There were negotiations, too, between Mr Henson and Mr Newman, Head of the soon-to-be-disbanded Wesleyan school, about the possible purchase of certain items. "A moveable pavilion and a quantity of sports apparatus", for example, was thought worth buying for £8.10.0, and the services of Harvey, the Caretaker at the High School, were retained at a cost of 16 shillings per week. "The boy", however, was not needed; nor was the school notice board which was situated strategically near the railway station. There is specific mention of Mr Henson's taking over from Mr Newman "a large umbrella stand", and I wonder, in passing, whether this is the large wrought iron umbrella stand which I inherited and which still does duty as a stand for pot plants in the foyer outside the present Headmaster's office.

And so the move was made. Mr Henson, the male members of staff, and the boys transferred to Wingfield Road, and the Boys' Secondary School, as it was now called, opened in its new premises in September 1912, whilst the Girls' Secondary School enjoyed the additional space that had been created for it at the Victoria Institute.

If the school's future as a single institution or as separate establishments was the principal preoccupation of the Education Committee during the years 1902-1912, staffing and salary levels was also an important issue. Staff changes were numerous. The school was growing and so additions to the teaching staff were needed. Mr Pease was appointed in 1904, and then Miss Sainsbury, who was promoted two years later to the post of Senior Mistress. Miss Thomas was an additional appointment in 1905. The significant appointment of Johnny Heal, to the position of Second Master, came at the end of 1907. (He was to teach at the High School for 36 years, dying in office in 1943.) And so, by 1912, the staff of the Secondary Day School consisted of Mr Henson, Mr Heal, Miss Sainsbury, Mr Gardner, Mr Lock, Miss Bazley, Miss Johnson, Miss Parsons, and Mr Hallett; but whilst some of these teachers were, or were to become, long-serving, others came and went rather too quickly. Appeals to the Committee for an increase of salary were frequent; some were granted and others rejected. There was a suggestion from the Committee itself that the salaries being paid were too low and that the undue movement of staff was because better pay could be obtained elsewhere. Nothing was done, however, and hopes were pinned on the establishment of a scale of salaries for teachers in secondary schools that would obviate the need for the sorts of individual negotiation that obtained at the time.

When the decision was taken for the boys, with Mr Henson and the male members of staff, to form a separate Boys' Secondary School in Wingfield Road, the necessity for the appointment of a Head Mistress to the Girls' School became pressing. The advertisement for the post was held up, however, as again the salary being offered was thought to be insufficient "to attract a mistress of the standing and ability required". It was redrafted, with a salary offered of £200 p.a. (Mr Henson's salary was £300 p.a. and Mr Heal's £200 p.a. in 1912) At this point, for reasons at which one may guess, "Toby" Sainsbury resigned, her resignation being received with expressions of regret and assurances that "the Committee had at all times complete confidence in her, and that her services had given entire satisfaction". The successful applicant for the post of Head Mistress of the Girls' Secondary School, from 85 applicants, 4 of whom were interviewed, was Miss E M Moore of Redland High School, Bristol, where she had been successively Head of Middle School, Senior Mistress, and Acting Head Mistress.

A Methodist Boarding School:
Trowbridge (Wesleyan) High School: 1884-1912

Just as the Grammar School of 1859-1867 is a divergence from the main stream of the development of secondary education in Trowbridge, so too is the Wesleyan High School that existed between 1884 and 1912. But it is important because it is this school's building in Wingfield Road that fronts the complex that is the John of Gaunt comprehensive school today. The High School brochure issued just before the turn of the century says:

> "The School was opened in January, 1884, on premises situated at the end of Duke Street, Trowbridge. The first Head Master was Mr R W Jackson, MA, (Lond), and his management was so successful that the Directors decided to erect buildings specially designed for their purposes. The site chosen on the Wingfield Road, on the out-skirts of the town, has proved to be admirably adapted for a Day and Boarding School."

The new buildings opened and the Wesleyan school moved into them in 1890. There they remain to this day, in outward appearance largely unaltered, and on a site that is still open, attractive, and convenient to the town of Trowbridge.

The original premises in Duke Street, joined by playgrounds and passageways to Dorset House in The Halve, and later to become the Garrick Club, are long gone. They were established by the Western Counties Wesleyan Middle Class School Association, Ltd, "to give to the youth of Methodist families, and others who wish their sons to avail themselves of similar advantages, the opportunity of a good all-round education free from special ecclesiastical bias"; and the second, perhaps less educationally acceptable, of the two stated objectives of the school was "to obtain for the shareholders dividends at the rate of £5 per cent per annum on their paid-up capital in the Company". It was the school's difficulty in meeting this particular aim that led the Wesleyans eventually to sell the property in Wingfield Road to the Trowbridge Education Committee for £3,500.

The lay-out of the Wingfield Road building is important in that what it offered and what it lacked very much affected the way in which Trowbridge Boys' High School developed thereafter.

In 1893 Mr Jackson left to form the West Wilts College at Sefton House (now Gordon's Hotel) in Wingfield Road, and his place was taken by T Russell Maltby, MA, who came from Kingswood School. The Head Master from 1903 to 1912, when the sale took place, was Walter Newman, MA, and in the present school's records is a photograph of Mr and Mrs Newman, with their six young teachers in suits and waistcoats, high-collared shirts, boots and gowns, charmingly posed outside the central front door, taken, presumably, to mark the closing of the High School in that year.

Mr and Mrs Newman and the staff of the Wesleyan High School, 1912. (Messrs Morgan, Underwood, Witty, Atkin, Kingham and Jones).

The school building of 1890 looked then much as it does today. It faced north, and in 1890 there were no additions to the west or east of the main frontage as there are now. The door under the central tower was the entrance, and the window to the left of that door (as one looks at the building) was the Head Master's study. Immediately to the left of that room was the School Room which stretched back half the depth of the building. (This space is now a girls' cloakroom and a storeroom.) Behind the School Room was a small lavatory and then the large and small classrooms, roughly where rooms W 33 and W 35 are now. The central hall and staircase remain today as they were in 1890, and to the left of the stairs, where there is now the "meter room" and the Head Master's Secretary's room, was the Masters' Room.

To the right of the main door was the Head Master's drawing room, with the dining room to the right of that, where the general school office is situated at present. In 1890, however, it was larger than this office and it spread back beyond what is now a corridor into the PE storeroom. The modern boys' changing rooms (or part of them) were, in the original building, a complex of pantries (two), scullery, storeroom, laundry and boot room – all of them behind the dining room – and the present men's changing room and shower, to the right of the stairs, was the kitchen. So, on the ground floor, the building was part school, part Head Master's house, and part dining and domestic accommodation for the boarders, because the Wesleyan High School, though it took day boys, was essentially a boarding school.

On the first floor were two large dormitories, stretching from the front to the rear of the building. The West Dormitory is now room W 4, and the Long Dormitory, which was much the larger of the two, W 14, W 16, and W 18; between the two were bedrooms, two large rooms at the front, over the study and drawing room, with smaller bedrooms and a lavatory at the back. At the top of the house, on the second floor, were the small rooms occupied by the domestic servants – two bedrooms to the right of the landing, as one reaches it from the stairs, the larger at the back and the smaller at the front, the linen room in front of the landing, and the sick room to the left. Also to the left was the box room, a long, thin room with a doorway to the open air above the quadrangle. This acted as a fire escape, and it is thought it was equipped with a canvas chute or some other means of descent. The box room still exists, as do the sick room (which contains the school's records) and part of the linen room (used by the examinations secretary). The other rooms, the major part of the linen room, and much of the landing, however, were merged into one large room, which came to be known as the Conference Room, after the fire of 1984.

In 1890, of course, the big double-doors to the right of the main frontage, and the modern assembly hall, did not exist, nor, more importantly, was there any east wing – the Sixth Form Common Room with W 22 above it, as it is today. When the school was erected in 1890, the building ended at the second set of windows after the main door – both to east and to west – and the end wall facing Avenue Road was windowed and gabled in the same style as the front. Instead of an east wing, there was an L-shaped wall some twelve feet in height that sheltered a large hut that served as a gymnasium.

The number of pupils attending the Wesleyan High School was never large. Even when it moved to Wingfield Road six years after its foundation, it had fewer than 40 boys. Five years later it had 59 – that is, 37 boarders and 22 day boys – but during the 1900's, though numbers increased somewhat, the proportion of boarders to day boys fell from what had been a majority to less than one in three, and well before 1912, as we have seen, it was clear that the school was scarcely viable financially. In its last term, there were 70 pupils, of whom only 15 were boarders.

Mr Jackson's West Wilts College closed in the mid-1890's and increased

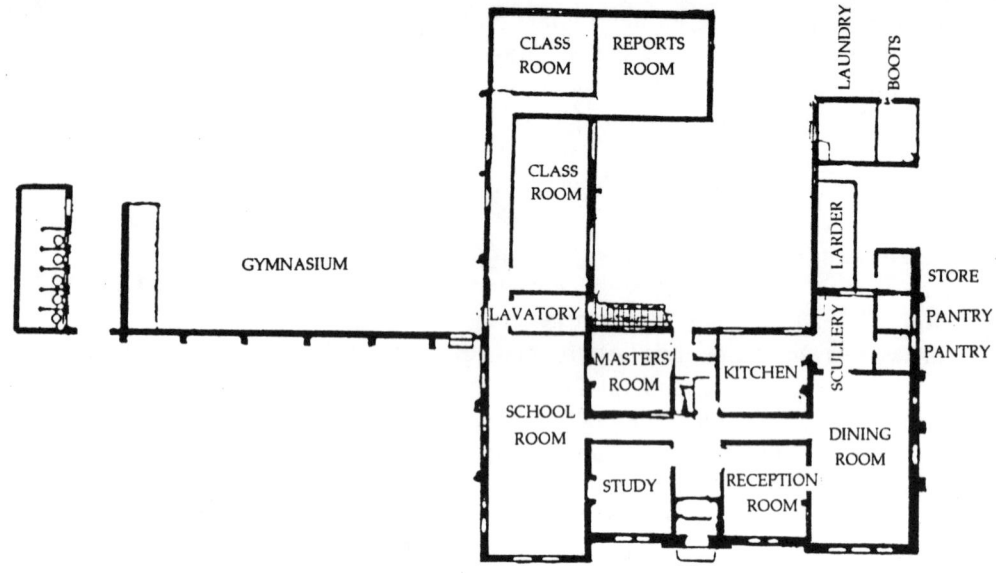

*Above: Plan of ground floor of Wesleyan High School, 1894.
Below: Wesleyan High School, 1894.*

Above: Covered gymnasium at back of New Schoolroom, c. 1900.
Below: Pupils at work in New Schoolroom (now Sixth Form Common Room), c. 1900.

numbers of pupils were anticipated at the High School. In preparation for these, a large new wing was built, and opened in May 1897. This new accommodation, though it was later modified and altered, is substantially the wing that houses the present Sixth Form Common Room, and it took the place of the gymnasium hut. It provided a new School Room, fifty five feet long and twenty two feet wide, with block floor, incandescent lights, and two large open fireplaces. On the first floor were the sick room, Fifth Form study room, a bathroom and lavatories, and in the corner, between the new wing and the main house, was the doorway that the Sixth Form now use as access to their Common Room. At the back of the new wing, a low, lean-to shed was erected that served as the school gymnasium in place of the former hut. To the left of the new wing, and slightly separated from it, were the outside lavatories. The site also included "the back field" and "the large field"; the former was behind the school and was slightly larger than the area covered by the buildings and the front lawns together, whilst the latter was adjacent to both of these on the west side and something like double their area. The area of the whole site was just over six acres.

Such, then, was the Wesleyan High School, with its inscription: "TROWBRIDGE HIGH SCHOOL", and the centrally placed date: "ANNO DOMINI 1890", as it was when Mr Henson, his staff, and the boys of the County Day School took it over in 1912.

To Wingfield Road:
Trowbridge and District Secondary School for Boys: 1912-1914

The new school, the Trowbridge and District Secondary School for Boys, opened on 16 September 1912, but by that date not all was quite ready. Mr Henson was to move from his house in Westbourne Road, "Finedon", the second house up on the left from Wingfield Road, into the Head Master's accommodation in the main school building as soon as a few minor alterations had been carried out. A new kitchen range still had to be installed, and the legal details of his tenancy had to be finalised with the County Council, for example.

The conversion of a boarding school to a day school involved changes more fundamental than those to the Head Master's house, the cost of which came to £1,200. The new wing that had been built in 1897 was substantially altered by the division of the ground-floor School Room into two classrooms, whilst, on the first floor, the boarding school's domestic facilities gave way to a large, well lighted art room. This meant that the wing's gabled elevation at the front disappeared, though its appearance at the back remained unchanged. Two classrooms were also created in what had been the Long Dormitory, with a substantial changing room and store room between them, but for the time being the West Dormitory remained unchanged and unused. The provision of these new rooms meant that some of the original classrooms could be adapted for other purposes. In the arm of the building that originally housed the old School Room (the lavatory and the large and small classrooms), a woodwork room was constructed where the present girls' cloakroom and store room are. There was a cloakroom beyond that, then a science lecture room or classroom (W 33), and, at a right angle to this room, a chemical laboratory (W 35). The School Room and the large and small classrooms were no more. Not least, the "outdoor offices" were made more airy. One thing that the Education Committee could not rise to, however, was the laying on of electricity. Despite impassioned pleas for the provision of this new form of energy, gas and solid fuel remained the order of the day.

At the front, the grounds were laid out to lawns, flower beds, and a shrubbery adjacent to the main road, whilst at the rear there was a small playground. Behind the playground was "the back field", roughly covering the area on which the Lancaster and Hertford buildings and the single tennis court now stand, rented out to the school by a Mr Usher for recreational purposes. Over the next few years the fate of this field was to cause the school, the Management Committee, and the Education Committee some anxiety. In 1912 its rental was £15 a year.

Thereafter the lease lapsed without anyone being quite aware that it had happened. Mr Usher proposed to sell the field; the price was considered to be too high; a further rental was agreed; and finally, to leap ahead a few years, it was eventually bought for £750 in 1919 after Mr Usher's death, "as it would be calamitous if it should pass into other hands". The securing of that small field occurred at precisely the time that other developments were taking place on land at the end of Gloucester Road, and, together, the two acquisitions were to form the basis of the present school's spacious and attractive site.

Mention is made above of a "Management Committee". The Education Act of 1902 made the Education Committee of the Trowbridge Urban District Council responsible for secondary education in the area, and it was effectively the Governing Body of the County Day School. But with the separation of the schools in 1912, the Education Committee delegated some of its powers to a Management Committee, which held its meetings alternately at the boys' and the girls' school, and increasingly it was this Committee which debated issues and reached decisions, for them to be ratified, somewhat later, by the full Education Committee. As we have seen, the founder Chairman of that Committee, from 1903 to 1915, was J Poynton Haden, and his influence upon the management and development of the schools was significant – much like that of a Chairman of Governors today. He was followed in office by E Fear Hill (1915-1920), W Walker (1920-1924), and W Nelson Haden (1914-1927). From 1927, the two High Schools had their own Board of Governors.

Freed of the limitations imposed by the cramped accommodation at the Victoria Institute, the Secondary School for Boys grew rapidly. In July 1912, there had been 51 boys at the Institute; in September, the new school opened with 103, and this increased to 128 a year later. The 103 was composed of 38 who came with Mr Henson from Castle Street, 40 (39 day boys and a boarder) who stayed on as former pupils at the Wesleyan High School, and a new intake of 25. Mr Henson himself taught mathematics and scripture on a limited teaching timetable; Mr Heal taught Latin, English and history; Jevs Gardner was a scientist who also taught music, acted as Games Secretary, and who had been appointed to the County Day School as long ago as 1906; Mr Lock was the geographer; and Mr Gorvett was a part-time instructor in woodwork. To these teachers from the former school were added Willy Fassnidge, Special French teacher, and, in January 1913, Idris Matthews, a former pupil of the County Secondary School, who was responsible for a Preparatory Class and who took art throughout the school. In April 1913, Mr Palmer, another scientist, was recruited. This, then was the staff when, in its fifth term after reorganisation, the school was inspected by HMI in June 1913.

The inspectors were very complimentary about the leadership and organisation of the school, about the quality of the teaching, and, above all, about the excellence of the accommodation that the new buildings afforded. Their comments under this head should, perhaps, be writ large, for 1913 at the Boys' Secondary School is virtually the only occasion in the 100-year history of these several schools when gloom and dismay were not expressed about the poor quality and inadequacy of the buildings. The accommodation was "entirely satisfactory", and "an excellent provision". When numbers increased, the West Dormitory (W 4) could be made into two additional classrooms, and the only slight worry that the Inspectors had was the lack of a gymnasium. But this deficiency could easily be remedied by the erection of a shed at one side of the back playground to serve as gymnasium and workshop, thus, at the same time, freeing the classroom in the main school that was then having to be used as a workshop as a room for the boys in the Preparatory Department. At the time of the inspection, they were having to be taught with class II for some of their lessons, and this was another cause of mild concern.

J W Henson, Head Master, 1897-1937.

There were Preparatory Departments, sometimes referred to as Junior Schools or Junior Classes, at both the secondary establishments in Trowbridge. The age of admission to these departments was lowered in 1912 to 8 years, but the Education Committee had made it clear that the fees charged should be sufficient to make them self-supporting, as they attracted no grants. In 1913, the fees for pupils in the Preparatory Department were double the five guineas per year that pupils in the main school had to pay – and this was also the case in the girls' school. The Inspectors noted the existence of this junior form in June 1913, and recommended its development. It consisted at that time of 13 boys whose average age was 9 years 8 months.

The other matter to engage the attention of the Inspectors was the curriculum and the quality of the teaching staff. Both were considered to be satisfactory. If a weakness could be found, it was in "expression" – in the teaching of English and in the pupils' ability to express themselves clearly in writing. However, the whole tone of the report was commendatory. The Education Committee were pleased and their congratulations were passed on to Mr Henson.

In 1913, about 40 boys took lunch daily at the school. Half bought the meal supplied by the school kitchen at a cost of 7d, whilst the other half provided their own, and, again, the inspectorial team was full of praise for the civilised nature of the eating arrangements. Games took place on Wednesday and Saturday afternoons, and a licence was applied for so that the Boys' School could operate a wireless telegraphy station. These small matters, however, were overshadowed by the school's change of name in January 1914. On the 26th of that month the school officially became the Trowbridge and District High School for Boys (or, in a somewhat abbreviated form, the Boys' High School) – the name by which it came to be known by generations of Trowbridge families. In Committee, some discussion took place initially about the need for a change because of confusion between the titles of the boys' and the girls' schools. Mr Henson had received letters that were intended for Miss Moore; this was because the names of the schools were so similar, or because letters had been ambiguously addressed; and what if the letters had been urgent? the delay in reply could have been damaging; etc. etc. But it was soon admitted that the real reason for a change in name's being sought was the enhancement of status that it implied. So it was agreed, and the ostensible reason for the alteration was conveniently forgotten when, eighteen months later, the girls' school, too, changed its name to bring it into line with the boys!

Arrival of Edel Moore:
Trowbridge and District Secondary School for Girls: 1912-1915

Edel Moore was a product of Cheltenham Ladies' College where she was a pupil under Miss Beale, that pioneer of women's education. In 1912, at the age of 39, she came to Trowbridge as Head Mistress of the Secondary School for Girls, and over the next 20 years she set her stamp indelibly on what was to become the Trowbridge Girls' High School. She lived at "Emsworth" (no. 63 Wingfield Road, the house next to what is now Gordon's Hotel). All who knew her speak of her with very great respect, and today, more than 60 years after her retirement from teaching, she is remembered in the special Edel Moore prizes that are presented annually at the John of Gaunt School awards ceremony, and by the plaque commemorating her Headship that is set into the centre of the wall at the rear of the stage in the Gloucester Hall. She was, by all accounts, a formidable and remarkable lady.

The new Secondary School for Girls opened a little earlier than the boys' school – on 6 September 1912. It remained, as we have seen, in the Victoria Institute, and valiant attempts were made to smarten the building up so that it would be worthy of its new role. The premises were entirely repainted and decorated for the occasion, principally in pale green, with dark green dadoes, and with the staircases done out in pink, with brown dadoes. This was not quite the same as being in totally new accommodation, but with the boys gone, with more room to manoeuvre in, with a bright, clean building, and a new and enthusiastic Head, the signs were propitious.

Other organisations used the Victoria Institute – the evening classes, for example – but arrangements were made to separate them from the girls' school, and a general re-allocation of rooms, such as the conversion of the old lecture room to a dining room, took place. The 54 girls of early 1912 in the mixed school had risen to 72 by September of that year, to 82 nine months later, 92 by September 1913, and over 120 by April 1914. This latter figure is significant in that Edel Moore had been promised that, when the number of pupils reached 120, the school would have a new building. The war, of course, made such a promise impossible of implementation. As her teaching staff, she had Miss Parsons, Miss Hague, and Miss Johnson, with Mr Hallett coming in part-time to teach art. Miss Hague was newly appointed, but all the others had taught in the mixed school, and, at the last minute, Miss Crisp of Corsham temporarily replaced Miss Johnson, she having been ordered by her doctor to rest until Christmas. "We were full of hope and energy," Miss Moore recalled, many years later; "we chose our motto (Vigor et Integritas) and emblem (a daffodil), and started our societies." A lady who entered the school in 1914 vividly remembers the first assembly she attended.

> "Miss Moore explained the school motto to us – and the stress she put on the word 'integrity'. She told us she had chosen the daffodil as the emblem of the school, because it was clean, upright, and vigorous, and she wanted us to be like that. It impressed me very much."

Within the first four months of its existence, the school faced a visit from HMI, and immediately, quashing any hope there may have been of the Victoria Institute's having at last found favour as a suitable building for a secondary school, very serious doubts were cast upon its adequacy, even after the face-lift and improvements that had been lavished upon it. These alterations were recognised, but the inspectors ominously added that

> "the general design of the buildings, and the fact that they are shared by evening students, make them far from ideal for the purposes of a Secondary School for girls, and it is hoped that the Local Authority will, on the first opportunity, take measures to provide as suitable premises for the girls as they have recently provided for the boys."

They reinforced this later in their report by saying that it would be "essential for new premises more consonant with the modern requirements of girls' education to be provided at no very distant date". The problem of the unsuitability of the accommodation at the Victoria Institute was just not going to go away. When they reported to the Education Committee, one of the inspectors, Miss Greene, rather cunningly suggested that, when new fittings were being considered for the school, they should be both inexpensive and portable, so that "they might easily remove to a new school building". The Committee, however, was having none of it and tartly replied that a new building was not contemplated, "nor was it within range of practical politics"! Six years later it had changed its mind.

What the inspectors saw of the staff and the teaching and the tone of the school, however, they very much liked. They were enthusiastic about the two new appointments, Miss Hague and Miss Crisp, and were admiring of Miss Moore's vision and ability. "The Head Mistress has high ideals of what a girls' school should be, and possesses in no small degree the practical capacity to give effect to her aspirations." There was, though, a problem of under-staffing. They thought the prospectus's description of the school as providing a commercial education misleading as the curriculum included "all the ordinary subjects of a Public Secondary School for Girls". Form II (Form I at the Boys' School), the junior department, they thought would expand when properly organised, but at the

Miss E M Moore, Head Mistress, 1912-1932.

time of the inspection it shared its room, and most of its lessons, with the next form up, Form III. With the very important exception of the suitability of the premises themselves, then, there was much that was approved of in the Girls' Secondary School in December 1912.

As we have seen, the number of girls on roll increased rapidly. The 72 with which the school opened rose to 92 a year later, and then to 121 in 1914. Fees were a modest 5 guineas a year (soon to rise to 6 guineas), which included all stationery and books that were needed, and this, together with grants from the Education Committee and the Board of Education in London, was the budget that the school had to work to. But annually a number of free places were awarded – 9 in 1912 and 12 from the 46 candidates who sat the internally set and administered examination in 1915, for example. The Education Act of 1907 had introduced the free place system in order to give bright children in elementary schools, who might not otherwise have been able to afford a place, chance of secondary school education. All grant-aided secondary schools had to award free places of a number not fewer than 25% of the previous year's intake, and for this they were reimbursed. The scheme remained unaltered until 1932, when, because of the national economic situation, a means-tested scale of fees was introduced. In addition, exhibitions could be awarded to pupils who lived more than three miles from the school for travelling or lodging expenses, and in cases of exceptional hardship, where a father was out of work or in the services, perhaps, fees could be reduced or waived altogether. The same system obtained at the boys' school. The Management Committee, and, later, the Governors, looked closely at the results of the entrance examinations, at how many free places should be awarded, and to whom.

This increase in pupil numbers had to be reflected in an increase in the size of the teaching staff over and above the shortfall identified by HMI in 1912. Miss Crisp was added to the permanent staff when Miss Johnson returned to her duties, and Miss Cook replaced Miss Johnson when she resigned in March 1913. Miss Grundy came to teach domestic subjects, Miss Oyler was appointed as Senior Mistress, and Miss Spinks took up her duties – all three additions rather than replacements. Early in 1914, Miss Bloor replaced Miss Parsons, at first in a temporary capacity but, later, permanently, when Miss Parsons resigned and, shortly afterwards, died, the school thus losing a long-serving and one of its very earliest teachers. And in September 1915, Miss Champ replaced Miss Hague who went to study medicine at Birmingham University.

Some of these teachers of eighty years ago are still remembered by those whom they taught: Miss Oyler, a historian, tall and upright and rather austere, who lodged at the little toll house on The Down; Miss Crisp and Miss Champ, teachers of French and maths respectively, who were liked and respected as enthusiasts for their subjects; and Mr Hallett, the art teacher, "who never let us do flowers or anything pretty – it was all design and perspective and architecture, which was useful when one got to college".

The school's position in the centre of town was always a problem, not least in that there was no possibility of any playing fields being available anywhere near. For some time a field at Holbrook Farm had been rented from a Mr Forrest as a games field for the girls at a cost of £3.10.0 for two terms and a further £4.0.0 for the cricket season, and a shelter of sorts had been erected there for the convenience of pupils as early as 1910. Later, the King family who lived in Adcroft House leased to the school a field at Prospect where the new Adcroft Surgery now stands; a lady who was a pupil during those First World War years recalls that "we played hockey and cricket and very little tennis. We went in crocodile form from the centre of the town to our sports field every Wednesday afternoon." It was not a long journey – from the Victoria Institute along Market Street and Silver Street, left into Church Street, right up Union Street, left up a little passageway called The Posts into Charlotte Street, and then right into Prospect. "Our tennis courts were in the Town Hall gardens, but only the Sixth Form played there; the others were not allowed." The state of the grass on the tennis courts, in fact, was the subject for repeated complaint by the school to the Education Committee.

One or two events of the years 1912-1915 reflect the temper of the times and the struggle of the school to adapt to its new situation. With the crusading zeal of a new Head, Miss Moore tried to introduce a health certificate to be signed by the parents of all pupils, but such was the discontent aroused that it was withdrawn rather hurriedly; creepers were bought to cover the walls of the cottages that backed on to the school; the school joined the Patriotic League; and two Belgian girl refugees were given places, free of charge, late in 1914. A year earlier, Miss Moore had bought the first two pupils' honours boards, in plain oak – the first of many. (One was inscribed with the school motto: "Vigor et Integritas", the caption: "Captains of the School", and the words "He that is first among you, let him be servant of all". There followed a list of the girls selected as captains of the school: Kathleen Richmond in 1912, followed by Christine Wiltshire, Dora Burgess, and one girl chosen for this honour every year until 1938 – Audrey Griffin, Irene White, Vera Silcocks, Grace Purnell, Marjorie Reeves, Joan Hussey, Joan Reeves, Dora Wesley (twice), Marion Rose, Daphne Sims (twice), Mavis Lush, Enid Davis, Phillis Thomas, Benita West, Edith Thomson, Joan Ottiker, and Betty Lucas and Mary Harris jointly in 1937-38. The second board was to record academic distinction; Kathleen Richmond and Lillie C Long gained county university scholarships in 1913, intermediate qualification in 1914, and degrees from the University of London in 1916. Winifred Cray, in 1924, was the first Oxbridge graduate. The distinctions gained by Irene White, Vera Silcocks, Audrey Griffin, Ethel and Emma Long, and Marjorie Reeves followed. These honours boards graced the walls of the Gloucester Hall until about 1984, when lack of space compelled their removal.)

And then, in July 1915, following Mr Henson's suggestion for the boys in

Wingfield Road, the school was officially renamed the Trowbridge and District High School for Girls.

An early honours board.

Growth and Expansion:
Trowbridge and District High School for Girls: 1915-1922

The Girls' High School came into being at a very difficult time indeed. Bessie Smith was a pupil then, and she describes her memories of eighty years ago at first-hand and in graphic detail.

"I went to the High School during the first World War so many luxuries were denied us. I was extremely proud of my straw boater, but in a very short time this was replaced by more modern headgear....As it was war time, the atmosphere of war was felt everywhere. 'Dig for Victory' was the slogan at that time, and dig we did. Wherever land was available, it was dug. A large field behind the Rectory was divided into plots for allotments, and Trowbridge Girls' High School applied for a plot. Lots were drawn and we drew the worst plot – 14 lug of root-filled land. A group of us worked, cleared the land, and produced marvellous vegetables throughout the war. Frequently we had patriotic assemblies, had pep talks, and sang the national anthems of the allies. We used to sing the Marseillaise in French and the Russian national anthem, 'God the All-Terrible', which is now never heard. Victories and defeats were marked by little flags on a wall map, and we were fired with patriotic enthusiasm. Prizes were given in the form of certificates, and money was invested for us in the form of war-loan certificates. I still have five of these prize certificates headed with the verse:

> *No easy hopes or lies*
> *Shall bring us to our goal*
> *But iron sacrifice*
> *Of body, will, and soul.* "

But while Bessie and her fellow pupils worked at their lessons and dug their allotment, Miss Moore struggled with what must have seemed the insoluble problem of too many girls and too little space. The way in which the school increased in numbers was remarkable. The 54 girls of 1912 had become 136 by 1915, and then, in successive years, 148 (1916), 160 (1917), 209 (1918), 238 (1919), and 265 (1920) – a five-fold increase in eight years – and, of course, the buildings, not very suitable in the first place, simply could not accommodate the numbers. In October 1917, Miss Moore stated that the Girls' High School was severely overcrowded and that accommodation in addition to that provided by the Victoria Institute must be sought urgently to house 3 or 4 of the lower forms. A year later she was to report that her staff were overworked and consequently discontented. This was partly because appointments were constantly being made in an attempt to catch up with the number of pupils that had to be taught, but it was also partly a consequence of the conditions under which teaching took place and the travelling about that, by then, had become a feature of teaching at the Girls' High School.

The Victoria Institute and new extension.

In 1917, a first attempt at some alleviation of the problem was attempted. The Golf House from Bradford on Avon (in reality, a large hut) was bought for £65 and erected at a cost of £38 "on the vacant land now forming the school yard". It was rather grandly known as the New Extension and was heated by gas radiators. Later in the same school year more premises were looked at as possibilities for extra accommodation – the Temperance Hall in the middle of town, Rodney House (now the offices of Bishop, Longbotham and Bagnall), The Cedars, Adcroft House, Bellefield House (opposite the fire station), and other properties – and the admission was finally made by the Education Committee that "it might be wise to consider what premises might be purchased for a new Girls' School which it was felt would have to be provided after the war". Before further thought could be given to this ultimate admission of the Victoria Institute's unsuitability as a school, however, a property for short-term rental was found. Rooms above the London City and Midland Bank in Fore Street, a very short distance from the main school building, could be had for 3 years at £55 per year, plus rates, and 2 rooms next door on the top floor of Boots could also be rented for £15 per year, plus rates. The lease included a small garden at the rear in which a shelter was to be provided, additional lavatories were needed, as was heating, and a couple of doorways had to be altered. So now, the renting of these premises having been agreed, the 209 girls of 1918-1919 could all be housed – 110 in the old school and 99 in the new accommodation.

It is no surprise to find the Board of Education saying, in 1919, that "the Trowbridge Girls' High School premises are now totally unsatisfactory and that new premises are required". The Education Committee agreed, and the search was resumed. Rodney House again, Adcroft House again, Bellefield again....Rodney House was suitable, but Adcroft House was better. And then, in June 1919:

> "The Committee proceded to view a field situate at the top of Gloucester Road and adjoining the premises of the Boys' School. It was resolved...that the Committee consider this field to be the best and most suitable site for the Girls' School and recommend the Wilts General Education Committee to purchase the whole field, the area of which is stated to be 6.435 acres, and hold any spare land for future developments. This, together with the Boys' School and Playing Fields, would form a compact block from Wingfield Road to Gloucester Road, the latter road forming the approach to the Girls' School."

Miss Moore must have thought that the end to her problems was in sight, but, for her, it was not so. She was to retire, and thirteen more years were to pass, before vision became reality.

By 1919, too, the staff of the Girls' High School had changed. Miss Oyler had gone and been replaced as Second Mistress by Miss Thomas (thought by her pupils to be "very approachable"), and of those who taught at the school in 1916 only Miss Champ remained. Miss LaTouche ("a very fine sports mistress" according to Mrs Rodway, the former Bessie Smith) had been appointed for gymnastics and had been joined by Misses Smith, Miller, Reeves, Brown, Godefroy, Harries, Bromley, and Wright. Mr Hallett was still there as a part-time teacher of art. He had taught his subject in a variety of local institutions for many years and had first been appointed to the staff of the mixed secondary school in 1902. Sadly, from being fresh and innovative in the early days, his methods were now deemed to be "antiquated and unsatisfactory", and a change was shortly to be made.

The junior girls of the High School in the Town Hall gardens, with Miss Bloor (seated) and Miss LaTouche (standing), 1916. Bessie Smith is fifth from right seated on chair.

It is clear that Edel Moore did not suffer fools gladly. She is reported as having been very strict indeed, coming down heavily on any girl in her charge who did not pull her weight in class or who misbaved either within or without school. A pupil of these years remembers having to line up with the other girls and being "inspected" by Miss Moore to make sure that their boots were clean and in possession of all their buttons. Welsh and a devout Christian, she had the virtues and, perhaps, some of the puritanism of that background. Girls of secondary age will even today occasionally test the most tolerant of Head Mistresses, and some of the pupils in those early years of the Girls' High School undoubtedly acted in a manner of which Miss Moore did not approve. Two were suspended for bad behaviour late in the summer term of 1917, one being expelled and one being allowed to return in September on promise of a mending of her ways. A little later, there were complaints that must have been of concern to the Head about the behaviour of some of those who travelled to and from school by rail. And then, late in 1919, what started as a comparatively trivial disciplinary matter blew up into a full formal enquiry by the Trowbridge Education Committee that involved the Wiltshire General Education Committee and, marginally, the Board of Education in London.

A girl called Maud had been misbaving in school and was warned that she was risking expulsion. Her father intervened, received no satisfaction, and was told that his daughter should leave at the end of the summer term, so he took his complaint further and was backed up by other parents who had complaints of their own. The outcome was nothing less than the ordering of a formal enquiry into the conduct and administration of the Girls' High School. The complainants wanted it to be conducted by the Wiltshire General Education Committee, but that body decided it was a matter for the Management Committee in Trowbridge. Only specific charges would be heard; whether or not Miss Moore should be legally represented was a matter for her; and one HMI would be invited in an advisory capacity. (In the event, Mr Cookson, who had inspected the school in 1912, attended.) So, from a routine disciplinary matter within school, a formal enquiry at a very high level, based upon multiple complaints, had emerged, and one can well imagine that it was a matter of serious concern and no little worry for those principally involved.

Both sides – Miss Moore and the staff, and all the complainants – were legally represented; each case was dealt with separately; and four cases were persisted with, the others being withdrawn. After sitting for six hours, the nine-member panel issued the following, unanimous, statement:

> "After the fullest and most patient investigation, Miss Moore was completely exonerated and all the charges against her failed. In the opinion of the Committee, neither Miss Moore nor any member of her staff exceeded their due powers of discipline. Nothing transpired at the enquiry which in any way detracted from the admittedly great work which Miss Moore had done in building up a most successful and efficient school."

If the parents concerned felt dissatisfied, the relief experienced by the staff of the school, and, in particular, by Miss Moore herself, must have been considerable.

Not all was gloom and acrimony. The summer holidays in 1919 were extended at both the boys' and the girls' school for three days – and one hopes they were sunny days – to celebrate the Peace.

Fields are easier to deal with than discontented parents, and the troublesome matter of the girls' playing field was settled reasonably satisfactorily and certainly amicably. In the 1919-1920 school year, the tenancy of the games field at Prospect was relinquished as, for some time, its state had not been acceptable. An agreement was reached whereby hockey in winter and cricket in summer could be played on the nearby County Ground and Trowbridge Cricket Club Ground, but this was quickly followed by an arrangement whereby the girls would be able to use the recently acquired field at the end of Gloucester Road for games. In September 1920 that field was being cleaned and rolled, and a small hut was provided to serve as a pavilion and shelter. In a very small way, perhaps, the Girls' High School had taken over its new site.

Girls' High School hockey XI, 1916.

The staff of the school in 1919/1920 was still both growing and changing, but after 1920, whilst change continued, growth was halted. The number of pupils on roll reached 265 in 1921, but from then, throughout the 20's, a plateau was reached and numbers remained very constant, between 247 and 257. Correspondingly, an increase in teacher numbers to match the number of pupils ceased. In 1920, with Miss Moore and Miss Thomas there remained Miss Champ (mathematics), Miss Miller (French), Miss Reeves (music), Miss Brown (English and maths), Miss Bromley (French), and Miss Wright (geography). Miss Dobson

(English) joined them in 1919 and Miss Pearson (mainly for the Preparatory Class) the following year. In 1920, too, Miss Bracher replaced Miss LaTouche (gymnastics) and Miss Grummitt took charge of the Preparatory Department in place of Miss Godefroy. She went to Pate's Grammar School in Cheltenham, whilst Miss LaTouche obtained a post as lecturer at Bingley Training College. And in 1921 Miss Essex Lewis replaced Miss Harries in Domestic Subjects, and Miss Davies took over from Miss Smith in science. There can be no question about the strain involved in teaching at the Girls' High School during these years. The conditions under which these young women taught were bad, and it is scarcely surprising that so many of them, after a short time, found less demanding work elsewhere.

Nevertheless, it must have been a considerable blow when, in June 1921, Misses Brown, Champ, Miller, and Wright all tendered their resignations for the end of that term. For a third of the assistant teachers to go at one time was unusual and disturbing, and it gave rise to speculation and rumour – so much so that the four wrote to the Management Committee in the following terms:

"It has come to our knowledge that certain rumours are being circulated to the effect that we are leaving the Girls' High School as a result of a disagreement with the Head Mistress. We should like to state that there is no truth whatever in any such rumour and that we have never been on any but the best of terms with Miss Moore. We trust that the Governors of the school will do everything in their power to contradict rumours of this kind that come to their notice."

More appointments were made. Miss Barnes (French), Miss Watson (science), Miss White (geography), Miss Lanson, and Miss Side joined the school; and later in 1921 we hear of substitute teachers standing in for several members of the regular staff who were ill. A further change, anticipated by the inspectors' report earlier in the year, took place in art in the summer of 1921. Miss Bromley had been groomed to teach some junior art, and a visiting mistress was to be brought in for one day per week to teach the senior girls. Miss Barber was appointed to this post, and the long-serving Mr Hallett, having been told that he would not be required after Christmas, resigned immediately.

If the constantly changing staff of the school reflected the terrible conditions under which teaching and learning took place at the Victoria Institute and in the Junior School above the Midland Bank, there was much to take pleasure in in the report of the inspectors who examined the school and its working for three days in March 1921.

The year had begun well. Miss Moore had gained her MA (Oxon) to add to her degree from Trinity College, Dublin, and had been officially congratulated on her achievement. Mrs Usher had presented the prizes at the Prize Giving in the Town Hall; a dramatic presentation - "Alice in Wonderland" and scenes from "Cranford", produced by Miss Pearson and Miss Grummitt – had been well received; and plans for the speedy erection on the new site of a Hut (which eventually became The Hut, to rank in TGHS history with The Hedge) gave promise of better things to come. And, in March, the inspectors had kind things to say.

> "The Head Mistress has done very good work for the school....By thoughtful management she has successfully raised the whole standard of the school, which reflects great credit on her powers of organisation. She is ably seconded by a very capable Senior Mistress, and she has succeeded in gathering round her a strong staff, well qualified for the most part, who cooperate loyally with her....The standard of work is steadily improving and is in many respects good. In particular, history and English are strong subjects....The various school societies are flourishing, and there is an active Old Girls' Society. A School Magazine is regularly issued....The school is exceedingly well managed, and the Governors are to be congratulated on the success which has attended the devolopment of a girls' school in Trowbridge."

Elsewhere, Miss Thomas, the Senior Mistress who was responsible for history and English, and Miss Champ, mathematics, were singled out for particular praise.

Of course, the accommodation was condemned – again. At the time of the inspection, teaching was actually taking place in the kitchen as dinners were being prepared! Domestic subjects were seen as being weak, and an improvement in the arrangements for teaching Latin was suggested. On the other hand, the acquisition of the Hut at Gloucester Road was thought to be an excellent development.

This was an ex-army hut. It had been obtained by the Wiltshire General Education Committee for Day Continuation Schools, but the starting of these had been deferred, and the Committee thought, correctly, that Trowbridge Girls' High School could probably make good use of it. It was a substantial building of four large sections that was set up immediately inside the Gloucester Road gates and it ran down parallel and adjacent to the back gardens of the houses in Gloucester Road and Avenue Road. In 1921, it consisted of an assembly room, five classrooms, a cloakroom, a dining room, and a teachers' room. After it had been suitably adapted and the surrounding land drained, because the whole area was very wet, it was intended that it would serve as the junior section of the High School, with the Preparatory Department transferring there also. As is customary in such situations, the pace at which the erection and adaptation took place caused anxiety, but matters progressed, and the girls of the Junior School were able to transfer from the Bank to the Hut which opened for business on 3 October 1921. A Caretaker was needed, so a Mr Lucas was appointed, his wife being available to help with meals. In the entrepreneurial way that caretakers have, he was soon applying to build a fowlhouse and hen-run on spare ground behind the building (refused), and then to develop a small garden (allowed). More will be heard of the Hut, which was to survive for more than half a century!

These matters apart, Miss Moore's energies at this period seem to have been engaged by issues that have much exercised me in my time – girls' welfare, bicycles, and trespass on school property! Some girls travelled a considerable distance in order to attend the secondary school in Trowbridge, and, despite a good public transport system in the 1920's, daily travel from home to school was simply not practicable. They therefore lived in lodgings, and one of the Head Mistress's concerns was the suitability of some of these lodgings. Enquiries were put in hand to find out how schools in other towns handled the problem, and the suggestion was made that licensing and inspection of these premises would possibly be desirable. Bicycles were a different sort of problem. (Today it is Sixth Formers' cars that cause difficulty.) It was agreed that some sort of shelter would be supplied for cycles at Gloucester Road; in town, an arrangement was arrived at whereby the girls at the Victoria Institute stored their bikes in the Market Hall, except on market days, and this proved to be an acceptable solution to that particular difficulty. And finally, trespass. This was a great waster of time and energy during the years of my headship at the John of Gaunt School, but a large, unfenced and ungated site is a magnet to local people. Cars, cycles and pedestrians, of course, have had to be turned away, but so, too, from time to time have golfers, fishermen, horsemen and horsewomen, icecream vans, a horse and cart, travellers' caravans, and a tame goat on a lead. It is consoling, therefore, to find that Miss Moore had the same problem some sixty years earlier. "A letter from the Wilts GEC was read," say the Management Committee's minutes, "asking what steps the Committee would take to prevent damage and abuse of the Gloucester Rd site on the part of the public it was impossible to protect the field from trespass and abuse until the land was fenced and to express the Committee's hope that this would be done at an early date."

Young Marjorie Reeves cycled the 5.5 miles from Bratton to the Victorian Institute, and home again, every day from 1918 to 1923, and if she remembers her school as being "terribly grim and unadorned, intitutional to a degree", she recalls her teachers with great affection.

> "Miss Thomas, of course, was the vital influence in turning me into an historian. She was a brilliant teacher with an elegant style and a gift of communication. She used methods which for those days were most

innovative. When she was Sixth Form mistress, she took us away for an historical weekend at Wells. This was a completely new experience for all of us. After she left, Miss Dobson, I think, became Sixth Form mistress. I don't remember much about her teaching but she took a great interest in our personal development and future plane. When I came up to Oxford, she gave me a set of Liberty silver coffee spoons – which astounded me! Miss LaTouche: red hair and a very graceful figure is my surviving impression. Mr Hallett's drawing lessons were ghastly. We drew formal shapes with a sharp pencil (which could not be rubbed out) on white paper. The results were dreadful ....The other teacher, besides Miss Thomas, who really stimulated me was Miss Croome-Smith, the botanist. I learnt no science but was inspired by botanical classifications. Miss Croome-Smith ran a flower competition each summer which my sister and I nearly always won."

But, as is the case with other former pupils of the Girls' High School, it is Miss Moore who is remembered most vividly.

"Miss Moore was the great presence in the school .... Her Somervillian education not only made her (to us) a real scholar but gave her a kind of solid integrity of judgement which meant that her decisions were respected and accepted. She arrived every morning by taxi and, being very lame, laboured slowly up those endless stairs to her room at the top. Her assemblies and her scripture lessons to the Sixth Form were memorable. All the present fuss about school assemblies and corporate worship has reminded me of one of her practices which (I now realise) left an indelible mark on me. Every end of term, at the 'break up' assembly, in a solemn voice which I can still hear now she always read Phillipians, chapter 4, verses 4-8. It was especially verse 8 that we remembered.'Whatsoever things are true, whatsoever things are honest, whatsoever things are just, whatsoever things are pure , whatsoever things are lovely, whatsoever things are of good report; if there be any virtue, and if there be any praise, think on these things."'

Despite this moral guidance, Marjorie Reeves, future Vice-Principal of St Anne's College, Oxford, and her young friend, Joan Hussey, future Professor of Byzantine History at the University of London, when set to clean out the store cupboards in a cookery lesson one end of term, in a fit of boredom took the lids of every tin and jar they could find and thoroughly and sytematically mixed up the contents. They remained undetected, and their subsequent careers appear not to have been adversely affected by the escapade.

Mistresses and Masters:
Trowbridge and District High School for Boys: 1914-1922

The Boys' High School opened quietly. The building in Wingfield Road had always been known as the High School anyway; no change in curriculum or in admissions policy was involved after the change in title, and, although life at school was now very different because of the war, the effect of the Secondary School's becoming the High School was scarcely noticeable.

However, war had now broken out in Europe. Signs of the times were the setting up of a miniature rifle range at the school, and the departure of members of the staff to the armed forces. A decision had been taken late in 1914 that any employee who joined the services would have his job kept open for him and would be able to return at the end of hostilities. Mr Luckman, who was to become one of the Boys' High School's very long-serving teachers, was appointed in 1914 to teach English. Later he went on to be senior French teacher and Acting Head Master for a few months in 1947. He was one who fairly quickly left for active service, joining the army and being awarded the Military Cross. William Phillips, too, saw military service and rejoined the school after the war to continue teaching French. Some decided not to avail themselves of their right to return, and so eventually permanent replacements had to be found for Mr Matthews and Mr Chandler who stayed in the forces.

One of the results of these upheavals was the arrival on the teaching staff of many short-term appointees to fill in for those who had joined up, and they were often young women teachers or the wives of male members of staff – Ada Lindsey, Enid Edwards, Florence Heal, Edith Williams, Lucy Phillips, Mai Slattery, Alma Brosnan, Elsie Goodwin, Alice Scott, Dorothy Rogers, and Hilda Gauntlett.

Jack Pafford, who later, as Dr J H P Pafford, became Goldsmiths' Librarian of the University of London, went as a pupil to the County Day School in 1910, transferred to Wingfield Road in 1912, and towards the end of the first World War became School Captain, representing the High School at football, cricket and boxing. His memories of those who taught him, as of many other things, are vivid and generous. Molly Parsons, for example, "was a dear". Something of a fuss-pot, she was a devoted, kindly, and motherly figure who used to say: "Little boys shouldn't think; they should know" – the exact meaning of which he is still trying to work out. And Fanny Bazley was also at the Victoria Institute. Her family were vets who lived somewhere between Hilperton and Staverton, and she taught French. She was apparently an enthusiast for the international phonetic alphabet, illustrative charts of which hung at the front of her room. This caused some confusion to young Jack in that he thought for a long time that those phonetic symbols showed the way in which French people actually wrote their mother tongue.

> ROLL OF HONOUR
> GREAT WAR 1914-1918
>
> W. J. BAKER
> W. T. CHIVERS
> B. COTTLE
> J. C. DRINKWATER
> R. S. FULFORD
> G. HUNT
> M. KNEE
> S. LONGSTAFF
> B. MAGUIRE
> G. MANNING
> R. J. MATTHEWS
> F. NELSON
> G. R. PALMER
> G. PIKE
> W. J. SCOTT
> H. SMITH
> G. R. WINTER
>
> WHO DIES IF ENGLAND LIVE?

Above and opposite: Plaques outside present Head's office.

At the Boys' High School, he remembers many of the temporary ladies who were appointed during the war – "Bronco" Brosnan, Mai Slattery, and Mrs Heal among others. Apparently Miss Brosnan held little seminars for some of the senior boys at which, fruitlessly, she tried to persuade them to pacificism, and he liked Miss Slattery who was "vehemently Irish". Miss Gauntlett seemed to him to be rather quiet and shy, and she taught only the lower forms. (She, of course, stayed. She taught English and Latin to the younger pupils, acted as Secretary to the Head Master, retired because of ill health in 1942, and died in 1945.)

He believes that the academic standard of the school during those war years was not particularly high, but he was happy there and remembers those who taught him with affection. The best teacher by far, he recalls, was Willy Fassnidge, but he was only in Trowbridge for three years before moving as French master to King Edward VI Grammar School at Southampton. Jack and his friends were in some awe of the Second Master, Mr Heal, at least as a disciplinarian, and he remembers him as often being sarcastic and having a biting tongue. Idris Matthews taught at the school for three years before being temporarily replaced by his brother, Arthur, when he left for military service, and Dr Pafford, aged 93, still feels a degree of guilt about how he and the other boys treated Arthur Matthews who was disabled in some way and found discipline difficult to maintain. That Jack Pafford made his mark at the school is shown by the significant part that he was asked to play in the presentations to Jimmy Henson and Jevs

IN MEMORY OF OLD BOYS OF THIS SCHOOL WHO GAVE THEIR LIVES 1939 – 1945.

AVONS M. J.	FLETCHER D.	PICKERING J. H.
BALCH W. H.	FORDE W. F. V.	PICKFORD H. S.
BULL L. J.	FRANCIS L. L.	POCOCK N. L.
BUSHELL J. M.	HAMILTON E. M.	REDMAN I.
CASE R. A.	HAMMOND H. E.	ROBBINS L. A.
CHIVERS M.	HARDIMAN K. W.	SARTIN K. P.
CIVILL A.	HAZELL A. L.	SILCOX R. A.
CLAYDON R. G.	HEATH G.	SIMS A. M.
CONNOR D.	HEAVYSIDE J. W.	SIMS B. L.
DALLIMORE L.	HISCOCK L.	SLATFORD F. H.
DALLIMORE R. E.	HOOPER L. W.	SMITH A. M.
DEACON E.	JAKINS G. P.	STAFFORD H. W.
DREW A. B.	KEENE F. E. B.	TOONE J. H.
DUNN P. W.	MATTHEWS R. J.	TYRRELL J. H.
EVANS A. E.	MOORE A. T. C.	VENTON M.
FAULKNER J. R.	PEARCE W. F.	WAIGHT A. W.

WESLEY A.   WILLIAMS R.

GREATER LOVE HATH NO MAN.

Gardner on the occasion of their retirement some twenty years later.

After the staffing upheavals caused by the demands of the armed services, there followed a long period of quite remarkable stability at the Boys' High School. (Some degree of staff movement is healthy for a school; the number of changes that obtained at the Girls' High School, however, was unhelpful. At the other extreme, lack of movement of the sort that pertained at the Boys' High School can lead to problems of the sort that were highlighted by HMI in 1929.) Mr Lock left in 1915, after three years, and a few appointments were made that proved to be short-lived. Very strikingly, however, a significant number of men were engaged who were to form the backbone of the teaching staff of the school for many years to come, from just after the first World War, in fact, until the mid or late 50's. Walter Luckman has already been mentioned as joining the school just as war broke out, and in 1919 Henry Downing (mathematics, 1919-1954), Wilfred Griffiths (geography, 1919-1953), and Reggie Beams (history, 1919-1959) were appointed; in 1920, Tom Powell (mathematics, 1920-1960), and Herbert Lambert (history, 1920-1957); and in 1921, Patrick O'Flaherty (science and art, 1921-1950), and John Burns (classics, 1921-1953) came to Trowbridge.

These eight men, between them, gave almost three hundred years of service to the school, so the character of the Boys' High School and the future of many thousands of Trowbridge boys was in large part inevitably determined for almost forty years by the professional standards that they set. Mr Henson himself was at the school for forty years, Mr Heal for thirty-six, Mr Gardner for thirty-one, and Miss Gauntlett for twenty-six, which leaves only Mr Phillips and Mr Westwick as relatively short-term appointments of those who were on the staff in 1922. At the end of the period under review, then, the teaching staff of the Boys' High School was: Mr Henson (Head), Mr Heal (Second Master), Messrs Gardner, Luckman, Downing, Phillips, Griffiths, Beams, Lambert, Powell, O'Flaherty, Westwick, and Burns, and Miss Gauntlett. During the same period, the number of boys in the school had increased steadily from 151 to 253.

Mr Henson's preoccupation with accommodation was not, during the early years of the High School, of the same magnitude as that of Miss Moore.

Nevertheless, there were problems. As we have seen, the number of pupils was increasing, and there was a need to find more classroom space. This was available in what had been the West Dormitory of the old Wesleyan High School. The difficulty was access. A solution appeared to be the building of an external staircase to this room, up the west outside wall of the school and into the dormitory through a new door on the first floor. A request for this to be done was first made in 1914, the work being costed at £6. But the war intervened in this, as in other plans, and despite frequent pleas for the construction of this staircase nothing was done until 1919, when, quite suddenly, a tender was accepted and the access built. Photographs of the time show it as being a straight, open-treaded staircase running up to a hut-like construction that sheltered the door into the first-floor classroom – as, by then, the dormitory had been converted into a classroom anyway. Just to the side of it, where the Wingfield Hall is now situated, was an ornamental garden, trellis work, and a croquet lawn, and at the front of the school, on the site of the present staff car park, was a grass tennis court. This particular staircase is long gone, of course, but its successor, which winds its way round corners and over low roofs and acts as a fire escape for W 4, still uses the same access to the first floor of the building as did the staircase of 1919.

T W Snailum remembers the croquet lawn. As a boy at school during the first World War, he was one of those "who were sometimes allowed to use this amenity, and when we played croquet against the ladies, we were alleged to hide the ball, to our advantage, under the ladies' long skirts." He was very friendly with Jimmy Henson's younger son, Reggie, whose passion was wireless telegraphy, and together they heard the news of the outbreak of war in 1914. Friendship with the Head Master's son brought with it a number of benefits, one being access to the school laboratories during holiday periods, and it was during a sortie into the labs that he and Reggie Henson managed to get an old motor cycle engine going by extracting hydrogen from water, by electrolisis.

Other maintenance matters that concerned the Head Master were the need for a re-asphalting of the back playground because the surface had deteriorated where a hut had once stood, the breakdown of the heating apparatus during a cold spell, with the consequence that some boys and teachers were away ill and the re-opening of the school after Christmas was delayed until 27 January 1917, and the desirability of laying on electricity to the labs. Electricity would have many advantages over gas in the laboratories, Mr Henson thought, and so, with these advantages in mind, as well as "the possible electrical lighting of the school building at some future time", the Education Committee were asked to pay for the laying of a cable. After many delays, all these matters were dealt with in 1919.

Throughout the War, as the number of pupils increased, so did the problem (yet again) of lack of accommodation rear its head. The urgent need for an outside staircase (mentioned above) was constantly reiterated, and the West Dormitory had already been converted into a classroom. By 1918, the Head was refusing admission to the High School to some pupils on the grounds of overcrowding; the Management Committee accepted the difficulty of the situation, but ruled that, even at the risk of an unacceptable degree of overcrowding, no pupil should be refused admission to either the Boys' or the Girls' School. Two years later, manual instruction had to be dropped from the curriculum as there was, physically, no room in which to do it; art was soon to follow; and the science lecture room had to be turned into a classroom. The provision of a hut was only a partial solution to the problem. This was a hut that was obtained from Trowbridge Barracks and that was erected across the yard and parallel to the rear of the main building, close to the bottom of the small field. It provided two more classrooms and some cloakroom accommodation. It seemed unlikely, nevertheless, that HMI would again praise the excellence and suitability of the accommodation at the Boys' High School when they paid their next visit, scheduled for March 1921.

Boys' High School football XI, 1919.
Standing, left to right: Leonard Fare, Sawyer, Burrows, C G Ingram (capt.), Mr P Henson (trainer), Francis, Hill; seated: McGuire, Leonard Lansdown, Reginald Henson, Clifford Sleightholme, Blanchard.

In the eight years since the last inspection, the number of pupils on roll had more than doubled, and the inspectorial team noted this as a mark of parental esteem. Speaking for his colleagues, HMI Battiscombe reported that they

> "had conducted a full inspection of the Boys' High School and were most gratified with the good work done in the school which had pleased them considerably. They found the work and general development most promising and well organised and the tone eminently healthy."

The teaching staff, they felt, were well qualified on the whole, and those who were insufficiently qualified for secondary teaching were urged, "as a matter of principle", to do something about it! It was thought to be a pity that the teaching of Latin was "fizzling out" in the upper school and it was hoped that this trend could be halted. (John Burns' appointment followed hard upon this recommendation, he coming from Forest Hill House School, London, and being the holder of an honours degree in classics from the National University of Ireland.) The school's teaching accommodation was noted as being 9 classrooms, 2 of which came from art and manual instruction with the consequent loss of these subjects to the curriculum. Laboratory accommodation was insufficient, and the lavatories were too few for the number of boys in the school. There was no gymnasium, but the inspectors agreed that this was of lower priority than some of the other deficiencies. Their comments on finance and the possibility of advanced courses to be run jointly with the Girls' High School are dealt with elsewhere. The report that they issued, then, about the state of the Boys' High School in 1921 was largely commendatory; there were, however, some criticisms and some statements that were guarded rather than totally favourable.

The lack of regular and continuing attendance of boys at the school caused some concern during these war and post-war years. In 1916, Mr Henson had been asked to explain the low average attendance at the High School. The following year, presumably as a result of concern expressed on this score, the Management Committee decided that the parents of any pupil admitted to the school would have to guarantee his attendance for at least three years, and, again, a year later, the rule that all pupils would be required to stay at school until the end of the term in which they attained their sixteenth birthday was established. Nevertheless, the Board of Education had reason to complain in 1922 that this regulation was being ignored in far too many cases at Trowbridge. The enrollment of pupils who decided to leave school early could simply not be afforded.

Another matter that must have been of interest at the time was the presentation to the school by the War Office in connection with the War Savings Association of a captured seven inch German trench mortar in 1920. It was placed between the hut and the small field where it could be climbed on, or, occasionally, toppled over. There it remained until 1932, when the building of a new classroom led to its removal. The mortar was then camouflaged by logs and put behind the cycle shed until, in 1937, Mr Smith, the then Head Master, disposed of it in view of its poor condition. Exercising an authority which I can only envy, in 1921 Jimmy Henson arranged with the local railway company for a train to be laid on from Trowbridge to Melksham at a time convenient for the pupils' afternoon return journey to that town, and in the same year an offer from the Post Office to install a telephone at the Boys' High School was curtly rejected. And finally there were the brothers Bennetto. These were two Italian teachers who were studying at the University of Bristol and who were attached for one month in the summer term of 1922 to the Boys' High School in a supernumerary capacity. There seems to have been some nervousness about how they would cope, or how the boys of Trowbridge would cope with them, but the Management Committee reported with relief that the time spent at the school by the brothers Bennetto had proved to be "quite satisfactory".

It is interesting that so many of the issues that first came to the fore in these few war and post-war years remained with the Boys' High School for many years to come, all proving in the long term to be matters of significance. There was the abandonment of art and manual instruction, the under-provision of laboratory accommodation, the reliance for teaching space on a cramped and unsuitable hut, the continuing lack of a gymnasium and assembly hall, the early leaving of too many pupils, and the start of very long service by many of the masters who joined the school at this time.

Boys' High School staff, c. 1922.
Standing, left to right: Messrs Westwick, Lambert, Beams, Phillips, Burns, Powell and O'Flaherty; seated: Luckman, Downing, Heal, Henson, Gardner, Miss Gauntlett, and Griffiths.

Common Concerns:
The Two High Schools: 1921-1922

Both the Boys' and the Girls' High School had the privilege of a formal visit from His Majesty's Inspectors in 1921, and the inspectorial team took the opportunity to suggest an initiative that, had it been implemented, would have had far-reaching implications for the two schools. It was that an advanced course in art should be established at the girls' school, to go hand in hand with a similar course in maths and science at the Boys' High School, so that a pooling of resources and closer collaboration at senior level might be developed between the two schools. The suggestion was evidently seized upon with enthusiasm by the schools, and a great deal of work went into looking at the accommodation and general resource implications of these advanced courses. For example, it was decided that extra teaching staff would be required at the Girls' High School, but that the boys' school could manage with its existing staff. The intended start date was September 1922. Sadly, hopes were dashed. The maths and science course was thought by the Wiltshire General Education Committee to be too expensive to set up, and the scheme was consequently withdrawn. Almost simultaneously, the Board of Education let it be known that, in their view, the advanced art course was unlikely to attract pupils in sufficient numbers to make it worthwhile, and so this idea, too, proved to be still-born. Both schools felt disappointment at the thwarting of these ambitions, and it is likely that parental disappointment was reflected in the fall-off during the next decade in what, to this point, had been a steady and consistent increase in pupil numbers.

The failure to establish advanced courses at the two schools was a joint failure, and in that it was common to both schools it was unusual. It is clear that the Boys' High School and the Girls' High School were separate and distinct institutions, each with its own style, its own developing traditions, and its own independent, not to say autocratic, Head. So, although there was one over-arching Management Committee for the two schools, development in many ways was individual and particular rather than the result of joint planning. The advanced courses scheme, however, was of importance to both. A second interest that was shared rather than individual was that of the Preparatory classes, and a third issue of common concern during the early 1920's was the increasingly desperate state of the schools' finances.

The Preparatory Departments, or Junior Schools, as they were sometimes called, had always been self-supporting – since their creation in, or just before, 1912 –

as they attracted no grants from the Board of Education, and in this sense they were not involved in the financial crises of these years. They were, in fact, the only classes of their sort in the county, and whilst the General Education Committee thought them "desirable", they were not prepared to subsidise them in any way. Fees, therefore, were high – £12 per annum in 1920 as compared with £6.6.0 for pupils from the age of 11 onwards. Even at this figure, the Boys' High School had had difficulty in paying an adequate salary for a teacher in the Department, and, principally on economic grounds, the suggestion was made early in 1920 that the boys should transfer to the Girls' High School to form one mixed class as from the following September. And this was done. Miss Grummitt was in charge of the Preparatory Department which for a year was housed in what had been the art room at the Victoria Institute before it transferred again – to the Hut – in the autumn term of 1921.

Mr Gardner and a physics class, 1922.

When the Girls' High School was inspected, the mixed Preparatory Department was still very new and was still at the Institute, so it is not surprising that its curriculum and organisation left something to be desired and caused the inspectors some uncertainty.

"The Junior Department would appear to contain 2 Forms: Form I, 22 pupils, average age 8 years 9 months, and Form II, 21 pupils, average age

10 years 7 months. There is, however, only one member of the staff specially trained for the work of a Junior School, and most of her attention is therefore devoted, as it should be, to Form I. This is her first post and she has much to learn about the handling of her classes."

(In the margin of the report, against the words "only one member of the staff", Miss Moore has scribbled the tart annotation: "two – Miss Grummitt, Miss Pearson, but Miss P. takes some maths in the upper school".) The inspectors, too, were critical of what was being taught and the way in which the teaching was being conducted.

But none of this would have worried Kenneth Ponting, one of Miss Grummitt's young charges in 1920. Thirty years ago, he wrote:

"When I first went (to the Junior School) it was housed in the Victoria Technical Institute. I must confess that I do not know how it ever got to this building....I do, however, very clearly remember leaving it for the new hut then being built at the site of the present Girls' High School. It was decided, perhaps unwisely, that the pupils should carry all their books from the Victoria Institute to the new buildings. We proceeded in a long column, and somehow or another our books got hopelessly mixed on the way. We were given at least a day's holiday whilst the staff sorted things out."

So Kenneth and his friends won round one against Miss Grummitt and Miss Pearson! He continues:

"The hut made a happy school, but my most pleasant memory is the cricket match against Chippenham. Each side consisted of eight boys and three girls, and it was the first occasion that anything of this kind had taken place. We set off by train on a brilliant June day, and at Chippenham inflicted a heavy defeat on our rivals. We repeated it the following week on our own pitch. The boys could not claim much credit for this victory. There was very little to choose between the eight boys on each side, but when it came to the girls we had the great advantage. Whereas the Chippenham girls were included because the rules of the match said you had to have three, we, on the other hand, had one who was an absolute genius at the game. She was the highest scorer on our side, and bowled with devastating effect against the Chippenham boys, as well as getting the three girls out for no runs at all. I remember very clearly her bowling. Her name was Janet, and I have often wondered whether this first flash of brilliance on the cricket field led to other sporting triumphs."

Clearly, life in the Hut for the boys and girls of the Junior School was anything but dull. And what became of Janet?

The time came for young Kenneth to transfer from the Preparatory Department to the Boys' High School. With a friend, he went through the hedge that divided the girls' site from the boys', and paid a visit

> "to the then Head Master, Mr Henson, a most notable figure in local life of the time. We were taken to his study, and, looking us up and down, he said: 'I hear you want to come to school here.' We replied that that was indeeed the purpose of our visit. He examined us again for a short while, and then said: 'That's all right. Goodbye.' We left. Our interview could not have lasted more than three minutes."

So Kenneth and his friend took their leave, not to return to school but to spend the rest of the day birds-nesting in the fields between Trowbridge and Wingfield.

Michael Lansdown, too, has fond memories of the Junior School in the Hut in the early 1920's. Forms I and II occupied the two rooms nearest the gate, the junior classes of the Girls' High School most of the rest, with the large end room set aside as gymnasium and assembly hall. He remembers

> "joining in the chorus of amazement and approval when our favourite Miss Grummitt came into the room on the morning after having her hair shingled, (and) being impressed by Miss Pearson's daring in riding to school from Bath each day on a motor-cycle, with a leather helmet over her coiled plaits."

The amalgamation of the two Preparatory Departments would appear to have been successful, at least financially, as Miss Grummitt was awarded a modest salary increase late in 1922 "as this class has generated a surplus of £60 in this session".

If the financial standing of the Junior School was sound, that of the two secondary schools was anything but healthy as the 1920's dawned. Cash came from three sources: a Board of Education grant, local authority grants from Wiltshire County Council and the Trowbridge Urban District Council, and from fees; and the level of fees came to be a matter of almost constant debate as the economic difficulties of the 20's began to bite. By 1921, the tuition fees had been set under the Articles of Government of the two schools at not less than £5.5.0 per year, and in practice they were £6.6.0, but even this was proving insufficient. The dilemma was that, should they be set at a higher rate, pupil numbers would be likely to fall, and the Management Committee repeatedly swung between an anxiety to increase revenue through higher fees and a fear of reducing the number of parents who were able to afford to send their children to the schools. A rise to £6.7.6 and then

£9.9.0 was suggested, and in 1922 the more radical idea of an increase to £12.0.0, with £6.0.0 for those parents who did not pay income tax, together with a reduction in the number of free places available to no more than 40% of the total, and these only for non-income tax payers. This latter suggestion arose from the fact that the number of fee-paying students was falling, whilst those applying for free places was rising. This was not acceptable; nor was an alternative, to charge in-county pupils £9.0.0 and out-county pupils £12.0.0. For the time being, therefore, the schools had to tighten their belts and make what economies they could.

Some help had already been given by Wiltshire County Council. In 1920, the Management Committee had appealed for a special grant of £2.10.0 per head to set the schools on their feet financially and to wipe out the deficit that had accumulated over several years, largely as a result of their success in attracting more pupils. The inspectors reinforced this request, and in the summer of 1921 a special grant of £1,370 was made, which helped considerably, but which still left a deficit of about £500 to be dealt with.

As schools today know only too well, when economies have to be made, eventually the spotlight focuses on the teaching staff, and that is what happened at both the Girls' and the Boys' High School in 1922. At the former, it was decided that the teaching of cookery should be discontinued, that the services of Miss Essex Lewis, Miss Barber, and Miss Bromley should be dispensed with, and that two teachers should be engaged who would be paid at the lowest scale (£170 per year). Miss Mitchell, in fact, was appointed for drawing, painting, needlework and embroidery in place of Miss Essex Lewis, and Miss Warburton and Mlle Truchet joined the staff. At the Boys' High School, Miss Gauntlett's contract was cut to half time (on half salary) and Caretaker Lewis's wages were decreased by stages of 3 shillings per week from 63 shillings to 54 shillings.

One further effect of the tightness of money at this time was the greater care that was exercised over allowing pupils to leave school. The Board of Education had pointed out that in Trowbridge too many boys and girls were being allowed to leave school before they were 16, and it suggested that there should be a greater insistence on their staying until the end of the term in which they achieved their sixteenth birthday. For a time, the Management Committee became much sharper in the early 20's, perhaps as a result of the Board's censure, perhaps through self-interest, in their requiring pupils to stay at school for the full period, and in their refusal to allow parents to remove their children and opt out of paying the fees for which they had contracted.

Though their inception lies outside the strict dates accorded this chapter, the two school magazines should be mentioned here. At each of the schools, a magazine was launched in 1920 that was to continue for the life of the High Schools. They were totally independent of each other, but they both had the aims of recording the activities of the school and of providing a vehicle for pupils who wished to write.

In 1921, the inspectors noted with satisfaction that the Girls' High School regularly published a magazine. Ambitiously, it began with one issue per term, but fairly soon became an annual. Apart from the editorial which was written by Miss Moore, the magazine was the work, under supervision, of the girls. Much of it was devoted to original composition, in verse or prose, but space was given in each edition to news of the school and the activities of the different school societies. A Literary and Debating Club had long been in existence, but by the 1920's it had been joined by a Youth and Music Club, a Science Club, and, in 1927, by a School Branch of the League of Nations Union. Also to be found in most editions of the magazine were a Library section, mention of a French Club, and Form Notes, records and accounts of the tennis, hockey, netball, and cricket teams, and a section given over to news of Old Girls. A very early magazine, interestingly and typically, contains a short article by Miss Moore herself on "Women at Oxford". In her editorial of the same edition she writes: "The experiment that we began in November, of giving self-government to the Upper School, has been only partially successful. The higher forms have understood that self-government does not mean no government, but that has not been the case with the three forms whose privileges have been taken away." At about the same time, HMI remarked: "Recently a scheme of self-government has been introduced which is still on its trial, but promises to be effective as a training in school discipline and citizenship." Such radical thinking was unusual in secondary schools seventy years ago.

There is one other matter from the Girls' High School Magazine of these years. It was thought important to foster the competitive spirit within the school both for sport (where there was a Mistresses' Games Cup to be competed for) and for other activities, so, not unusually, a House system was created in 1920. The four Houses took the names of people of local significance – Addison, Clarendon, Herbert and Sidney. Within a few years the system had died, but it was revived again under a new Head Mistress and at the request of the School Council in 1932, when the Houses were named Addison, Clarendon, Herbert and Wren. What had happened, I wonder, during the intervening twelve years to cause Sidney to fall from favour and to be supplanted by Wren?

"The Wing", magazine of the Boys' High School, was started at the same time as the Girls' High School Magazine. In many ways similar, it was somewhat heavier in its format, and laid more stress upon sport, prose articles, and news of Old Boys. Its first editor was John Garrett who later went on to become Head of Bristol Grammar School, and his enthusiasm carried the magazine through its first few editions. As with the girls, what began as a termly venture soon became an annual, and editorial despair about the lack of contributions from those in the school from whom the greatest support might have been expected became more strident as the 20's progressed. There were, too, frequent editorial mentions of the demise of school clubs. Neither of these themes is uncharacteristic of school magazines in general, but they become something of a leitmotif of "The Wing" in the 1920's. On the other hand, sport – football and cricket – was clearly thriving in the school, and both inter-House and inter-school matches are recorded and reported in detail. Brooke, Farleigh, Forest and Gaunt were the Houses, created at first according to the initials of boys' surnames, but altered in 1925 to what was thought to be a more satisfactory system based upon the geographical areas in which they lived.

The other lively section of the magazine is that devoted to the meetings of the Old Boys' Society. Former pupils met regularly for what were quite clearly very convivial reunions; members of the teaching staff attended, and Jimmy Henson was usually the Master of Ceremonies. There is a striking and, perhaps, significant contrast between these accounts of masculine sociability and the more astringent contributions of Edel Moore in the sister publication.

2. 1875 Years:
Trowbridge and District High School for Girls: 1923-1927

Changes that are important to the management and administration of schools can occur without the pupils or their parents, or, indeed, the majority of the members of the teaching staff, being aware of any alteration to the normal routine of their teaching and learning. The years from 1923 to 1927 built up to such a change, for, on 31 March 1927, the Trowbridge Education Committee handed over its responsibility for the secondary schools in the town to the Education Committee of the County Council. On that date, both High Schools became "provided", or "maintained", schools, with the Wiltshire County Council being the provider, or maintainer, and its interests being safeguarded through a Board of Governors on which it had direct representation. This was for the future. Nevertheless, a reluctance to take decisions which would have significance for the future is increasingly and unsurprisingly recognisable during this period in the deliberations of those committees that, after the end of March 1927, would cease to exist.

There were two matters that must have concerned Miss Moore very greatly on a day-by-day basis during the years 1923 to 1927; they were the standard of the premises of the Girls High School and the staffing situation.

The really depressing news of March 1925 was that the new school, to be built on the Gloucester Road site acquired some six years earlier, was not even a possibility in the foreseeable future because of cost. Beside this, any good news that there might have been on the building front paled into insignificance. Nevertheless, there was good news. The Hut was beginning to look more comfortable: the entrance to it had been improved and Miss Moore herself had paid for the labour of a pathway's being cut to it, and later in 1923 an asphalt playground was created for the use of the pupils in what was still a very wet field. Whether Miss Moore's pony was allowed to enjoy the lushness of the field is not on record, but she certainly made application at this time to use part of it for the animal! And a pond in the field was fenced. A more important improvement was the moving of a pavilion in the field to a new position adjoining and at the rear of the Hut, so that it could be used for the preparation of meals and as a drying room. On the Upper School site at the Victoria Institute, other matters required attention. The heating boiler was declared beyond repair, so a new one was acquired at a cost of £108, and new gas lamps, of the cluster type, were fitted in seven of the classrooms. The bicycle problem was solved, too. Mr Stephens of the Castle Street Carriage Works was prevailed upon to allow the girls to park their cycles on his premises on market days, when the Market Hall was not available, for the sum of 5 shillings a day. But the problem of a split site, with neither building's really being adequate or suitable as accommodation for a girls' secondary school, remained, and the stresses that resulted in part from this situation were reflected in the very unsatisfactory staff turnover at the school.

The newly acquired Girls' High School site in Gloucester Road, 1925.

In the period from January 1923 to March 1927 the Boys' High School lost one teacher because of his promotion to a Headship in Oxfordshire and another through ill health. This contrasts strikingly with the situation at the Girls' High School – a situation to which Miss Moore must have been extremely sensitive. During the same period Miss Reeves was replaced by Miss Blackburn, who was replaced by Miss Peterkin, who was replaced by Miss Speir, who was replaced by Miss Reynolds; Miss Bracher was replaced by Miss Traylen, who was replaced by Miss Hoare; Miss Barnes by Miss Williams; Miss Thomas by Miss Barton, who was replaced by Miss Synge; Miss Davies by Miss Rankin; Miss Side by Miss Goldberg, who was replaced by Miss Legassick; Miss Grummitt by Miss Pim; Miss Warburton by Miss Shillito; and Mlle Truchet by Miss Borries. Some, like Miss Thomas and Miss Grummitt, left because they had sought and obtained promotion elsewhere, and at least one, Miss Warburton, left because of serious illness, but the reasons for most of these staff changes are now not known. One consequence, however, was that from the start of the summer term in 1924, Miss Barton for a short time became Second Mistress, to be succeeded, when she herself left the school, by Miss Dobson in September 1925.

Such a massive and continuing turnover on a staff of thirteen or fourteen teachers must have been very disruptive to the continuity of learning, and a member of the Education Committee, a Mr Thomas, raised the matter in a way that gained him some publicity in the Wiltshire Times of July 1924. He wanted to know why it was happening; several parents had spoken about the matter; when teachers came for interview, he said, "they smell a rat". The implication, though it was never overtly stated, was clearly that there was some difficulty in the relationship of the teaching staff with the Head Mistress, but at the time the discussion was allowed to rest with some comment about young, unmarried ladies being more ambitious and more mobile than older men with families.

Unfortunately, Miss Moore took grave exception to the remarks; they were quite untrue and she found them very hurtful. There was talk of a special meeting at which Mr Thomas would have to explain himself, despite his vigorous assertion that he was innocent of mischief-making or of being antagonistic. Eventually, the controversy was allowed to die, with the uncomfortable statistic hanging in the air of the average length of service of staff at the boys' school at that time being 6.125 years, as compared with 2.1875 years at the girls' school.

Miss Thomas, the Second Mistress, who had been acting Head for some months in 1923 as a result of Miss Moore's illness and operation, obtained a very good promotion at St Andrews in Scotland the following year. (Miss Grummitt also, incidentally, went to St Andrews.) She had been in her post, which could not have been an easy one, for six years, and is still remembered with affection by a former pupil whom she taught and who spoke to me about her. Before she left, she presented a framed picture to the Girls' Upper School and had a number of trees planted near the entrance to the Girls' Lower School. In this latter gesture, she was the forerunner of many others, particularly in recent years, who have marked their leaving one or other of the schools with a gift of trees, shrubs, or bulbs for the lawns and grounds.

A young pupil in the Preparatory Department from 1924 to 1927 was Margaret Adams (now Mrs Margaret Bruce-Mitford), and she has interesting memories of her teachers, her fellow pupils, and the social background of the school at this time:

"After two dame schools (Miss Foord's in the Wingfield Road and Miss Lansdown's in Hilperton Road) I progressed to the Preparatory Department of the Girls' High School at around the age of 9 and went into Form II whose form mistress was Miss Pearson (I believe). My brother started in Form I at the same time – form mistress Miss Pim. Other mistresses were Miss White, Miss Purnell, Miss Hoare, and Miss Borries, who became a legend. Our Head Mistress was Miss Moore who was a rather daunting figure. I recall one morning assembly when the girls had to come and be scrutinised to ensure that our gym tunics were the regulation length from the floor when kneeling. Mine was slightly too long, but I explained to Miss Moore that my mother had had it made that length to allow for growing. She twinkled quite understandingly at this practical point of view.

The children in my form were from the middle classes of Trowbridge and the surrounding villages: the farming Tuckers from Melksham and Staverton way; the Noads from Seend; and others from the Bratton and Westbury areas. From Trowbridge there was Michael Lansdown of Wiltshire Times fame, David Stevens, Betty Phillips (whose father was manager of Lloyd's Bank), the Huntleys (coal merchants), Janet and Anne Snailum (auctioneers), Patrick Troughton, who may be the actor [He isn't!], Kenneth Bonner (son of the Barclay's Bank manager), John Reeves (the iron master's son from Bratton) etc.

The education was reasonably stimulating and I recall being inspired by 'Morte d'Arthur' and 'The Faerie Queene', to the extent of ordering the latter for Christmas. My finest personal achievement was writing an essay about the picture of a boy in blue playing his pipe under a tree. It was accorded 9½ out of 10 with a special mention, but unfortunately I was off with a cold when it happened so could only enjoy temporary fame in retrospect. Other outstanding memories are productions of 'A Christmas Carol' at the end of the Christmas term and being taken for a nature walk when the pipes froze.

Also there was the announcement that a clever Sixth Form girl had won a scholarship to St Hugh's College, Oxford, and the school was given a half-holiday to celebrate. She was Marjorie, the elder sister of John Reeves (aforementioned), and she became a very distinguished mediaeval scholar, ending her career as Vice-Principal of St Anne's College, Oxford – my own alma mater....Miss Moore was an Oxford graduate herself and kept a high academic standard throughout the school.

Just before I was 11 I was taken away from the Hut (the name of the Prep School which was indeed housed in a large hut-like building) and sent to a boarding school at Burnham-on-Sea. This was following the social pattern of middle class families who would not let their children go into the High School proper because they would develop Wiltshire accents through mixing with the scholarship girls who, if bright enough, came up to the school from the elementary school in Newtown. St Monica's convent school in Warminster was a popular establishment, with Bath and Bristol schools being patronised by the better-off families. I went to Burnham because around that time I was failing to thrive, and the ozone of the very extensive mud in the Bristol Channel was reputed to work wonders on sickly children."

By 1926, the Wiltshire General Education Committee was demanding staff cuts at both schools in the interest of economy. Because of an increase in numbers in the Preparatory Department to 42 in 1925, Miss Purnell (mentioned above) was engaged to teach the youngest children on a temporary part-time basis. She would be employed for as long as the numbers in the Department required it. Her contract was terminated abruptly, however, after just one year as a result of these new demands, and the school declared itself willing also to release Miss Traylen, the drill instructress, for one day a week to teach elsewhere if such a post could be found for her. (This offer was, in fact, withdrawn when Miss Hoare replaced Miss Traylen.) Miss Moore pointed out quite forcibly, on the other hand, that in 1926 more of the teachers at the Girls' High School were at, or near, the bottom of the salary scale than had been the case three or four years earlier, and that special consideration should be given to the school because of the travelling between sites that the staff had to undertake.

First form band at the Hut, c. 1926.

The Preparatory Department itself, whose fortunes continued to see-saw, was another financial worry. At the end of 1923 it showed a sizeable deficit, leading to a suggestion that its future should be reconsidered; a reduction in the number of teachers committed to it was implemented and it was felt that this would improve the situation; it did, and July 1925 saw a financial surplus achieved; a year later this had turned into a deficit of £102.18.1, but a surplus was anticipated for 1927; and so the rise and fall in its fortunes continued.

There were to be fewer admissions at the bottom of the school after 1927, but, for the moment, the Preparatory Department survived. Young Michael Lansdown, a veteran of the Department, admired the smartness of Miss Mitchell who taught drawing, enjoyed the friendly jollity of Miss Traylen who took him for gym, and liked Miss Pim who succeeded Miss Grummitt and who first taught him that letter boxes in Ireland, her home, are green, not red. "One person I have not yet mentioned," he writes. "Miss Moore, then Head Mistress, was rarely seen in Gloucester Road, or so it seems in my memory. To me she seemed a remote and rather terrifying figure, already crippled and walking with a stick." Another pupil, Barbara Thomas, writing of the same time but of the Victoria Institute, says, "I can still recall the tap of Miss Moore's stick as slowly, painfully and indomitably she made her way from her room, at the top, to the gymnasium, which was used for morning assembly." Bessie Smith remembers her Head as being "very, very strict". "I was alright," she says, "because I behaved well and did my work, but Miss Moore was very hard on those who were not pulling their weight." And one final assessment: "Miss Moore was a fair and just Head Mistress who could unbend at parties and prizegivings." In 1927 she still had five years of headship ahead of her and a continuing struggle with the ill health that finally forced her retirement.

Towards a Change in Management:
Trowbridge and District High School for Boys: 1923-1927

Illness and injury struck the staff of the Boys' High School in 1923. Mr Powell was hospitalised with some degree of urgency, Mr Burns had a serious accident, Herbert Lambert was admitted to Winsley Sanatorium for treatment, and William Phillips suffered a breakdown that initially was thought likely to keep him off work for several months. In fact, he did not return for over a year. Powell and Burns were not away for very long, but the brothers Bennetto still had to come to the rescue. They were again at the University of Bristol doing another course that necessitated their being attached to the Boys' High School for a time, so in the emergency that the school found itself in, they provided teaching cover for the absent staff, thus avoiding the need for short-term appointments, at least to begin with. Both Mr Lambert and Mr Phillips returned for the start of the summer term, 1924, but, sadly, William Phillips was again ill in 1925 and finally resigned because of a breakdown in his health at the end of the school year, 1926. No replacement was appointed; even the services of a man called Morrison, who latterly had been substituting for Phillips, were dispensed with summarily in line with economies in the teaching staff that were called for by the General Education Committee and that also affected the girls' school.

It was in early 1926 that the Committee made clear its requirement for staff reductions at both schools. The demand itself, and the means by which it was suggested it might be achieved, have a familiar ring. The amount of teachers' "free" time could be cut down, or class sizes generally could be increased, or the viability of some of the very small post-matriculation classes should be looked at. Schools have been known to take a liberal view of their staffing needs from time to time, and it is not unreasonable, when they are caught, for them to be required to cut back by an anxious paymaster, but neither the Boys' nor the Girls' High School at this time seems to have been extravagantly staffed. Nevertheless, a gesture towards economy was made by Mr Henson, as is explained above. On the other hand, it was only a year earlier that Hilda Gauntlett had been restored to full-time teaching from the half-time post that she had held for 2½ years as the result of a previous demand from the County Committee.

One other personnel matter of interest at this time was the appointment of Jimmy Henson's elder son, Paul, to the staff of the school. Matthew Westwick had obtained the headship of an elementary school in Oxfordshire, and a replacement was needed in February 1924. Paul Henson had been a pupil at the

County Day School in the Victoria Institute and had gone, with his father and his younger brother, Reg, to the new High School in Wingfield Road. At the end of his time there he had done a little teaching in the school prior to going to the University of Bristol in 1919, and now he returned to teach maths and physics. Jack Trott, a pupil at the High School from 1927 to 1932 before going on to become Departmental Head at a large school in Southampton, recalls that Paul Henson had the reputation of being an excellent mathematician but an indifferent teacher.

"He often got up late in the morning and would miss one or two of his scheduled lessons. Mad on astronomy, he could easily be inveigled into explaining something about the stars and the planets, so our proper work tended to suffer."

Little Margaret Adams remembers that she used to meet the Head Master at Christmas parties,

"along with his nice but rather fearsome-looking wife. She had a piercing glance behind steel spectacles, and bristly, frizzy, white hair. They had two sons, the older of whom was felt to have some sort of shadow surrounding him; possibly he did not complete a university course he had entered upon. (In those days, children did not satisfy curiosity by the confrontatory question. Such facts as were available had to be picked up haphazardly, often leading to an incorrect conclusion.)"

Paul Henson stayed for five years before leaving to take up a commercial appointment.

So the staff of the Boys' High School in 1927 was: Mr Henson (Head), Mr Heal (Second Master), Messrs Gardner, Griffiths, Luckman, Downing, Beams, Powell, Lambert, O'Flaherty, Burns, and Paul Henson, and Miss Gauntlett. There had been few changes in the past five years.

1923 saw new prospectuses issued for each of the two High Schools. A new prospectus was not an annual event then as it is today, and the old publications were very much out-of-date. "It was understood that the prospectuses would be illustrated with exterior and interior photographs of each school, and would be of a somewhat more ambitious character than the old prospectus." They were, and 500 of each were printed.

1924 was the year of the British Empire Exhibition at Wembley, and a great school trip was organised by the two Trowbridge High Schools, in conjunction with their neighbours in Chippenham and Devizes. The railway company put on a special train, at a cost of five shillings and six pence for pupils and eleven shillings for adults, the schools were closed for the day, and a picnic tea was taken in the grounds. One hopes, and assumes, that the day was a success. There was clearly a good working relationship with the railway company in these early years of the schools' history, despite occasional complaints about the behaviour of pupils who travelled by rail, but the Stationmaster at Trowbridge received a dusty answer when he enquired in 1926 about the possibility of the dates of terms and holidays being altered "so as to avoid congestion of traffic on the railways at certain times of the year". As subsequent enquirers have discovered, the timetable for the school year can never please everybody and, once it is set, shifting it by even a day is a virtual impossibility.

Miss Gauntlet and IIB, 1924-25.

The first telephone was installed at the Boys' High School in 1925. A suggestion that this should be done had been rejected four years earlier, but now the nettle was grasped. The cost was £1.15.0 per quarter. The Girls' High School was similarly equipped at the same time, but, with an extension to the Lower School, the cost here was £2.19.0. Miss Moore complained that she could only hear the ringing of her telephone bell if she were actually in her room and she asked for a number of extension bells to be fitted. This matter, however, was shelved. Honours boards were bought for the Boys' High School, some fourteen years after they had been introduced by Miss Moore. The idea was discussed by the Management Committee, tenders were sought, and in March 1927 that of Henry Sumption was accepted – for the supplying and fixing of four honours boards in the sum of £6.3.0. We know that this work was done, but I have never seen the boards, I do not know where they were placed, or what eventually happened to them. And a new piano was bought for the school. It cost £45, the old piano being sold to Mr Henson himself for £2.

In the school grounds at this time there was a pond. It was in the top left-hand corner of the larger of the two playing fields (approximately where the main footpath through the school passes between the Hertford labs and the end of the Sports Hall today), and it led into a ditch that ran along the hedge that separated the two fields (from the Hertford labs, parallel and close to the footpath, through the Lancaster kitchen, close to the wall of the Wingfield Hall, down to the main road). In 1924, the pond was filled in and the ditch between the two fields bridged with sleepers; and some three years later estimates were being sought for the final removal of the hedge between the two fields, though this did not happen immediately.

"Good fences make good neighbours." The fence, or rather the hedge, that separated the school from the gardens of the houses in Avenue Road was not very good, and encroachments were being made by some of the householders on to school territory. The ditch had been blocked and gardens extended! So, early in 1926 the hedge was grubbed out, field pipes were laid, and what sounds like a formidable fence was erected of 4'6" Empire Fencing with iron stakes. Boundary disputes of one sort and another still occurred in my time at the school, but, to the best of my knowledge, there was no trouble henceforth on the Avenue Road front at least.

As has been said, after March 1927 the Management Committee of the Trowbridge secondary schools gave way to a Board of Governors that was directly and unambiguously answerable to the General Education Committee of the Wiltshire County Council. Perhaps this was timely, because at least one member of the soon-to-be-disbanded Management Committee seemed very uncertain of his role. His colleagues received "a questionnaire submitted by Capt H C Smith who desires to know what purpose he serves by attending meetings of the Management Committee, as up to date he cannot grasp why the Committee is in being at all". He then asked questions about the purpose of the Committee under thirteen heads: to whom is the Committee responsible? are there any standing orders? what are its financial powers and responsibilities? and so on. Though most of the answers that he was given were fairly obvious, this review of its function was probably a useful exercise and one that other committees could undertake profitably from time to time. Whether Capt Smith was a genuine seeker after enlightenment, or whether he spoke tongue-in-cheek, is now not clear. Whichever was the case, when it gave him his answer the Management Committee still had three years to run before it was able to thank its Secretary, Mr Ledbury, for his twenty-six years of devoted service (1893-1901 and 1909-1927), present him with a gift of £120 as a mark of its gratitude and respect, and hand over its duties to the new Board of Governors on 1 April 1927.

Contrasting Inspections:
The Two Trowbridge High Schools: 1927-1932

Initially, the Board of Governors of the two Trowbridge High Schools consisted of 17 nominees: 5 were from the County, 6 from Trowbridge Urban District Council, 2 from Melksham UDC, 2 from Westbury UDC, 1 from Trowbridge and Melksham Rural District Council, and 1 from Westbury RDC. In June 1931, as a result of the decision to close Warminster Secondary School at the end of term in July and have pupils from that town go to school in Trowbridge, the Board was expanded to include 2 members from Warminster UDC. The term of office was three years; a minimum of six meetings a year had to be held; and at least two Governors had to be women.

The Governors had powers over finance, producing estimates of income and expenditure for the two schools as required. They were responsible for appointing, and, if need be, suspending and dismissing the Heads, and for appointing and dismissing assistant teachers. It was for them to prescribe the curricula in general terms, arrange the dates of terms and holidays, and exercise supervision over the suitability of the buildings and the maintenance of plant and equipment. The Heads had always to be consulted by the Governors, and it was they who were responsible for the internal organisation, management, and discipline of the schools.

In practical terms, much of the Governors' time was spent in discussing such matters as the withdrawal of pupils from the school, the payment or the waiving of fees when pupils had left the schools early, the allocation of free places, maintenance grants, the irregular attendance or under-performance of pupils, accounts, requisitions, the awarding of incremental increases to teachers, and the appointing of new teachers (though the short-listing of applicants was a task delegated to the two Heads). Essentially, they kept things tidy. They were not initiators, seldom enquiring into what the curriculum was or where it was going, and not looking particularly to the future except insofar as it concerned buildings and book-keeping. It is clear, from the records of their deliberations, that the Governors were business men and respected members of the community rather than than educationalists or visionaries. Certainly, being seen to have acted correctly is the hallmark of their proceedings, and in this, though different from the Governors of secondary schools today, they were typical of their time. All members of the Governing Body sat on one of two House Committees – one for the Girls' and one for the Boys' High School – and much of the detailed work was done by the House Committees that reported thereafter to the full Governing

Body. The former Chairman of the Trowbridge Education Committee, W Nelson Haden, became the first Chairman of Governors, and, ex officio, a member of both House Committees.

The first thing that the new Body had to do was formally to reappoint to their former posts all the members of the teaching and non-teaching staffs, including the two Heads, and this they did. However, they had plenty of other things to get their teeth into, and one of the first matters to engage their attention was the commercial class, or classes. Some years earlier, the Management Committee had suggested to the Heads that a commercial class, with a teacher shared by the two schools, would be a good idea, but, even though a scheme had been drafted, the idea was shelved when the General Education Committee made it clear that there would be no extra funding for the class from them. Now the idea was explored again. At the request of the Governors, the Heads submitted a scheme which was open to pupils who had passed their first School Certificate Examination, or who had been at the school for four years, or who were at least fifteen at the beginning of the session in which they were to join the class. They were to be prepared for the London University Common Certificate Examination, the London Chamber of Commerce Examination, or the RSA Examination, and a suitable teacher was available immediately – a Mr Tillotson – who could spend one day per week at the boys' school and one day a week with the girls. So the initiative was launched in September 1927, with 13 boys and 17 girls, though many subsequently dropped by the wayside.

A good start seemed to have been made, and in the summer of the following year the first examination successes were recorded. The boys principally took the RSA book-keeping exams, and the girls the Diploma in Commercial Subjects of the London General Examination. At the inspection of the two schools in 1929, HMI poured cold water on the scheme. They questioned whether it was worthwhile, and condemned the course that the girls took as unsatisfactory. Two years at least were needed for such work. The experiment of rather crudely grafting vocational courses on to the traditional secondary curriculum could not be said to have been entirely successful and, at the Boys' High School at least, the commercial course was held in no great esteem.

The Governors, and their predecessors, spent much time in discussing the Preparatory Department. Thirty years ago, Michael Lansdown wrote: "As far as I know, this school was run by the Governors as a sort of private venture," and, broadly speaking, that is correct. It had to pay for itself; so a great deal of the heart-searching about it centred on the Governors forgetting from time to time the General Education Committee's insistence that under no circumstances could any aspect of the Department be funded by public money, and their being rapped over the knuckles as a consequence of their forgetfulness.

Prior to 1927, Miss Pim was in charge of the Department and Miss Borries spent two-thirds of her time there, so most of the pupils' fees went to pay the salaries of one and two-thirds teachers. (Materials and accommodation, of course, also had to be paid for.) But now Miss Moore did some rather careful accounting and discovered that the Preparatory Department should really only be paying for one and a half salaries, thus enabling it to stay more easily solvent. At the Girls' High School, the teaching week consisted of 40 lessons of 40 minutes each, and the Department claimed only 60 of these, the equivalent of 1½ teachers. Miss Pim taught 37, Miss Pearson 10, Miss Hoare 4, Miss Clutterbuck 3, Miss Reynolds 3, Miss White 2, and Miss Horton White 1. Despite this manoeuvre (and its credibility must be suspect because it takes no account of teachers' free periods) by the end of 1928 a state of crisis had been reached yet again; numbers were falling, costs were rising, and outside help was not possible. It was decided, therefore, to advertise the Preparatory School aggressively in the local press, to establish a Kindergarten class for pupils aged 5 and upwards, to charge £9.9.0 a year for pupils under the age of 7, and to maintain the fee of £12.12.0.for all others. This, at least in the short-term, was a successful move.

Throughout 1929 there were between 12 and 14 children in the Kindergarten and an increase in the number of slightly older ones, so much so that in the summer term 1¼ teachers were being deployed and the services of a pupil-teacher were also required. Ironically, greater numbers required more accommodation, and at the Girls' High School, whether in Castle Street or at Gloucester Road, extra accommodation was just not available. So in 1929, HMI, who approved in principle of the Preparatory Department, claimed that its development was being crippled by lack of space, and the Board of Education insisted that something should be done about this within a reasonable time and, in any case, within a year of the inspectors' visit, which had been in May.

What was done was the purchase and erection of a tent – an imaginative but scarcely permanent solution to the problem! It cost £19.10.0, and the wooden floor an additional £7.10.0. Miss Pim had gone – to Alexandra College, Dublin – and had been replaced by Miss Dawes who, within a month, had found the work "too exacting" and in her turn had been replaced by Miss Taylor. On the credit side, numbers now ran at over 60 pupils in three classes (the Kindergarten and two classes for slightly older children) so that the Department was declared full; the difficulty remained of how to accommodate them suitably on a permanent basis.

In the late 1920's the pattern of pupil entry, leaving, and attainment was similar in the two schools. If 1927 is taken as an example, 41 new boys and 40 new girls entered the schools in September, both of which were two-form entry, with 25 boys and 26 girls leaving at the end of the previous summer term. The destinations of these leavers make interesting reading. Of the boys, 2 went to Bristol University, 4 to other secondary schools, 2 became student teachers, 10 became clerks, 1 a dispenser, 1 a buffet attendant on the railway, 1 a fitter, 1 went into farming, 2 left for financial reasons, and 1 was out-of-work. The girls fared similarly, with 1 going to a training college for domestic science, 4 becoming student teachers, 9 transferring to other secondary schools, 4 becoming clerks, 3 nurses, 2 left the area, 2 were needed at home, and 1 left because of ill health. In the summer of 1928, 14 out of 28 boys were successful in the Oxford Local School Certificate and 16 girls out of 22 in the London General School Certificate examination, Miss Moore having changed from Oxford to London in 1923 as she believed that the papers of that board would be more suitable for the girls of the High School. It would be fair, therefore, to say that the academic pretensions of the schools were relatively modest. On the other hand, there were 17 girls in the Sixth Form in September 1927, the largest number for a long time, and the following summer three out of four candidates were successful at Higher School Certificate, with all eighteen girls passing School Certificate in summer 1929.

The number of pupils in the Girls' High School remained pretty well constant from 1924 to the end of the decade, ranging from 218 to 221, not counting the Preparatory Department, but they fluctuated more at the Boys' High School, dropping steadily from 236 to 200 over the same period. The need constantly to recruit extra staff because of rising numbers had long gone. Paul Henson left the staff of the boys' school, his period of notice being waived in view of his having already taken a post in commerce, and Albert Marchment was appointed for a year on probation to teach mathematics and elementary science. Unfortunately, his appointment coincided with a visit from HMI who decreed that, because of the fall in numbers, the school was over-staffed, and so he only remained in post for six months. The comings and goings at the Girls' High School, however, were as persistent as ever. In the period 1927-1929, of the fourteen assistant mistresses only four served for the whole three years, and several of the other posts changed hands more than once. Miss White (geography), Miss Pim (Preparatory Department), Miss Pearson (Preparatory and some maths), and Miss Borries (French) remained unchanged. Miss Dobson, the Second Mistress who taught English, was replaced in both capacities by Miss Curry. Miss Watson went to the Headship of a boarding school in Cork and was followed by Miss Wright as science teacher. Art suffered badly. Miss Mitchell left, to be succeeded by Miss Clutterbuck who had a nervous breakdown, and Miss Caslake who followed her was in turn replaced by Miss Coe. Miss Williams (French) gave way to Miss Horton White. In music, Miss Trafford took over from Miss Reynolds. Miss Rankin was told that her performance must be improved; she was encouraged to attend a refresher course, but resigned almost immediately. Her replacement in science was Miss Greeves. Miss Synge (history) was followed by Miss Knowles. Miss Shillito (Latin) was replaced by Miss Hamer, and Miss Legassick (mathematics) by Miss Morrey. Finally, in gymnastics Miss Hoare gave way to Miss Brewer who in turn gave way to Miss Bowen. Edel Moore must have been in despair – or, perhaps, by 1929 she was resigned to the situation.

Girls' High School staff, 1927.
Standing, left to right: Misses Mitchell, Synge, Watson, Legassick, Shillito, Hoare, Pearson, Reynolds, Rankin, Horton White, Borries, and Pim; Seated: Miss Dobsom, Miss Moore, and Miss White.

More positively, during the same period Walter Luckman was congratulated on gaining his MA from Birmingham University, Miss Knowles on her First Class Teacher's Diploma, and Miss Greeves on her MSc. Miss Synge, when she left, presented a framed picture of the Infanta Margarita Teresa which was to be awarded to the best form in history, and Miss Dobson gave a Charles II period chair as a gift to the school. She had joined the Girls' High School in 1919 and became Second Mistress in 1925. Four years later she applied for leave-of-absence for a year in order to study and do research (and, probably, to recharge her batteries after 10 difficult years); sadly but predictably her application was turned down. She resigned almost immediately, intending to leave in July 1929. However, during the summer holidays of 1929 Miss Moore was ill again and was unable to return to school until the end of October, so, unusually, Miss Dobson was asked to stay on for a couple of months as Acting Head, in which capacity she actually represented the school at the meeting of Governors in October.

"The new school buildings are in sight at last!" enthuses the girls' magazine of summer 1929. By that year, possibly as a result of pressure from the inspectors who had just visited the school, the building of the new Girls' High School had become something more than a distant and uncertain vision, and this is reflected in the staff changes during the next three year period. They were far fewer. The Pim-Dawes-Taylor changes in the Preparatory Department have been mentioned.

In addition, Miss Morrey and Miss Bowen left, to be succeeded by Miss Cameron and Miss Segger, in maths and gymnastics respectively. The only other change was occasioned by Miss Curry's gaining the Headship of Spalding High School for Girls and being replaced as English teacher by Miss Bumstead and as Second Mistress by Miss Wright.

Buildings, of course, were never off the agenda for long. Routinely, improvements and repairs took place. The boys' cycle shed was extended, and renovation was needed to the ceiling of the landing of the outside staircase. The Hut was extensively redecorated; a Sixth Form room was created at Castle Street; and rats were discovered at both the Girls' School sites. (These were dealt with by a "Rat Officer" who found them under the floor of the dining room at the Victoria Institute.) But principally discussion centred on the lack of a gymnasium and an assembly hall at Wingfield Road, and on the very urgent necessity for a new Girls' High School. An approach by the Governors to the local authority about a gymnasium for the boys was turned down flat in 1927, and a similar approach about a gymnasium and an assembly hall received the same response in 1928.

Nor was there much more promise, initially, of relief for the girls' school. The picture that the Governors painted in requesting a new school building was vivid enough, and, anyway, it was now almost ten years since the site for it had been acquired. At the Victoria Institute there were 94 steps from the lower ground to the upper floor, and there was the best part of a mile between the lower and the upper schools; these factors alone "materially impair the efficiency of the staff". A school split between two sites was not satisfactory; there was no assembly hall and no playground at the upper school, the public park having to be used for recreation; there was no accommodation for cycles at the upper school, and no dining accommodation at the lower school; cloakrooms were inadequate at Castle Street, and some classrooms were subterranean, others little more than corridors. As HMI put it in 1929: "There can be few secondary schools in the country where conditions are so adverse to the development of corporate life and all that it implies." Relief was to be forthcoming, but three more years were to elapse before the opening of the new High School in 1932. In the meantime, Miss Moore, by now quite unwell and walking with some difficulty, moved out of her office on the top floor of the Institute to what had been a staff room on the first floor.

Much has been said of the teaching staffs of the two schools. Non-teaching employees were not numerous in the 1920's, but then, as now, caretakers were people not to be trifled with. George Lewis, who by this time was a well known figure locally, had been in post at the Boys' High School since before the war, and in 1929 his duties changed significantly. Quite extensive work had just been done on levelling and relaying the Gloucester Road playing fields which had always been notoriously wet and uneven. This project completed, it was suggested that someone should be responsible for the playing fields of both establishments, the logical person being the Caretaker of the Boys' High School. This suggestion was adopted, an extra cleaner was employed to cover some of the work that Lewis had been doing, and he took over this dual groundkeeping job in March 1929. For all those to whom I have spoken and who remember him, however, George Lewis was important for a different reason. He operated a sort of semi-unofficial tuck shop from his Caretaker's quarters from which the boys could obtain essential sustenance during the day.

Mrs Greatwood was Caretaker at the Victoria Institute (to be replaced by Mrs. Griffiths at a wage of 21 shillings per week in 1930), and Mr Lucas, of whom we have already heard, at the Lower School in Gloucester Road. Lucas seems to have had a talent for getting into trouble! He is reputed to have been a somewhat irascible man whose pet hate was small children who swung on the heating pipes of the Hut and damaged them. Much of the building was to be distempered internally in the summer of 1928, and he had been instructed by Miss Moore to prepare some of the classrooms for the redecoration. This he had neglected to do, but with his letter of explanation for this omission he also boldly included a request for an increase of wages. This was refused by the Governors and he was reprimanded for his ignoring of Miss Moore's instructions. Undeterred, he next asked for extra payment for the work he had had to do in cleaning up after the decoration. This too was refused. Another request followed, this time for permission (again) to erect a hen-house on the school site. It was refused. And in 1929, Lucas had to be forcefully told once more, as the result of some further misdemeanour, that he simply must carry out all instructions given to him by Miss Moore. Further requests for an increase in wages followed; all were refused. One senses some sort of power struggle behind these skirmishings, but, despite his being repeatedly rebuffed, the Caretaker at Gloucester Road kept coming back for more. Eventually, when the new school opened on the Gloucester Road site, though he applied for the job, he was replaced by H T Symonds, Caretaker at Midsommer Norton Secondary School.

One or two matters of this period are interesting because they strike a somewhat antique note. In 1930, Miss Horton White wanted to move to live in Bath. For this, Governors' permission had to be obtained, and, though it was given, the point was made that it was "on condition that her residence out of town does not interfere with the proper performance of her school duties". Then there were the school caps. Michael Lansdown explains that throughout his time at the Boys' High School there was no uniform requirement, though there was a chocolate coloured blazer, and a red, brown, and silver tie; pupils wore whatever they wished, or whatever they had – except for the uniform hat. There was a junior hat which had broad brown and red stripes, separated by a narrow white stripe, that ran around the hat, and there was a senior hat that had vertical red and brown segments. It must have been the latter that caused young Woodman (later, Sqn Ldr R G Woodman, DSO, DFC) and his friends some embarrassment in Paris when they went there with Walter Luckman on a school trip at Easter 1930. His photograph of a group of Trowbridge High School boys on the banks of the Seine shows them sporting black berets. "We bought French berets because there was anti-red Bolshevik hysteria in Paris at the time and our red school caps attracted attention." So, for this particular group, the red caps gave way to black berets, at least temporarily.

Boys with berets in Paris, 1930.

There are few mentions in the deliberations of those who were charged with the management of the High Schools of discussions about curriculum or curricular innovation. What few there are invariably came from Miss Moore. She it was who changed the pattern of music teaching at the Girls' High School in 1927, opting for less emphasis on individual tuition for instrumentalists and more on group musical appreciation. Despite this move, the successes of girls at the Trowbridge Music Festival were frequently recorded, and Miss Reynolds and Miss Hoare were congratulated on the standard achieved by their pupils in singing and dancing. Again, it was Miss Moore who negotiated the loan of a set of drawings of the Italian School from the Victoria and Albert Museum for girls taking arts and crafts, and it was she who revived the annual Speech Day and Prizegiving that each of the schools held in the Town Hall. In the same innovatory vein, she introduced very early in her headship of the Girls' High School experiments in self-government for the pupils, of which mention has already been made. Like Miss Beale, under whom she had been a pupil, she herself was uncompromising and something of a pioneer.

A well known figure locally who lent his services to, and profited from, the two schools was Mr Slade. He was a farmer and he operated a milk-round in the area; St Augustine's School, in fact, is built on what used to be known as Slade's Field. His connection with the High Schools is that for many years he grazed his cattle on the Gloucester Road field, and after he gave up the tenancy because of the use of the field by the school, he maintained huts there until 1928 in which he kept farm implements. And on the fields of both schools he contracted annually to maintain the hedges and remove the grass as feed for his cattle. Slade appears to have been a good neighbour, and negotiations with him usually went well. Some of the householders in Avenue Road were perhaps slightly less satisfactory as neighbours. To their annoyance, the Governors discovered that wireless aerials had been hitched to some of the trees in the grounds of the Boys' High School by the residents of Avenue Road without permission. Stern warnings were issued. The aerials had either to be removed or permission sought for their retention. Some were removed forthwith, but permission was given for others to stay at a rent of one shilling per year.

An annual distribution of prizes to the meritorious had been instituted early by Mr Henson and Miss Moore at their respective schools, but they seem to have been relatively modest affairs, as befitted two small establishments. The first World War put an end to them, as to many other things, and it was 1927 before these celebrations were revived. In that year, Countess Cairns presented the prizes and gave an address to the girls in the Town Hall, with the Vice-Chancellor of Bristol University doing the same for the boys shortly afterwards. A Prize Fund was established to which parents were invited to contribute two and six pence each. Distinguished local people were called upon – the Master of Marlborough College, the Professor of Education at Bristol University, the Warden of St Andrew's Hall, Reading University, and Col Maxwell-Earle of Hilmarton Manor, for example – until a simpler sort of ceremony evolved because of the national economy campaign in the early 30's.

However, more serious matters of this period – indeed, the most serious matters for many years – were the inspections of both schools by HMI in 1929, and, at last, the establishing of firm plans for the building and opening of a new Girls' High School in 1932, with, simultaneously, the retirement of Miss Moore.

The full inspection of the Girls' High School took place on three days in mid May 1929, and Miss Moore and her staff must have been pleased by it. The Governors certainly were. They congratulated the school on its achievements when they received the final written report some months later. It revealed a dedicated and skilful teaching staff, well led by a Head who showed "courage, devotion, and organising gifts". Virtually everything that the school attempted was adversely affected by the physical conditions under which it had to work, and the inspectors' summary of these difficulties has already been mentioned. The curriculum and its delivery were praised, as was the attitude of the pupils and the general atmosphere of the school. There were criticisms, of course, but they were minor: the commercial class was not satisfactory; there was a tendency, still, for girls to leave as soon as they reached the age of 16, with a consequential depletion in numbers at the top of the school; and the professional competence of one of the teachers was questioned. (This teacher had been asked in the past to attend refresher courses during the school holidays; now the Governors made it a condition of her continuing employment, and the lady in question accepted the suggestion.) But all in all the report was positive and must have been received with satisfaction.

Before looking at the report on the Boys' High School, the similar, but differently labelled, organisations of the two schools, as they were in May 1929, can be compared. Subtracting the Preparatory Department, the class groupings with ages and numbers on roll were as follows:

	Girls		Boys	
11+	IIIA	26	IIA	26
	IIIB	25	IIB	16
12+	IVA	23	IIIA	33
	IVB	23	IIIB	20
13+	Rem A	26	IVA	34
	Rem B	22	IVB	17
14+	Lower VA	16	Lower VA	17
	Lower VB	9	Lower VB	14
15+	Upper V	20	Upper VB	18
16+	VIB	6	Upper VA	3
17+	VIA	3	VI	2

In the girls' school Latin was begun in Rem A, while Rem B did extra English and handwork; commercial subjects were done only in the B stream of Lower V, and at this stage many girls left during the course of the year; Upper V was the School Certificate class; and in the Sixth Form, B was for one-year students, A for the two-year Higher School Certificate course. With the boys, Latin was taught to the A forms from IIIA onwards; Lower VA and Lower VB, with over 40 boys at the beginning of the year, were taught for much of the time as a single unit; Upper VB was the School Certificate class; commercial studies could be undertaken in Upper VA, though younger boys were also admitted; and form VI was for Higher School Certificate.

The inspection of the Boys' High School took place on the first three days of May 1929, and it turned out to be a disaster. Either directly or by implication, the school management, the Governing Body, and the local authority all came in for severe criticism. If the inspectors' written report exudes a lack of enthusiasm for what they saw and heard, their oral report to the Governors at the close of their visit was scathing. The organisation of the school had been adversely affected by a recent fall in numbers – from 258 to 235 in September 1928, and to 200 in the following two terms; there was hope that this trend could be reversed, particularly with the impending closure of the school at Warminster, but it should not have been allowed to happen in the first place. The attention of the Governors in particular was drawn to the very serious leakage of pupils from the school before the age of 16; they were warned to be more vigilant. The distribution of staff was deemed to be far from satisfactory. At the top of the school, 5 boys occupied the full time of 2 teachers; Heal gave 7 periods to a single boy, 8 to 3 others, and had 10 free periods ("an absurd timetable"); elsewhere, 40 pupils were being taught together. The staffing situation, therefore, was seriously out of balance, and overall a reduction in the number of teachers being employed was recommended.

The inspectors also had severe reservations about the curriculum. The commercial course was badly flawed; art, which had been inspected separately some four or five months earlier, was weak, manual instruction – an important area for many of the pupils in the school – did not exist, and physical education was negligible, despite recommendations that had been made in 1926. Although some members of staff were praised for their competence, and the organisation of some subject areas met with approval, there was adverse comment generally about schemes of work, a lack of appropriate materials, and, in some cases, teaching ability. The Governing Body had, for a long time past, been attempting to do something about the lack of an assembly hall and a gymnasium at the Boys' High School, so it is no surprise that the inspectors should pick on these as serious deficiencies; but, additionally, the hut across the back yard was not thought to be suitable as accommodation for teaching, the lecture room was recommended for conversion to a physics lab, one staff room instead of the three tiny rooms in use by staff at that time was thought desirable, the lack of a library or any coherent system of organising reference books caused the inspectors surprise and dismay, and the state of the school lavatories was deplored.

All in all, therefore, His Majesty's Inspectors did not consider the standard of the Boys' High School in 1929 to be satisfactory. The impression that one has is that complacency and a comfortable life had become the order of the day rather than a desire to improve and make the best of what, in some ways, were difficult conditions. The local authority had to take some of the blame for this situation, as did the Governing Body, but the school's management was singled out for attention. HMI stated:

"The Head Master with advancing years was losing some of his vigour; as an organiser and as a Head to his staff he was not as efficient as he used to be....Governing Body after some discussion generally agreed and seemed to be of opinion that the Head Master should retire when he reached the age of 60."

(In fact, Mr Henson remained in post until he was 65!) And the Second Master came in for the same sort of comment.

If this inspection and report were intended to bring about improvement, then they were successful. The criticisms were accepted, and steps were quickly taken to put matters right where this was possible, so much so that, before the end of the year, the Governors felt able to reassure the General Purposes Committee of the County Council that all that was in their power to do had been done.

Albert Marchment's contract was terminated, thus reducing the number of staff at the Boys' High School; penalties for the parents of boys who left the school early were more vigorously enforced; the number of pupils rose; Burns, Lambert, and Hilda Gauntlett went on refresher courses during the summer holidays; shortly afterwards, Jock Burns went on a physical training course at Eastbourne; Pat O'Flaherty was put in charge of art; manual instruction was to be given in the hut across the yard, and a second classroom hut was erected next to it. This, together with other improvements intended to provide better staff and library accommodation, were to cost well over £3,000. No extra member of staff was to be provided for the teaching of manual instruction, and in order to meet another obstacle to his plans raised by the local authority, Mr Henson extended the school's morning session by 45 minutes on a Wednesday and started each morning 5 minutes earlier, thus increasing teaching time by 75 minutes per week.

That things actually did happen after the inspection of the Boys' High School in 1929 is indicated by the following extracts from HMI memos, unsigned and undated, of 1931 and 1932:

"The full inspection has been exceptionally productive of good result (sic) – and that very quickly....Even more important has been the effect on HM and Second Master. HM had clearly been taking things rather easily as his retirement came in sight, and the Second Master had come to be satisfied with a meagre view of his function as a teacher. The change in both is obvious."

And, the following year:

"The last full inspection shook things up a good deal, but one is inclined to feel that the HM who is nearing retirement is not taking life too seriously...."

So the inspection of the Boys' High School in 1929 was a traumatic but salutary experience for many people closely associated with the school.

In the next few years, the number of boys on roll increased significantly, not least because of the closure of the school at Warminster. This resulted in 1931 in 6 pupils joining the school part way through their courses and others starting with the new intake in September. There were some 66 pupils who travelled at this time from Warminster to Trowbridge (33 at each of the two schools), and again the aid of the local railway was invoked. A special train was put on daily, leaving Trowbridge at 4.05 and reaching Warminster at 4.30. Jack Trott, mentioned earlier, says that "no history of the school would be complete without some reference to our journeys to school". He speaks of Melksham, Steeple Ashton, Bratton, Westbury, Warminster, Heytesbury and Codford.

"Most of the students from these places travelled to Trowbridge by train, after first walking to the home station. In my case this was a walk of about three miles, which together with the walk from Trowbridge Station to Wingfield Road made a pretty good start to the day. When this was reversed at night, we had walked something like eight miles; starting at about 7.45 a.m. we often didn't get home until about 5.30. An evening meal, a wash, and homework didn't leave much time for hobbies or for play – perhaps it was as well that television hadn't been invented."

He goes on to give hair-raising details about what happened on the trains between Warminster and Trowbridge, with law enforced effectively but unofficially by the train prefects.

The increase in numbers (from 200 in May 1929 to 281 two years later) led to the appointment of an additional teacher, Mr Hollings, and the recommendations of the inspectors to that of Mr Bradfield for manual instruction in 1931. A new classroom was created in what had been the West Dormitory by dividing it, and such was the press of numbers that the original intention of using one of the spaces thus created as an art room had to be abandoned. Mosscrop replaced Tillotson at both schools as the teacher of the commercial class, and teachers had a 10% pay reduction as one result of the national economy campaign.

*Mr Lambert with the Boys High School cricket XI, 1929.
Standing, left to right: Norman Connor, Mr Lambert, David Payne, Ronald Brain, Jack Pearce, Roy Prosser, Geoffry Warren, Hawkins, Lionel Henson; Seated: middle: Guy Hussey, Bill Udy, Ken Sidey; front: Peter Dunn, Alen Thomas.*

At the Girls' High School, all centred from about 1929 onwards on the building of the new school. It was now definite; plans were drawn; turf was cut and foundations laid; and bricks and mortar began to form the outline of a building. The official opening was to be on 28 September 1932 (though lessons began a couple of weeks earlier), but before the new school came into being there had been a final brief flurry of staff changes. Miss Bumstead, who was still fairly new, had to be replaced – as the new school opened, in fact, by Miss Goodall – and an addition to the staff had been Miss Symmonds (maths) who joined the Girls' High School in a supernumerary capacity in September 1931 when the secondary school at Warminster closed.

The most significant, and the saddest change, however, came with the resignation of Miss Moore from the end of the summer term of 1932. She was able to get to school only rarely in that year, but continued to work from home and actually did a certain amount of teaching there. Increasingly ill and disabled by arthritis, she handed in her resignation in April, and at the end of the school year retired to her new home, 7 Southstoke Road, Bath, where she could receive the constant treatment that was by then necessary. It was her wish that there should be no big presentation ceremony on her leaving, though the Governors made a private presentation to her of Cezanne's "The Village" on 26 July. No one was in any doubt that the Girls' High School in Trowbridge was her creation. "She has made it what it is, and her personality has been strongly impressed upon almost every phase of its life." As she herself wrote: "School...has been the chief interest of my life for twenty years." Not an easy woman to work for, she is still remembered with great respect by those who knew her, not least for fighting her corner unflinchingly in what was still largely a man's world. Her old Head Mistress, Miss Beale, would have been proud of her, and I fancy that Mrs Hart, my Deputy at John of Gaunt some half century later, would also have very much approved of Edel Moore.

A New Broom and a Fading Light:
The Two Trowbridge High Schools: 1932-1937

The new Head Mistress of Trowbridge Girls' High School was Miss J I Field, BA (Oxon), BSc (Econ) (London). She was appointed from 142 applicants, six of whom were interviewed, and she came from the post of Senior History Mistress at King Edward High School for Girls, Birmingham, where she had been since 1927. Prior to that she had taught at St Mary's College in London and been a member of the Society of Oxford Home Students.

Her staff were: Miss Wright, Second Mistress (science and maths), and Misses Borries (French), Cameron (maths), Coe (art), Goodall (English), Greeves (science), Hamer (classics), Knowles (history), Pearson (Preparatory), Segger (PT), Symmons (maths), Taylor (Preparatory), Trafford (music), Horton White (French), and White (geography); and very soon a part-time domestic science teacher, Miss Cubitt, was to join them. Miss Wright had been promoted to the position of Second Mistress after the resignation of Miss Curry in 1931 for the duration of Miss Moore's headship of the school, it being thought at that time that this could not be long because of her continuing ill health, and she took on extra responsibilities during the period of the Head's absence. In 1932, Miss Wright was confirmed in this post for a further year.

As the buildings of the Girls' High School have so far occupied us quite considerably, and as from 1932 onwards they were to change but little, some detail of the design of the new accommodation should be given. The Wiltshire Times of 1 October is precise on the matter.

> "The school is built on a ground plan of 'E' formation, with a 340-feet frontage to the footpath leading from the top of Gloucester Road to Pitman Avenue. This gives the desired south-east aspect to the main frontage which includes all the classrooms – six on the ground floor and four on the first floor. To the left of the vestibule, just inside the central front entrance, is the headmistress's room, and beyond a secretary's office, with small waiting-room behind. To the right is the staff room. Facing the vestibule, on the wall of the corridor which runs the whole length of the building, is the honours board, on which are inscribed the names of girls who have won special educational distinctions since the school's establishment in 1912."
>
> "The classrooms on the ground floor are ranged three on each side of

the vestibule and offices, and at the south end are the biology laboratory, with small greenhouse for the culture of botanical specimens adjoining, while on the south wing of the 'E' is the balance room, to serve both laboratories, and at the extremity of the wing is a spacious chemistry laboratory. At the eastern end is the pupils' entrance, and immediately inside are the cloakrooms, and forming the eastern wing are more cloakrooms, and at the extremity the domestic science room. In the basement is the drying room for pupils' clothing." (This was at the end of the wing, under the domestic science room, and next to the boiler house.)

Crossing the corridor from the vestibule one enters the assembly hall, fitted with a stage for the presentation of plays, and in the centre of the gallery at the rear is the projection room for films. This assembly room is 70' by 35' and forms, with dressing room and gymnasium behind, the central branch of the 'E'. The dressing room serves both the assembly hall for stage plays and the gymnasium, and is fitted with shower baths....In the basement below the gymnasium is the dining room....Adjoining the dining room are the kitchen and servery....Above the vestibule, on the first floor, is the school library, with two classrooms on each side, and small rooms for medical inspection and music, while on the second floor is the art room."

The New Girls' High School, with trees planted in memory of Nelson Haden, 1932.

The new school building, thus described, is readily recognisable today. It was not, in fact, exactly as had been planned. The national economy campaign, which most memorably resulted in a cut in teachers' salaries of 10%, put a halt to all

County building projects, but, as it was already part-built when the campaign was initiated, this particular project went ahead. Nevertheless, some economies were effected. The dining room was to have been an addition to the ground-floor accommodation, and the space that it eventually occupied in the basement was to have been the bicycle store. This had to be relocated in the Hut, which remained where it had always been – by the Gloucester Road gate. The art room, too, was an economy; it was an attic rather than a purpose-built teaching area, inconveniently placed and difficult of access. And the open corridors were a third economy. They were totally unenclosed on both floors, and became wet and snow-bound in bad weather, as those who endured them tell with gloomy relish. I had always thought they were built in this fashion to accord with some notion of fresh air's being healthy and invigorating for young girls, but it was not so. The real reason was meaner and less idealistic! One other detail of the new building is worthy of mention. Above the main front door is the school crest, carved in stone. Some months before the official opening, the staff and pupils had assembled to see this tablet hoisted into place by Eva Selman, the Old Girl whose design for the plaque had been selected from amongst those submitted.

In 1932, there was nothing beyond the chemistry laboratory in the south wing – no third laboratory (G 81) or Remedial Department extension (G 83 and G 87). To the side of the hall was a staff lavatory on the right and a similar room for the Head Mistress to the left, with a cleaner's room next to it; the other present-day toilet accommodation in this area is a later addition.

Many items had been given to celebrate the opening of the new school. The oak panelling round the stage in the assembly hall was the gift of Miss Moore, and Nelson Haden, Chairman of Governors, provided a bronze plaque to record the fact. The Old Girls Association presented a Jacobean oak table and reading stand for the hall, and the assistant staff an oak seat for the vestibule. The Chairman's chair had already been given to the school by Miss Dobson; Mrs Lambert and the former pupils of year IV wanted to give either a clock or a picture for the year IV form room, and the students of the school gave a gift of a set of chairs for the library. The former Second Mistress, Miss Curry, gave 1,000 bulbs to be planted in the grounds; others, including the Governors, who also presented a portrait of Miss Moore, gifted trees and shrubs. Books, too, were given. Many of these gifts of sixty years ago are still in use today, though their origins are now remembered by very few.

Miss S M Fry, JP, MA, late Principal of Somerville College, Oxford, officially opened the new building, the first secondary school built in the County for girls only. The choir sang the school song, followed by Blake's "Jerusalem", the Chairman received a buttonhole and Miss Fry a bouquet of chrysanthemums from Dorothy Luckman, speeches were made, and the new school was open.

The boys beyond the hedge must have watched all these activities with interest and some concern. They had already – prudently – begun to take defensive

OPENING

OF THE

TROWBRIDGE HIGH SCHOOL FOR GIRLS

BY

Miss S. M. FRY, J.P., M.A.,

ON

WEDNESDAY, SEPTEMBER 28th, 1932,
at 2.30 p.m.

Programme for the opening of the new school.

SCHOOL GOVERNORS.

Chairman: Mr. W. N. Haden.

The Rev. E. A. Anthony
Mr. A. W. Austin
Mr. F. Beer
The Rev. J. Morley Davies
The Rev. S. D. M. Davys
The Rev. H. L. Dixon
Mr. H. H. Dyer
Mr. H. Flay
Mr. J. F. Gardiner

Mr. J. S. Marks
Mr. D. Marley
Mr. R. Morgan Smith
Mrs. Pullinger
Mrs. R. J. W. Reeves
Mrs. Swanbororough
Mr. W. C. Thomas
Mrs. F. Wootten

S. Holding.
Secretary to the Governors.

STAFF.

Head Mistress:
Miss J. I. Field, B.A., Oxon, B.Sc., London.

Second Mistress:
Miss M. C. Wright, B.Sc., Hons., Maths., London.

Mistresses:

Miss L. D. Borries, Diplome de Maitresses Secondaires de la Ville de Lausanne. Cambridge Secondary Teacher's certificate.
Miss J. J. M. Cameron, Nat. Sci. Tripos, Cantab.
Miss M. J. Coe, Oxford Art Teacher's Diploma
Miss S. M. Goodall, B.A., Hons. English, Birmingham
Miss F. M. Greeves, M.Sc., Durham
Miss M. D. Hamer, Classical Tripos, Cantab.
Miss E. M. Knowles, History Tripos, Cantab.
Miss O. M. Pearson, Certificate for Junior Teachers, University of Manchester
Miss M. W. Segger, Diploma of Anstey Phyical Training College
Miss A. M. Symmons, B.A., Wales
Miss F. M. Taylor, Diploma of the National Froebel Union
Miss M. E. Trafford, L.R.A.M.
Miss C. M. H. White, B.A., Hons., Modern Languages, London
Miss F. F. White, Camb. Secondary Teacher's Certificate

measures. The ditch that ran along the hedge separating the two communities was cleaned and deepened – "to facilitate drainage". K G Culverhouse recalls the situation: "The playing field of the Girls' High School adjoined that of the boys and mysterious gaps used to appear in the hedge. It was therefore decided to paint white lines a distance from the hedge on each side and the area between the lines became a no-go area for each school except for prefects who were supposed to patrol it. Another perk for the prefects!" As with The Hut, The Hedge looms large in the history and mythology of the two schools.

The new Girls' High School must have totally transformed life for pupils and teachers alike. Flight after flight of stairs had dominated the old Victoria Institute; the noise of the town, and particularly of the market, was an insistent background to all that was said and done; lack of space frustrated everything. A former pupil, Barbara Thomas, records the transformation:

> "The new school was completed in 1932. We had watched it grow when we had our games afternoon in the playing fields surrounding it and when we entered into our inheritance the first impression was one of space and light. No longer hemmed in by buildings, or shut in by high windows, we could see green fields and trees instead of buildings, roof tops and chimneys. There was warmth inside – real warmth, not the inadequate radiators of our old building. Yet, outside the classroom the wind and rain found us hugging the walls to shelter from the elements, as there were no enclosed corridors."

> "For the first time we had a library we could sit in and use, although I believe only the Sixth Form were allowed to remain there for studying. The newly equipped gymnasium was an inspiration even to those normally uninterested in activities of that nature....The science and physics labs were the pride of their users....Perhaps the biggest change in the routine came at morning assembly. Never before had the entire school been able to join together for the morning service. There seemed many more staff and too many girls at first, but in a short time the younger ones were no longer in awe of the upper school girls, and we tolerated the lively and excitable third and fourth formers."

Much has been written about the Preparatory Department that began its life as a mixed class in 1920 and that for virtually the whole of its existence occupied the Hut by the Gloucester Road gate. After years of fluctuating fortune, it closed in 1935.

As late as 1932, the future had looked rosy. The opening of the new Girls' High School building meant that there was room for expansion in the Hut. The income from 68 pupils was more than enough to cover the salaries of 2½ teachers (Miss Pearson and Miss Taylor, plus nineteen periods a week from Miss Segger,

Miss Trafford and Miss Coe – for gymnastics, music and art), so the services of Miss Crudge, a non-Burnham assistant, could be retained as well. Unfortunately, by 1933 things were looking less cheerful. A permanent reduction in numbers now appeared likely because of complications following the abolition of free places and the instituting of the County Entrance Examination. From 68 in 1932, numbers fell in 1933 to 60, by January 1934 to 58, and to 36 by October of that year. Miss Field was asked to prepare a report on the future of the Department, the conclusion of which – inevitably – was that it should close. It could simply no longer be afforded. Miss Pearson, who had been at the school for fourteen years, had her contract terminated in the summer of 1934; Miss Taylor and Miss Crudge finished the following year. The closure of the Preparatory Department, in fact, only anticipated national requirements by a few years and it left the accommodation in the Hut free for alternative use.

During this period, 1932-1937, the numbers of pupils at both schools increased steadily – from 259 to 287 at the Girls' High School, and, more steeply, from 275 to 326 on the other side of the hedge. This led Mr Henson to ask for more staff, so Oscar State was appointed for gymnastics in 1934, and Frank Webb for science and maths the following year. State only stayed for a couple of years before moving on to Bath Technical College, to be replaced by S B Wilson, and in 1937 Hollings went to the inspectorate, with Frank King appointed in his place for English and history. The two most significant changes, however, were the resignations of Jevs Gardner and Jimmy Henson after 31 and 40 years of service to the school respectively, their departures effectively marking the end of an era at Trowbridge Boys' High School. D Brabbon was appointed to teach science; L G Smith became the new Head Master.

Changes at the Girls' High School were more numerous, though not on anything like the scale that had pertained at the Victoria Institute. Miss Hiller replaced Miss Goodall in English in 1937; Miss Greeves gained promotion to Mexborough Grammar School in Yorkshire, to be followed in Trowbridge by Miss New; Miss "Geography" White (as distinct from Miss "Haughty" White) suffered a breakdown and gave way to Miss Luffman; there was a Cameron-Jenkins-Morris change in science, and a Segger - Elliott succession in gymnastics. When the new school opened, a part-time domestic science teacher had been appointed. A year later, the art teacher, Miss Coe, resigned – not in disgust at her cramped accommodation in the attic, but in order to get married. This provided an opportunity for a re-shuffle, so Miss Cubitt became full-time teacher of domestic science, with a new appointee, Miss Davies, joining the school in a part-time capacity for art. In 1935, Miss Cubitt moved from Trowbridge to Nairobi; Miss Ayre replaced her.

Two other staffing matters are worthy of note during this period. What must have been the first teacher exchange for the school took place. The historian, Miss Knowles, went for a year to the Northfield Seminary, Massachusetts, and her counterpart there, Miss Davis, joined the High School.

> "In September, 1936," says the school magazine, "Miss Lincoln Davis came over to discover England. Before school opened she had run up to Scotland and back and was planning a tour to Greece as it seemed so near!....I have one very pleasant picture of her, sitting with her knitting needles flicking and flashing, among girls who must all have been complete strangers to her, tranquil and at home."

So Lincoln Davis became, albeit temporarily, a well liked and respected member of the teaching staff. And Miss Wright was confirmed in her position of Second Mistress, but only on a year-by-year basis. In September 1936, the post went to Miss Borries after the Head had given notice that in future it would be rotated rather than awarded permanently to one person.

With their new buildings, the girls were able to be much more ambitious in all their extra-curricular activities, and in drama in particular. Clubs of various sorts had been established and had flourished under Miss Moore; now they expanded. The Literary and Debating Society, the Science Club, the Music Club, the League of Nations Union, Dr Barnardo's Young Helpers League, and others were active, with a healthy membership and programmes that some sixty years later still look attractive and challenging. Some of them were based on the newly reinstituted House system, as were internal sports activities. Hockey, netball, tennis and rounders were now all possible both within the school and, increasingly, in inter-school competition. From the very earliest days, cricket had been one of the major games played by the girls at the High School. (Indeed, Mr Buchanan had withdrawn his daughter, Gladys, from the school in 1920 because he disliked the rules that restricted leave-of-absence, did not favour the school hat, and objected to the playing of cricket.) After 1932, however, there is no further mention of cricket, and it appears to have died as a games option.

The annual Speech Day was now a larger and grander affair, held as it was in the new assembly hall. Miss Gray, the first High Mistress of St Paul's School, London, did the honours in 1933, and she was followed by the Head Mistress of Colston's Girls' School, Bristol, Countess Cairns, the Marchioness of Lansdowne, and the Dowager Countess of Radnor, all of whom presented prizes and addressed the pupils (doubtless) in terms suitable to the occasion. "The Taming of the Shrew" (with Margaret Adams, now returned from her private school, as Bianca) was the first dramatic presentation in the new hall, in 1934; others followed. Laurence Housman read selections from his own work. And in addition to educational trips at home, the girls now began to travel abroad. Miss Borries was the instigator of these adventures, with a group going to Paris at Easter 1936, and another group setting up a pupil-exchange programme with a school at

Rheydt, near Cologne, the following year. Of these pre-war years at the two schools, and of the girls' exchange with the German school, Bob Randall writes:

> "The threat of war was ever with us, it seemed. True, in the interests of friendship between nations, there was a visit from a party of German girls from Rheydt, with a reciprocal visit by a group of girls from the Girls' High School. One of the girls, Brigitte Klavitter, stayed with us, and my sister Joan stayed with her parents in Germany. Rudolph Hess invited the girls to have tea with him. I acquired a pen-friend from the area, Fritz Reiter, subsequently killed, I believe, on the Russian front. Yet nothing rolled back the clouds."

War was still a year or two away, and in the meantime the girls of the High School had a varied and stimulating menu of extra-curricular opportunities.

More prosaically, the train from Melksham was not satisfactory, but the railway authorities were helpful in re-timing it so that the girls were no longer late for morning prayers. Negotiations with the Caretaker were less positive. Mr Symonds' performance was repeatedly questioned; he was reprimanded for felling a tree in the school grounds without permission, though, a few months later, several more had to be felled – officially – as they were found to be dangerous; finally, he was sacked in March 1936 following a neglecting of his duties that resulted in radiators and heating pipes bursting in the Hut over the previous Christmas holidays. Fortunate in many ways, the Girls' High School had so far been singularly unfortunate in its Caretakers. Mr Todd succeeded Symonds in the post.

From being petitioners in the matter of buildings, the Girls' High School now found itself able to distribute largesse, the boys being the beneficiaries. They were allowed to hold their Speech Day in the new hall of the girls' school for the first time in December 1933, and the practice continued thereafter. Even greater interest, however, centred upon the future of the Hut. Adjustments had been possible after the opening of the new Gloucester Road building, but in 1935 the closing of the Preparatory Department coincided with there being about fifty more boys on roll in Wingfield Road than there had been some three years earlier, these two factors combining to make the provision of extra accommodation for the boys both essential and practicable. Possibilities were explored. The Hut could be split, half going to the boys' site and half being retained by the girls. It should all stay where it was, but be given over entirely for use by the boys. Eventually, a compromise was reached. The total accommodation consisted of one large room with a changing room and store, five classrooms, one cloakroom, and one cycle store. The latter two rooms were to be thrown together to form a larger cycle store for the girls, and the next two classrooms were to go to them, redesigned, as a large needlework room and a small staffroom. The rest was to be used by the boys – three classrooms and an assembly hall/gymnasium. Extra lavatories were to be provided and a path built from the boys' school to the near end of the Hut.

Immensely welcome though it was, the new Girls' High School building was not perfect. The very poor accommodation for art has been mentioned, and there were also the matters of the windows and the verandahs. Only six months after the opening of the school, Miss Field drew attention to the dangers of the folding windows on the corridor side of the classrooms. When opened and folded, they projected half way across the corridor at about head height and posed a real threat to the unwary. I remember them well! They were still there, still cracking pupils' heads, in 1991, so Miss Field was clearly unsuccessful in her protest. (The present Head, with no respect for tradition, has had them permanently secured and has thus eliminated the hazard.) The disadvantages of the open verandahs, too, were obvious. They gave an attractive, cloister-like look to the buildings, but were abominably vulnerable to bad weather. The Head's appeals for them to be enclosed initially met with no response until, late in 1937, five bays on the first floor (on the left as one faces the back of the building) were provided with a full outside wall at a cost of £85.

The extension of the site of the two High Schools was effectively accomplished very early in 1935 when the County Council acquired ownership of two fields adjoining the existing playing fields. The next couple of years saw them levelled and fenced, with a few of the trees on the banks felled, cleared of some of their hedges and ditches, and generally prepared for use as school playing fields. A shelter and a shed for games equipment was was put on the higher field; the hedge between the two schools was made good. It was, therefore, in the late 1930's that the present school site, with its two major buildings, and its extensive fields and lawns and gardens, really begins to be recognisable.

Of course, there were other matters which, though important at the time, now have a mere curiosity value. The Trowbridge Radio Relay Exchange applied for permission to erect two poles so that they could carry light wires over the school grounds. They were refused. Miss Segger was congratulated on the excellent report given her department by the specialist PE inspectors who came to look at it in 1934; Miss Trafford, too, was officially commended for the pupils' achievements at the Devizes Music Festival. And the administration of school dinners, then as now, took up an inordinate amount of managerial time and energy.

Finally, examinations had to be sat and passed if pupils' ambitions were to be realised and the school's reputation maintained. Results varied year by year, as results are apt to do, but those of the summer of 1933 can be taken as fairly typical for the Girls' High School at this time: two candidates successful out of two in the Higher School Certificate of the University of Bristol; thirteen successful candidates at the London General School Certificate, of whom four matriculated, two gaining distinctions, both in French; and three candidates added further subjects to existing certificates.

The national economy campaign of 1932 brought the free place system to an end. There was now a County Entrance Examination under which County Junior Scholarships were awarded to a number of pupils who had no fees to pay at all. These were not to number more than 30% of the previous year's intake. Others who reached a satisfactory standard in the Entrance Examination were awarded places, but on a sliding scale of fees – three, six, nine, or twelve guineas annually. So, to take 1933 again as being a typical year, 57 new pupils were admitted to the Boys' High School, 20 with County Junior Scholarships, 30 who paid 3 guineas, 2 who paid 6 guineas, 1 who paid 9 guineas, and 4 who paid 12 guineas. For many boys and girls, waiting for the results of the County Entrance Examination, later known simply as the Eleven Plus, was an anxious time because, as Paddy, in Maureen Duffy's novel *That's How It Was*, tells so vividly, the opportunity of High School education would have gone had either the exam been failed or had it been passed with a fee of any sort to be paid.

The Boys' and Girls' High Schools had decided to share a Secretary, so in the Spring of 1934 a Miss Holman was appointed for a day and a half at each school for secretarial duties. A year later she had resigned and was succeeded by a Miss Edmund who lasted only a few weeks, to be followed in her turn by Mrs Thomas. She, it was hoped, would provide secretarial assistance on a more permanent basis. A more significant departure was that of George Lewis who had been Caretaker at the Boys' High School, and joint Groundsman of the two schools latterly, for twenty three years. It was decided that, with his going in October 1936, the jobs of Caretaker and Groundsman would be split, so the appointments of W G Stevens as Caretaker and S F Jones as Groundsman were made; their wages were £2 per week in each case, rising to £2.5.0 after six months.

The special allowance of £20 a year that the Second Master, L W Heal, received in that post was the subject of much debate during 1935 and 1936. The Governors felt, prompted, doubtless, by Mr Henson, that the post of Second Master was worth £40 rather than £20 a year, and an appeal for his allowance to be increased not just to £40 but to £50 in view of his many years of service to the school, was made. Initially the suggestion was rejected, but eventually a concession was made and Heal's special allowance was raised to £25, with further increases agreed of £5 every two years until a maximum of £50 was reached. Beyond this, despite protests from the Governors, County would not go. Miss Wright's allowance was increased from £20 to £25 at the same time, but her successor as Second Mistress, Miss Borries, was appointed at the original figure of £20.

A depressingly repetitive theme during these years, as it had been for many years past, was the difficulty posed for the boys' school by the lack of both an assembly hall and a gymnasium, but again, as in the past, all appeals by Henson and his Governors fell on deaf ears. Teaching accommodation at Wingfield Road was now very tight and, in certain areas, sub-standard. For example, the huts across the back yard were really quite unsuited for the purpose to which they were put. After the inspection of 1929, one part had been pressed into service as a woodwork room (the left hand section as one faced it from the school), the central section was what passed for a library, and the right hand hut was the Sixth Form room. The Sixth Form often worked in the library, with the noise of the woodworkers to one side, the clatter of the typewriters of the Commercial Sixth on the other, and the uproar of the junior footballers just behind them on the small field. As if this were not sufficient handicap, the rooms themselves were quite inadequate. Michael Lansdown recalls how Mr Henson used on occasion to address the school, assembled in the yard, from the steps of these huts, and how the Sixth Form, unprepared for this manoeuvre, found themselves trapped in the library, unable either to get out or participate in what was happening. The steps from which the Head spoke were made of wood; by 1934 they were rotten and dangerous, so they were replaced by a more substantial concrete flight of steps. But more significant changes were on the way.

The closing of the Preparatory Department in 1935 had brought some extra rooms to the boys, but it was Jimmy Henson's retirement in the autumn of 1937, and, with it, the freeing of the main school building from its function as a dwelling house, that made the biggest difference. For the first time a real library became a possibility. This was created in what had been the bedrooms at the front of the house – the area that many years later at the John of Gaunt School we used for Sixth Form private study and that we designated W 6 and W 8. The woodwork room in the hut across the yard was then extended by taking into it what had been the so-called library. This still left a hutted classroom next door.

Thomas Jevons Gardner and Joseph Warner Henson retired at the end of the summer term 1937, the one after 31 and the other after 40 years at the school.

Jevs Gardner, who was also known to the boys by another nickname, was an unusual man. In 1929, the inspectors wrote:

"The senior science master, though a non-graduate, is widely read, and in teaching his subject he shows a resourcefulness that is quite unusual. Yet past examination results have been poor....There is a good deal of home-made apparatus for teaching physics – most of it the outcome of the personal skill and ingenuity of (Mr Gardner)."

Almost all those who were taught by him and who still remember him say that he was not a good class teacher of adolescent boys and that his discipline in particular left a great deal to be desired; they all admit, too, to treating him

Retirement presentations to Mr Henson and Mr Gardner by former pupils A B Turner (in blazer) and J H P Pafford (concealing presentation binoculars behind his back!)

rather badly. But again they all say the same about him as a person – that he was a very kindly man who always strove to do his utmost for his pupils and who, unlike some of his colleagues, was clearly interested in them as people. Jack Trott says," He was a very practical man who had made much of the apparatus that he used in class, and affirmed that his projector, made out of a blackened biscuit tin and a cocoa tin, together with a second-hand lens he had picked up in Bath, worked better and was more reliable than that provided by the local authority." He was "something of an odd-job man", according to Jack Pafford, an opinion born out by his having at one time been games secretary and teacher of music. Michael Lansdown recalls that it was he who played the piano when, infrequently, a formal assembly was held. The partition between the two classrooms on the ground floor of the east wing would be pushed back, Jevs would come in with a pile of science catalogues which he used to raise the height of the seat at the piano, and he would play for the singing of a hymn. Not so much a pedagogue or odd-job man, perhaps, as an enthusiast, an amateur, an ingenious physicist. At the retirement party, it was Jack Pafford who presented a pair of field-glasses to Mr Gardner as a leaving-present.

    How does one sum up the career of someone who taught for forty five years, forty of them at the same school and as Head of that school? There can be no doubt that, in the early days at least, Jimmy Henson was responsible for the good name that the school acquired in the town. He made it what it was. One former pupil describes him as "erudite, firm, and kind". Another says that he was a good disciplinarian, in full control of his staff and the boys, and a good administrator and teacher. "You were left in no doubt about who was boss." But it is perhaps inevitable over a span of forty years in the same post that something of the freshness and the challenge goes out of one's approach to one's job, and a sort of complacency sets in. Certainly, one former pupil to whom I have spoken remembers Mr Henson with something less than respect, and this accords with the opinion of the inspectors in 1929, which has already been mentioned.

Tales, many of them apocryphal, abound about the eccentricities of Head Masters. Can it be true that pupils in form IIA, if they stood on the radiator in their form room on a Saturday morning, could actually look across from the upper part of the window into the Hensons' bedroom and see their Head Master asleep in bed? (Bob Randall swears it is true. "His wrath when he awoke and saw the faces at the window was immense. He came storming up, dressing-gown over his pyjamas, and caned the whole class.") And is it true that when he taught trigonometry to LVB he was followed into the classroom by his cat, Felix, who jumped on to and settled on the desk of some boy who was then excused all written work for the rest of the lesson? Whatever the truth of these matters, Jimmy Henson's retirement on 27 July 1937 was an occasion of some moment.

On 17 July, the Old Boys Society made a presentation. A B Turner, a former School Captain, presented the Head with a grandfather clock dating from 1830, a cheque, and a book in which were written the names of the subscribers; Mrs Henson was given a black handbag. A former pupil wrote a glowing tribute for the ceremony, saying that "we remember Mr Henson as a good singer of such songs as 'The Old Shako'. He has reached high Masonic rank and has been hail fellow with many townies." Elsewhere, he was described as "one of the most beloved Headmasters of all time. He never did things which we don't like Headmasters to do; he never crept around with rubber soles on; he always managed to do the right thing in the right place." All this took place on the front lawn after tea, 170 guests sitting down to tea in two classrooms, the whole thing supervised by Mrs Henson. A cricket match between the Old Boys and the school began in the afternoon and finished in the evening, but a sing-song that had been arranged had to be cancelled because of the late finish of the match.

During the following week, W Nelson Haden, Chairman of Governors, together with Miss Field and Miss Moore, presented Mr Henson with a silver salver; the staff of the school gave him an antique bureau and his wife a cut-glass stuart posy bowl; and on 27 July, the boys made a presentation to him of a barometer, with a silk umbrella for Mrs Henson, and a tin of salmon (large) for Felix, the Hensons' cat.

The Pre-War Years:
The Two Trowbridge High Schools: 1937-1939

L G Smith, MA (London), BSc (London), a married man, aged 34, who came to Trowbridge from St Marylebone Grammar School where he had been Senior Physics Master, was the new Head of the boys' school. His assistant staff numbered fifteen; with their dates of appointment to the school, they were: Messrs Heal (1907), Luckman (1914), Downing (1919), Griffiths (1919), Beams (1919), Powell (1920), Lambert (1920), O'Flaherty (1921), Burns (1921), Bradfield (1930), Webb (1935), Wilson (1937), Brabban (1937), King (1937), and Miss Gauntlett (1916). Mosscrop (1931) was a part-time teacher of commercial subjects. Leslie Smith very quickly let it be known that changes would be made, the first being his intention immediately to bring the boys' school into line with the girls by working a five-day week, Monday to Friday, and dispensing with Saturday morning school. Matches would henceforth be played on Saturdays. He noted, too, the lack of changing and washing facilities in the school, but this defect could be remedied by the alterations that he envisaged in the layout of the main building.

The central section of the Boys' High School building changed in 1937 from being domestic accommodation, the home of the Head Master and his family, to becoming a working part of a boys' day school, and the principal alteration that this involved has already been mentioned – the conversion of the first floor rooms at the front of the building to a school library. There were other major changes, however, some of which provided changing and showering areas, and these directed the use to which the building was put in the future.

As one faced the central front door of the school, the four principal rooms, clockwise from the left of the door, were the Secretary's office (now the Head's office), the staffroom (now divided into a meter room and the Head's Secretary's office), the old kitchen which now became a staff cloakroom, toilet, and shower (still serving the same purpose today and containing, I suspect, the same fitments!), and the Head's office (now the Admin. Officer's room). To the left of them, what had been the original schoolroom, which later became the woodwork room and, later still, a classroom, was converted into a changing room, a cloakroom, and a lavatory and cloakroom combined; these stretched back to the physics lab (W 33) and the chemistry lab (W 35). Entry to these two latter rooms was from the yard as the corridor that now gives access to them was a later addition. The dining room remained where it had been – in the area of today's general office, somewhat extended – but behind it the complex of larders and pantries and other domestic rooms gave way to a second changing room, showers, a toilet and the heating room, accommodation not very different from today's provision in that wing of the ground floor.

Upstairs, the old West Dormitory contained two classrooms; next to them was a small Sixth Form room (W 2) with the new library across the corridor. The first classroom in the old Long Dormitory (W 14) was separated from the doorway that gives access to it by a partition, and this was now raised to ceiling level. At the other end of the wing was another classroom (W 18), and the space between these two rooms, awkward in 1937 as it still is today, was changed from a bathroom and lavatory to a small classroom and projection room. Across the yard was the workshop and, adjacent to it, a hutted classroom. There was other accommodation, as we have seen, in huts further up the site.

New broom that he was, Mr Smith also had windows mended, repairs effected to the roof, and electric bells operating in the workshop across the yard and in the Hut. He made noises about the desirability of a school uniform for the boys, of whom there were now 278, with a small increase likely in September 1938; but before the new school year, a full inspection of the Boys' High School took place.

The inspection of 1938 resulted in a report far less critical than had been that of 1929, and what criticism there was centred on the deficiencies of the buildings. Although the benefits of recent alterations were acknowledged, HMI were still unhappy about much of the accommodation. The "excellent provision" of 1913 had become a "serious inadequacy" by 1938. "It is no exaggeration to say that in almost every department the serious inadequacy of the accommodation makes the efficient conduct of the school either much more difficult or quite impossible." There was no assembly hall; the two laboratories in the main building were too small and were ill-equipped, and the third, in the Hut, had no gas; the gymnasium was also in the Hut, was too small, and was unsuitable in other ways; the art room (a part of the first floor of the east wing) was sub-standard; the workshop was in a hut across the yard and was subject to extremes of temperature; the dining room was too small to be used for the serving of cooked meals; and the classrooms, though sufficient in number, were scattered, three being in huts and several only having access through other rooms. All in all, then, it was a grim picture. Suggestions as to what was required were made, and the need for a comprehensive, long-term plan of the building requirements of the school was stressed. Ambitious plans for the future were indeed produced following the inspectors' visit, but the outbreak of war shortly after ensured their demise.

There was some concern – still – about the number of boys who left the school before they were 16, but anxiety on this score was less than it had been in the past. The academic qualifications of the teaching staff overall were considered to be rather low; on the other hand, "the teaching generally is good and in several cases it is outstanding". For the future, it was recommended that teachers, experienced or not, should serve a period of probation after appointment before being confirmed in their posts. The 9 boys in the Sixth Form were fewer than was desirable, but an increase here looked likely, and with 8 going to higher education in the past three years (4 to universities and 4 to training colleges) the situation was satisfactory.

Leslie Smith was probably reasonably happy with and unsurprised by the results of this full inspection. What he had already achieved in less than a year was recognised; some positive features were identified; and weaknesses of which he would already have been very much aware were highlighted with a view to remedial action's being taken. In addition to the major weaknesses mentioned above, there was huge concern over the buildings, the fact that some 69% of the pupils left without gaining the School Certificate, and comments like the following: "The almost complete absence, apart from games, of any out-of-school activities, hobbies, or training for leisure is a regrettable feature". But, like house surveys, inspectorial reports tend to emphasise the defects rather than extol the merits.

The issue of school uniform for the boys produced some heat – not from pupils, or parents, or Governors, all of whom approved of the proposals, but from the Trowbridge Chamber of Commerce and the National Association of Outfitters. The Head Master had put the supply of uniforms out to tender, the contract being won by Salaman of Leicester, who agreed to supply grey flannel suits in different sizes, including an embroidered badge, caps, ties, and blazers in the new school colours, yellow and blue. Uproar resulted. It was held that the contract should have gone to local tradesmen. The Head's action was dictatorial, and dark suspicions surfaced. The NAO, quoting a similar case reported in the Bath and Wilts Chronicle and Herald, wrote that "there (was) a commission or rake-off on those goods....It was a spirit of Hitlerism that was entering into the schools today." Nevertheless, Mr Smith and his Governors weathered the storm, and school uniform was introduced in September 1939.

There were changes, too, in school organisation. Parallel forms were introduced in the first and second years, with an arts or science bias – L for Latin and S for science – differentiating the two forms from year three upwards. The commercial class was disbanded, with Mosscrop's contract being terminated at the end of the summer term 1938. And new buildings became a possibility. Money – £3,000 – had been put in the budget for 1938/39 for the building of a new dining hall and kitchen, the hope and expectation being that this very welcome initiative would not prevent some of the other improvements recommended by the inspectors from taking place also. With no cooked lunches possible in the existing accommodation, it looked as though, with a new dining hall, some 50 could be provided daily at an estimated cost of 6d. So things were happening at the Boys' High School.

Bob Randall recognised the changing climate of these pre-war years.

"When the new Head Master, Mr Smith, came, the colours were changed to blue and yellow, and grey flannel trousers were introduced as the school dress....The school remained in my time a mixture of the traditional original school and a mixture of huts, but before the war, work started on the site of the old garden on a dining hall, and a welcome addition to the school facilities in the late thirties was the installation of showers – a deficiency which had previously dismayed visiting teams, especially after a muddy game of soccer. With the first term of war, a big new wireless was provided for instructional programmes."

At the beginning of 1938, there were 277 pupils on roll at the Girls' High School, with about the same number expected in September. Miss Elliott and Miss Knowles (gymnastics and history) resigned, to be replaced by Miss Whitehouse and Miss Senior, but what seems to have been a quite unexpected development was the resignation of the Head Mistress, Miss Field, when she was appointed to the headship of the Cambridge County High School.

Joyce Field had only been in Trowbridge for six years. She had come in very favourable circumstances; her achievements, even so, were considerable. In addition to driving the school forward in ways made possible for the first time by the new building, she had been responsible for the forming of a Parents and Teachers Association, and had taken a particular interest in such areas as the curriculum, the welfare of her girls and her staff, the library, and the garden. There is a positive feel about the time of her headship. Nevertheless, to me at least, she remains a shadowy and elusive figure. Those who remember her speak of her as being "austere" and "reserved", but Margaret Bruce-Mitford found her extremely kind in both her professional and her private concern for her when she was in some difficulty. Miss Field eventually retired to Bradford on Avon, initially to a house in Newtown and, later, to sheltered

*Miss J I Field,
Head Mistress, 1932-1938.*

housing at Bethell Court on the Winsley Road. Here she is remembered as tending to keep herself to herself. She died in hospital in the early 1980's.

Her successor from 1 January 1939 was Kay Dawes. Miss K M S Dawes, BA (Oxon), had been a mathematics lecturer at the Froebel Educational Institute in London since 1937, and, prior to that, Vice-Principal of Wychwood School, Oxford, a small boarding school for girls. She inherited the following staff: Miss Borries (Second Mistress and French), and Misses Wright (maths and science), Ayre (domestic science), Davies (art), Whitehouse (gymnastics), Hiller (English), Hamer (classics), Senior (history), Luffman (geography), New (biology), Trafford (music), Horton White (French), Morris (maths and science), and Symmons (maths). Miss Morris became Mrs Holman late in 1938 and the Governors had to search about to see whether they had a rule relating to the employment of married women. They felt able to renew her contract provisionally until the end of the summer term 1939, then for a further term, at which time Mrs Holman resolved their difficulty by resigning. She was replaced by Miss Legh. Miss Luffman left, to get married also, and Miss Edwards was appointed for geography. An addition to the staff late in 1939 was Miss Buckland, whose appointment on probation was agreed by the Education Committee after considerable delay, to allow courses "alternative to those on the academic side" to be provided – an indication of the widening ability-range of entrants to the Girls' High School – and in September Miss Wright was restored to her position of Second Mistress, vice Miss Borries.

Despite these moves, the principal thought in everyone's mind during 1938 and 1939 was the threat of war. Preparations had to be made. As early as June 1938 discussions took place between Heads and the local authority about air raid precautions. First aid equipment was provided; surveys for the siting of trenches took place in the playground of the girls' school and on the playing field of the boys', with instructions about the pattern to which they should be dug; trench-digging implements were purchased; and the Boys' High School closed for a couple of days for the billeting of children from East and West Ham to be arranged. All members of staff at the two schools were either trained, or were in process of being trained, in first aid, and the boys' school was designated as a wardens' post for West Trowbridge. It was decided some months before the actual outbreak of war that, in the event of a national emergency, both schools would close for a week whilst those evacuated from other areas were absorbed into the county, that the buildings would be used as reception premises for evacuees pending their allocation to billets, and that the teaching staff would help the officials conducting the evacuation. War was declared on 3 September 1939.

The Governing Body decided new procedures for the conducting of their business in war time. The meetings of the House Committees were suspended, full Governors' meetings were to be held once a term, and an Emergency

Committee was formed to take urgent decisions at short notice. Evacuees arrived – 21 to the Boys' and 49 to the Girls' High School; doors and walls were sandbagged; discussions took place about whether windows should be protected by tape or fine wire mesh; about an acre of ground at each school was set aside for use as allotments; and it was decided that Speech Days would be very simple affairs for the time being, with no entertainment provided. The two Heads now had problems to contend with of which neither they nor anyone else had had any experience.

Exigencies of Wartime:
The Two Trowbridge High Schools: 1939-1947

The strains of life for a working-class family in wartime Trowbridge, and the pressures felt by a child hoping for a grammar school place, are strikingly recalled in Maureen Duffy's novel, *That's How It Was*. The book is a novel and not an autobiography, but it is as impossible not to recognise Miss Dawes in it as it is not to be carried back to the depressing atmosphere of war that affected everyone's lives in the early 1940's – the shortages, the blackout, the presence of "the Yanks", with the children pestering them for money and other favours, and, in "Wortbridge", County Hall hiding under its camouflage canopy – "a netful of brown and green seaweed". The significance of school to her, of its being another and a more real world into which she could escape every day, is powerfully remembered in her introduction to the book.

> "Entering Trowbridge High School for Girls I was absorbed into a different world every morning....The education we were given was in the most enlightened liberal humanist tradition which exactly suited my needs and temperament....Life at home was nasty, brutish and might be short; it was no wonder that the pleasures of learning, of music and the visual arts took me over. Above all of course there was literature in Latin, French and English. We were encouraged to write poetry, short stories and essays, some of which found their way into that first publication outlet for so many writers, the school magazine. Poetry in particular was a source of the intensest pleasure."

Maureen Duffy's tribute to those who taught her is a generous one. It being wartime, however, Miss Dawes' preoccupations were sometimes peculiarly mundane. "Fortunately for me," she wrote,

> "during the war Trowbridge got evacuated families, not, as had been expected, unaccompanied children. So we did not have to share our buildings, and I was not faced with planning a shift system and getting girls in for half a day. On one occasion, however, we had to bed down some hundred or more mothers and children on blankets on the hall floor. Five expectant mothers were segregated in the changing rooms. Crying babies were expertly extracted by one of the Boys' staff, soothed by the Gym Mistress and returned to their mothers."

There is not much of educational theory, liberal or otherwise, in such a situation.

At both High Schools, developments of all sorts were put on hold for the duration of the war, and energies were bent to protecting the buildings from bombs and to securing the safety of the pupils and staff during school hours. Wire netting and anti-splinter paint covered windows; sandbagging took place; more evacuees arrived, this time from Tottenham High School – 48 boys and 19 girls, together with five members of staff; the names of the schools were removed from external notice boards so that potential invaders might be confused as to where they were; and the army authorities sought permission to site a hut for the storage of explosives just behind the big bank at the south west corner of the Girls' High School – a proposal to which the Governors did not see fit to agree!

Firewatching duties had to be carried out at both schools during hours of darkness. This proved not to be a problem at the boys' school as it was a wardens' post, with three wardens on duty every night and sixteen members of staff either Civil Defence Workers or members of the Home Guard; the situation at the girls' school was less easy as there was no compulsion for women to undertake these duties. Nevertheless, volunteers were forthcoming for at least a skeleton presence. A scheme was introduced whereby help could be given to farmers by boys at school, and Mr Smith was able to report that, in the summer of 1940, 24 pupils did 80 pupil weeks of work from their camp on the Strattons' farm at Kingston Deverill. The schools themselves remained open and provided a makeshift programme during the summer holidays for those who wished, or needed, to attend; and Miss Dawes, as an experiment, decided to keep poultry on the premises to supplement supplies for the canteen. In 1941, the necessity for strict school uniform was waived for the boys for the duration of the war, and 909 Squadron of the Air Training Corps was formed, with 73 cadets under the command of Flying Officer Smith, Pilot Officer Beams, and Pilot Officer Webb. (Their promotion to the ranks of Flight Lieutenant and Flying Officers soon followed.)

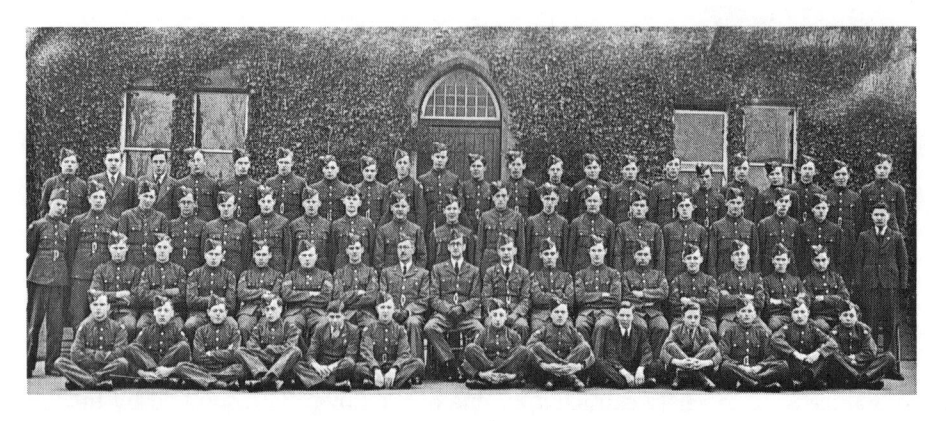

ATC Squadron 909, with (left to right) F/O Beams, Flt Lt Smith, and F/O Webb, c. 1942.

Many former pupils and members of staff will have their own memories of the Trowbridge High Schools in wartime. Kenneth Rogers, recently retired from the post of County Archivist, was one such pupil, and he told me of the vivid memory he has of one day standing on the school playing field, looking up, and seeing a squadron of Fairey Swordfish flying over the school, each with its torpedo slung beneath the fuselage, on their way, he believes, to attack the German battle-cruisers Gnaisenau and Scharnhorst, and the Prince Eugen, as they left the safety of Brest to steam northwards to home waters.

A War Savings Campaign, organised by Mr Lambert, was promoted; a Red Cross Fund opened; senior pupils from both schools provided voluntary labour for the affixing of contex containers to some 3,500 gas masks; and news constantly and depressingly came in of former pupils who had died whilst serving in the armed forces. Bob Randall remembers that time.

"First aid instruction was given. It seemed possible that the school could be bombed. In the event, there was very little damage done by bombing in Trowbridge. The Guards' camp off the Frome Road suffered a bit, but with few casualties; the then disused canal towards Staverton was breached; and, worst of all, in an early-morning raid, two girls seeking refuge from London were killed when the British Legion Club by the Town Bridge was hit."

That was an incident witnessed at first hand by Lennie Lambert who was on Home Guard duty on the Bridge at the time.

So the early 1940's were unusual years for those charged with running schools, as they were for almost everyone in the country, but by late 1944 or early 1945 the clouds were beginning to lift, and, although the war was not yet spent, thoughts were turning to the future and the resumption of a more normal sort of life. The school-based Air Training Corps, for example, closed down at the end of 1944; the blast walls that had been built for protection at both the girls' and the boys' schools were demolished; and the Governors felt able to abandon their Emergency Committee in favour of a re-establishing of their peace-time procedures early in 1945.

Wartime or not, His Majesty's Inspectors still went about their business, and their business took them, in October 1943, to the Girls' High School. The number of pupils on roll at this time was just over 370 – at which level, or a little below, it remained consistently throughout the decade – so there had been an increase in the number of staff employed in the two or three preceding years. Misses Wright, Borries, Hiller, Hamer, Senior, Trafford, Horton White, and Symmons remained from 1939 or before, and Miss Drummond (as a second teacher of domestic science) and Miss Cooper (for junior English and history) had been added. In art, Miss Davies had given way to Miss Cunnington and she, in turn, to Mrs Kinnear; Miss Ward had replaced Miss Whitehouse in gymnastics, and Miss Crawley-Boevey followed Miss Edwards in geography; Miss Barrington succeeded Miss New in biology, and another Miss Ward replaced Miss Cook who herself had replaced Miss Buckland. Miss Wood took over from Miss Ayre in domestic science. The commercial class still survived, and since as long ago as 1934 it had been in the care of a Miss Matthews of Bath after Mr Mosscrop had had his contract terminated; she was now replaced by Mrs Loram.

The report submitted by HMI after their visit was "satisfactory" (that anonymous, insipid, uncommitting term so favoured by teachers in reports on their pupils), but sufficiently so for Miss Dawes and her staff to be congratulated by the Governors on the result of the visit. The inspectors liked the buildings, except for the art room, and the uses to which they were being put; minor improvements were needed to the library and the gym, and the look of the buildings generally would have been enhanced by a better use of pictures. The length of lessons was thought to be too short, pupils were still leaving too early in too great numbers, and too few were going on to higher education. The dropping of some subjects at an early stage was seen to be a weakness – Latin particularly, and maths in the fourth and French in the fifth years being examples – and the beginning of commercial work before general education had been completed was also criticised. On the other hand, the recent introduction of the Oxford School Certificate examination for weaker pupils was thought to be a good idea, the range of clubs and extra-curricular activities was commended, and the relationship between staff and pupils was felt to be happy. Some excellent teaching was seen, particularly in PT, domestic science, and by the younger teachers generally; and the planning of work, except in mathematics, was deemed to be sound. Mathematics, both in its organisation and its delivery, was criticised, and Latin, history, and French provoked some unhappiness.

Miss Dawes' defence of her staff was vigorous – and probably justified. Miss Senior, the teacher responsible for history, was very good indeed, and the inspectors had done her less than justice. Miss Hamer (Latin) was a quiet, rather nervous person who would certainly under-perform when being inspected. Many girls in the school came from illiterate backgrounds; French in particular, therefore, posed difficulties for the teacher. And the maths teaching was better than the report suggested, both Miss Wright and Miss Symmons being successful in their own ways with certain sorts of girl. The general tenor of the report, however, must have given pleasure and was a cause for optimism.

In the next three or four years, more staff changes took place, a number of them with important implications for the future. In 1944, Miss Thomas came to teach English in place of Miss Hiller, art went, first, to Miss Strain and then to Miss House, and the second domestic science post passed from Miss Drummond to

Miss Wilkinson before being taken by Mrs Dobson and then by Miss Hazell in 1946. In 1945, Miss Cadwallader replaced Miss Hamer, Miss Metheringham replaced Miss Crawley-Boevey, Miss Haines took over from Miss Legh, Miss Goldie-Smith and then Miss Sanders from Miss Barrington, Miss Turner from Miss Ward in gymnastics, and Miss Richards from Miss Cooper. Miss Morris arrived in 1946 to replace Miss Senior, and Miss Urquhart and Miss Quine in 1947 in place of Miss Turner and Miss Wood. So, at Easter 1947, the staff of the Girls' High School was: Miss Dawes (Head Mistress), Misses Wright (Second Mistress), Borries and Horton White (French), Trafford (music), Symmons (maths), Hazell and Quine (domestic science), House (art), Thomas (English), Cadwallader (Latin), Morris (history), Metheringham (geography), Sanders (biology), Haines (science), Urquhart (gymnastics), Richards and Ward (general subjects). Mrs Loram and Miss Bailey were part-time teachers of commercial subjects and science respectively.

The war had put a stop temporarily to many of the peacetime activities of the girls' school such as the traditional Barnardo's fete, and a School Society was formed in 1943 as a sort of umbrella organisation for those few extra-curricular initiatives that were still possible. But 1944 proved to be a bad year. Caesar, the school cat died, and was mourned appropriately by a contributor to the magazine. The school allotment, too, was devastated by marauding sheep from a neighbouring farm, and, although compensation was paid in the sum of £5, this was felt to be scant recompense for the many hours of work that had gone into its cultivation. The following year, the House system, which had been allowed to fall into abeyance, was revived, this time with Gloucester, Kent, Windsor, and York as the chosen names; and a further sign of renewed activity was the application by the school for a licence for music and the performance of stage plays.

The Secretary whom the two High Schools had shared since 1935, Mrs Thomas, resigned in 1942, forcing the issue of a separate, full-time Secretary for each establishment that the two Heads had been urging for some time. Miss White replaced her almost immediately at the Boys' High School, but the problem was not so easily solved by Miss Dawes. After some delay, Mrs Paine was appointed, and, following her resignation, Mrs Dugmore took the post. The position of Caretaker, too, was unsettled. Mr Brookman resigned in 1943, to be replaced by Mr Richman for a couple of years before the post went to Mr Gay in 1945.

A radical administrative change was brought about by the 1944 Education Act, one of its provisions being the abolition of fees for secondary education. This was actually effective from 1 April 1945, but the Governors chewed upon it for a long time afterwards. One of their duties had always been the levying of damages upon parents who withdrew their children from school before the end of the year in which they attained their sixteenth birthdays, and they had been able to call upon legal assistance to deal with parents who were unreasonably obdurate. Now, however, all was changed. They could still ask parents to pay, but whether they did or not was henceforth a matter of conscience, not of legality, and the problem with which the Governors struggled was whether it was worth their while to make demands which they no longer had any legal means of enforcing. And, in the same year as this dilemma arose, posts of special responsibility were created in schools. In the first instance, these went at the Girls' High School to Miss Wright, Senior Mistress, and Miss Senior, but by 1946 they had been extended to include Miss Wood and an allowance shared by Miss Ward (gymnastics) and Miss Thomas.

The period 1939 to 1947 began at the Boys' High School with the opening of the dining hall and kitchen, the first permanent new buildings to be erected on the site since 1897. It closed with the resignation of Leslie Smith when he moved from headship to the inspectorate.

In addition to the main Wingfield building and the separate dining hall and kitchen now built behind it, a so-called gym and a couple of classrooms were still being used in the Hut up on the site of the girls' school, and across the back yard were the yellow galvanised workshop hut and a hutted classroom that stood next to it. A new and less than glorious addition to the accommodation occurred with the acquisition in 1945 of yet another hut that had been put up during the war by the fire service. This was situated over by the Avenue Road fence just beyond the workshop hut; it had been empty for some time and had been used on occasion by the ATC. Now the school gathered it into its collection of such buildings, and it eventually became the music room.

The effect of the war principally felt by the Boys' High School was, unsurprisingly, that on the teaching staff. At a very early date, both Mr Smith and Mr Luckman attempted to join the armed forces, but the Head's application was blocked by the Governors on the grounds that his presence at school was more important than his going to the services, and Walter Luckman was refused permission by the County authorities. A little later, Leslie Smith wanted to go as a teacher of physics to a technical establishment, again at governmental request, and again it was felt that his presence at the High School took precedence. An ageing teaching force meant that, in fact, few were conscripted from the boys' school, but Frank King joined the RAF, Douglas Bridgeman, who was an addition to the staff for modern languages in 1942, went within a very few months to the services, Donald Brabban went to essential work in an ordnance factory, and another scientist, Frank Webb, was seconded to a training college under the Emergency Scheme in 1945. King, Brabban, and Bridgeman returned; Webb, though his job at Trowbridge was protected, did not.

Replacements had to be found for these absentees, some additional teachers were needed to deal with a rise in pupil numbers similar to that at the Girls' High School, and a couple of unexpected vacancies also occurred. As had happened a quarter of a century earlier, a number of ladies were recruited at different times and for a variety of subjects, to cover the shortfall. Ursula Evans, Mary Ashworth, Ethel Whittaker, Amber Bryant, Vera Hall, Dorothy Longman, and one man, Walter Discombe, all served on the staff for short periods, but all had left by early 1946. Ken Rogers and his brother, Norman, remember these ladies. In particular, they remember the efforts made by Mrs Whittaker to improve her pupils' speech through elocution lessons. Extra staff were needed on a permanent basis, however, and as well as Douglas Bridgeman, Thomas Snook was recruited in 1944 for science and maths, Arthur Gotch in 1945 for PT, and Wilfred Kemmery in 1946 for English.

The two unexpected vacancies mentioned above were created by the loss to the school of L W Heal and Miss Gauntlett. Hilda Gauntlett had suffered ill health for some time before she officially retired in March 1942; she died some three years later. A Trowbridge girl, she had been educated at Duke House School and then the County Day School before going to University College, Aberystwyth. After graduating, she taught for five years at Dolgellau and then returned to Trowbridge in 1916 to teach mainly English and Latin to the junior forms at the Boys' High School, and to act unofficially as Jimmy Henson's secretarial assistant, for the next twenty-six years. Johnny Heal died in office in May 1943. Like Miss Gauntlett, he had given a lifetime's service to the school, and if he is remembered for his severity and sharpness of tongue his dedication to the reputation of the Boys' High School can not be doubted. He was followed as Second Master by Walter Luckman.

Grave of J W Henson in Hilperton churchyard.

Jimmy Henson, now in his fifth year of retirement, died in October 1942 and is buried in Hilperton churchyard. His long-time colleague, T J Gardner, who retired with him in 1937, had died a year earlier – in 1941 – after a serious cycling accident. And in June 1946 yet another death – that of W Nelson Haden, Chairman of Trowbridge Education Committee from 1924 to 1927, and then Chairman of Governors from 1927 to 1946 – came as a severe blow to the High Schools. A good Chairman of Governors is a friend and a guide to a school and its Head; Nelson Haden was certainly both of these, and the schools owed much to his ability and generosity over a very long period. He was followed in the post by Frank Beer.

Despite these losses and the exigencies of wartime, life at school went on as normally as was possible. With the availability of the new dining hall, the number of pupils requiring a hot dinner rocketed; intended to serve 80, more than 180 out-of-town boys were being provided for by 1945 and the kitchen had to be virtually rebuilt. Mr Smith was appointed a magistrate in 1944, Paul Henson became a Governor, representing Warminster UDC, in 1945, and rugby was successfully introduced as second winter game for the boys in 1946. In its inaugural season, the school first XV played twelve matches and won them all. Vice-captain of the team was Peter Riddiford who, thirty years later, was to become Chairman of Governors. The Old Boys' Society was reconstituted, with a well attended smoking concert as its first event. Former pupils, staff, and members of the Sixth Form enjoyed a convivial evening in October 1946 organised by Mr Bradfield, with Mr Griffiths at the piano, Jock Burns singing "Cockles and Mussels", and the whole presided over by Mr Smith.

Speech Days, too, were back as occasions of some ceremony (though the boys still had to use the girls' hall for these events) and in his report at the Speech Day of 1944 Mr Smith mentioned the long journeys that some pupils had to make to get to school. This provoked a discussion about the desirability of setting up some sort of hostel accommodation for the boys, those few girls affected being adequately provided for by suitable local lodgings. The opinion of parents was sought, but lack of any sort of unanimity led to the suggestion's eventually being dropped. And Messrs Luckman (Second Master), Downing (maths and careers), Lambert (history and cricket), Brabban (science and football), and King (English, drama, and athletics) received allowances for holding those posts of special responsibility. (Lennie Lambert's pride in his cricketing pedigree was well known. It was his boast that he had played against W G Grace, and that "I was the middle victim of a hat trick!")

One continuing feature of school life throughout the war was "The Wing", the school magazine. It appeared regularly, twice a year, as a forum for those with ambitions to write, and to provide a record of the school's activities. Football, cricket, and swimming featured regularly, the popularity of the latter having been boosted by the opening of the baths in Trowbridge in 1939. Previously, pupils had had to cycle over to the Laverton Baths at Westbury. One or two clubs – for chess, music, and debating, for example – were able to survive during the war, and the House system continued. The names of the Houses – Brooke, Farleigh, Forest and Gaunt – had been thought up by Mr Heal in the early 1920's. As has been said, boys were originally allocated to them on the basis of the initial letters of their surname, and then, in 1925, according to where they lived. Forest had been for those who lived in Melksham, Holt and Hilperton; Brooke (from Brooke House, a fifteenth century manor some two miles from Southwick) for those from Warminster, Westbury and Southwick; and Gaunt and Farleigh were for Trowbridge boys. Now, however, though the names remained, allocation to the houses was random. And news of Old Boys was an important aspect of "The Wing" during these war years.

Just prior to his resignation, Leslie Smith had the task of negotiating the application of the Development Plan to the Boys' High School with the local authority. There was a Plan for the Girls' High School, too, but as their buildings were much more recent than those of the boys, this was comparatively modest; two staff rooms were thought to be necessary, and probably two more classrooms. Detailed drawings were made of what the expanded Boys' High School would look like, and discussions were entered into about the minutiae of the extensions.

The plans show a complex of laboratories and workshops stretching from the corner of the east wing nearest to Avenue Road up the site in the general direction of the Hut. Beyond them, and nearer the Hut, was to be the new gymnasium linked to the main building by a covered way. To the west of the house was to be the assembly hall and stage, close to where it is today but at right angles to the present hall, stretching out into the gardens and games field. Other rooms were intended to link this with the new dining room and kitchen, with classrooms beyond. A central feature, opposite the dining hall, would be a lawn with a surrounding cloister. The first floor of the building was to be remodelled and extended, with the art room and library much as they already were, but with a number of new classrooms and study rooms. It was an ambitious and attractive scheme.

The Governors, advised by the Head, were invited to submit their views on the plan, which they did, their suggested revisions turning out to be a fairly comprehensive demolition of the original conception for a new building. The total number of classrooms should be increased from 9 to 11 – one for each class in the school, of which there were 10, and one for the Sixth Form. The position of the assembly hall should be switched from the west to the east end of the building where the labs and workshops were shown on the plan; thus situated, it would shield the school from the houses in Avenue Road, and vice versa, it would be close to cloakroom facilities, and it would not there encroach upon gardens, lawns, or playing fields, which were already an attractive feature of the school. The two staff rooms shown on the plan – both the front and the back room to the left of the central door – should be combined to make one large staff room, and more changing and showering facilities were needed. Other smaller changes, too, were suggested. But in the event, of course, none of these ambitious developments came to fruition. When expansion did eventually become possible, it was piecemeal and as a separate building based on the recently opened dining hall and kitchen – the accommodation known today as the Lancaster building.

> "During his ten years at Trowbridge, Mr Smith has succeeded in making the school even more successful than it was under the long regime of his predecessor. He has enjoyed the fullest confidence of the Education Committee, who have often consulted him upon educational problems, and of the school Governors, and his relations with his staff have been of the happiest character. Now he has been singled out for promotion as one of His Majesty's Inspectors of Schools, an even more responsible position than that of Head of this school."

Thus spoke Frank Beer, Chairman of Governors, on the occasion of the annual Speech Day in April 1947 when he stood in for the intended guest of honour who was indisposed. Leslie Smith, as Mr Beer implied, was a most competent professional, and it was with a real sense of loss that all connected with the school saw him depart for his new duties in Cornwall at the end of the spring term. He and his wife were entertained by the staff to a farewell luncheon at the George Hotel, a presentation being made by Captain Luckman of a silver coffee pot. Mr Smith, unfortunately, could not respond as he was suffering from laryngitis. The boys of the school gave him an electric clock, but the liveliest send-off was probably that of the Old Pupils' Societies of the Girls' and the Boys' High Schools, at which function presentations were made, a recital of songs was given by former pupils, and dances, old-time and modern, were enjoyed by those present – the whole proceedings being managed by Jock Burns as MC.

A new scientist, Len Newell, arrived on 1 March 1947 to replace Donald Brabban who had left in February to go to Gaddesden Emergency Training College and Mr Smith was succeeded as Head of the Boys' High School by G V S Bucknall, MA. As he was unable to take up his post until September 1947, Walter Luckman stood in as Acting Head for the summer term. The staff that Mr Bucknall inherited when he did arrive was: Messrs Luckman, Downing, Griffiths, Beams, Powell, Lambert, O'Flaherty, Burns, Bradfield, Wilson, King, Bridgeman, Snook, Gotch, Kemmery, and Newell.

F W (Stan) King taught English at the Boys' High School from 1937 to 1949, and from his home in Swindon he sent me a long and fascinating account of some of his memories, an extract from which makes an appropriate postscript to this chapter on the Trowbridge High Schools in war time.

"In September 1939, staff were recalled from summer holidays to assist with evacuation activities. We had previously canvassed the town for likely billets for children and mothers who would come to Wiltshire if war was declared. Many days were spent waiting for arrivals at Trowbridge railway station. The girls' school on the other side of the playing field was a reception point. Children and mothers were fed and put to bed there when they arrived from London late in the evening, and they were taken to their billets next day. When school assembled, air raid precautions had to be established. Each boy and master had his own station to go to in an emergency. Some were unlucky enough to be given a 'place of safety' in one of the open trenches which had been dug alongside the hedgerow which divided our playing field from the girls'. In winter, they collected quite a deal of water, but fortunately there were few air raid alerts during the winter of the phoney war, 1939/40.

After Dunkirk, many British soldiers were quartered at Trowbridge Barracks. During this rest period, the Head Master invited any soldiers who so wished to use the school field to recover from their ordeal across the Channel. I can well remember many men lying fast asleep in the sunshine along the hedgerow that skirts the Wingfield Road. Later they indulged in impromptu cricket matches, but were soon posted to more strenuous military duties. During this period, we frequently had air raid warnings several times a day. These made it difficult for boys sitting their O level examinations. They were quickly evacuated from the exam room (near the old cycle shed) to their shelters in the trenches outside, and ordered to say nothing to each other while the emergency lasted. This was indeed a difficult task for the masters concerned with such disciplinary duty. I believe my literature exam lasted – on and off – for over three hours whilst we waited for the All Clear to be sounded.

I recall an incident that happened in the summer of 1940, a few weeks before the Battle of Britain began. The Luftwaffe was carrying out various recce raids over the southern counties, but not without some losses. I had taken our cricket team to Bruton one glorious summer's day, and in the middle of the game a German aircraft came into sight, hotly pursued by a Spitfire. Everyone stopped playing – even the two umpires forgot their duties – and watched. After a few moments of an exciting dog-fight, the two aircraft disappeared, with the Spitfire still on the attack. My fellow umpire, a master from the opposing school, looked down the pitch and shouted, 'Shall we resume play, Mr King?' to which I replied, 'Certainly, sir!' and to everyone's satisfaction the peaceful calm of an English summer's afternoon returned. A splendid example of British sang-froid!

Immediately after the end of the war – in 1946 – it was agreed to introduce rugby football into the school for one term in the winter season. I was very surprised by the height and weight of the first teams we fielded because they had lived for five or six formative years on their rations. Perhaps the school dinners helped. We were also lucky to receive a supply of jerseys, shorts, and stockings, as well as a rugger ball or two, from army units that were being broken up in the vicinity. Thus we were freed of the worry of finding clothing coupons which were still very necessary at this time of austerity. Athletics was flourishing, too, thanks largely to the coaching prowess of Jock Burns. He produced an all-England hurdles champion in Johnny Adlam and several others who gained second or third places at the Schools' Championships at Eton, Kingston upon Hull, Carshalton, and Bath."

Fifty years on, the harshness of the reality of life in war time is softened to a sort of period charm.

New Blood and a New Impetus:
The Two Trowbridge High Schools: 1947-1954

Nearly half a century after he took up his Headship at Trowbridge, Geoffrey Bucknall writes:

> "I inherited a staff with an average age of over 50 (which caused problems with the taking of games!). I think there were only 2 under 40, with Len Newell in his early 30's as the youngest. The Senior Master, Luckman, had joined the staff in September 1914, joined the army after a term, and came back in 1919 after 4 years and more in the trenches. Fortunately, with one exception, they were very capable and got on well together so that I also inherited a very friendly atmosphere. Gradually, of course, they all retired, and by a combination of good luck and good judgement we managed to replace them with (almost without exception) very good men who also fitted in well both with the older ones and with each other."

Mr Bucknall's statistics are absolutely correct; in 1947 the staff was very elderly, with 2 masters in their 60's and 7 others in their 50's, and it was issues of staffing in particular that came to dominate these post-war years at both the Trowbridge High Schools. At the Girls' High School, 2 teachers with many years of service to their credit were to leave, and something of a crisis developed over the Headship, with Miss Dawes' long-term illness; at Wingfield Road, the established order was also to change, the old guard beginning to disintegrate with 3 retirements and a death in office.

Pat O'Flaherty, an Irishman of volatile temperament, who combined, unusually, the teaching of science and art, retired in 1950. He died in 1963. At the Boys' High School for almost 30 years, he had on occasion been at odds with authority and he clearly made an impression on many of those whom he taught. He had qualifications in both his teaching disciplines, but they were Irish qualifications, and this, combined with the fact that his first 12 years of teaching were in Dublin, led to difficulties over his being accepted as a qualified teacher and over his Irish service's being recognised for salary purposes. Eventually, as late as 1949, Mr Grimston MP intervened on his behalf, and O'Flaherty then received a substantial back payment of salary. His retirement, which was delayed from November until the end of the school year because of the difficulty of replacing him, actually created two vacancies – one in science and a second in art. A young Gareth Roberts, who many years later was to become Chairman of the Wiltshire Education

Committee, filled the science post, J F Hand that in art. Mr Hand remained at the school for two years and then seems simply to have not returned after the summer holidays. His contract was consequently terminated, and George Johnston was appointed in his stead in 1953.

G V S Bucknall, Head Master, 1947-1968.

It was in 1953 that the school lost two more of its very long-serving teachers, Weg Griffiths and Jock Burns, the latter suffering a heart attack in school and dying the same night. Teacher of Latin, he had often been prominent in the staff's social activities, but his real claim to fame was as an athlete. He apparently at one time held the all-Ireland 440 yards (though some say the quarter mile hurdles) record. Jack Trott says drily that he was "a likeable man in many respects, but I learned almost nothing from him because his Irish accent was so thick that I could rarely understand his English." Like several others on the staff, Jock Burns lived in Wingfield Road – in the turreted house next to the catholic church. (L G Smith lived at no. 42. Mr Bucknall followed him at this address, selling the property to Frank Lavery when he moved to no. 60. This house, in its turn, passed to Gerald Gibson. And Reggie Beams lived, even in my time, at "Eype", no. 44 Wingfield Road.) The school also lost the services of Weg Griffiths, Senior Geography Master, who retired, slightly early, at the end of the summer term, having given 34 years to the boys of the High School. He was succeeded by H W Hardy; W E Bingham replaced Burns.

And finally, of the very long-serving members of staff, H J Downing retired in 1954. Tubby Downing was the school's senior mathematician and he was picked out by inspectors and pupils alike as being a quite outstanding teacher who seldom needed to raise his voice or indulge in needless eccentricity to gain attention. After teacher training, he had served in the Royal Navy during the first World War and then taught for the next 35 years at Trowbridge Boys' High School. It has been said that he, more than anyone, was responsible, through his competence, for the school's manifest bias towards mathematics and the sciences in the time that he taught there. Gerald Gibson, from St Marylebone Grammar School as L G Smith had been, replaced him.

Presentation on the retirement of H J Downing, 1954, with, left to right: Messrs Beams, Downing, Bucknall, Luckman, Powell and Lambert.

These were changes of great significance. O'Flaherty, Burns, Griffiths, and Downing were all at the school for 30 years or more, so their going marked the end of an era. The woodwork teacher, F W J Bradfield, also retired in 1948 (after a mere 18 years at the High School), being replaced by E R Webster. Thomas Snook was replaced by F S Harris for chemistry in 1949, Stan King by Rhys Prosser for English in 1950, and A F Gotch by John Colin for PE in 1951.

Part-time teachers came and went in both art and music, in which subjects they were principally employed. Art saw 4 such between 1947 and 1949, and music 5 up to 1951, but finally two appointments were made of whom more will be heard – Vic Belcher in art and Frank Lavery in music. Mr Lavery was to become a tremendous influence not only in the High School but, later, in the John of Gaunt School, until his retirement in 1982, and he it was who inherited as his first music room the hut by the Avenue Road fence – not the old hut erected by the fire service during the war, for this had become too dilapidated for further use, but its successor, acquired in 1949, that was somewhat smaller and equally unappealing as teaching accommodation.

A different sort of appointment was that of D Sharman in 1948. He was the school's first lab assistant – aged 15, salary £78 per year! Eventually he was called up to do his national service and was replaced by a boy called Rogers. One must assume that these assistants were useful as, too late, the Girls' High School decided that they would like one too. By 1951 the next round of financial restrictions was biting and the local authority was not able to sanction the appointment of a lab assistant to the girls' school at that time.

So, by 1954, the full-time staff of the Boys' High School had taken on a new look and was significantly different from that of 1947. It was: Geoffrey Bucknall (Head Master), and Messrs Luckman, Gibson, Lambert, Harris, Prosser, Hardy, Newell, Beams, Powell, Roberts, Johnston, Bingham, Webster, Wilson, Bridgeman, Kemmery, and Colin; and of the assistants, Luckman as Senior Master, Gibson, Lambert, Harris, Prosser, and Newell received allowances for their posts of special responsibility.

The pupil population of the school remained at between 320 and 340 during these years, so additions and improvements that were made to the premises were due to existing inadequacies rather than to a need based upon extra pupil numbers. The kitchen of 1939, much extended in 1945 to increase its capacity from 80 to 180, was again rebuilt, this time for a capability of 250 meals daily, and it became operational in 1949. Tacked on to it in 1950 were two new classrooms (L 21 and L 25), the second stage of what is known today as the Lancaster building, which was erected piecemeal over many years from the isolated dining room and kitchen of 1939. This addition, costing £3,657.5.0 and built by Holdoway and Sons of Westbury, enabled Geoffrey Bucknall to shuffle some of his classes around and to bring one of them in from the distant Hut closer to the main school building. And the third stage of the Lancaster building was to be the addition of laboratories; these were asked for in 1954 and a half promise extracted from the local authority that they might be forthcoming in 1955-56.

Other improvements, or repairs, took place. The heating boiler was defective and had to be replaced (a story that I know only too well); workmen erecting the new classrooms damaged the playground and repairs were necessary here, too (another story that I recognise); and the lavatories were found to be disgusting (again, not unusually so). On the other hand, a sensible and coherent lettings policy, particularly as regards security and the proper use of equipment, for both the premises and the grounds was framed for the first time, and Mr Bucknall purchased a school flag, to be flown, presumably, from the flag pole which had existed on the gable to the left of the main door from the building's very earliest days. This pole was found to be unsafe and was removed when the roof was being repaired in 1990.

From written evidence and from personal memory, one has the impression in these years of the school's surging forward again, prompted by the enthusiasm of a new Head and released from the restrictions of wartime. Drama became a feature of school life.

> "Something I introduced was school plays," writes Geoffrey Bucknall. "We started with one-acters for juniors, middles and seniors, and then, the boys having acquired some experience, Rhys Prosser began producing full-length plays. Ones that come to mind are 'King Lear' and 'Coriolanus', 'Juno and the Paycock', 'A Man for all Seasons', and 'The School for Scandal'. When we started, clothes rationing was still in force, so Peggy [Mrs Bucknall], who acted as wardrobe mistress all through, helped by a sequence of mothers, appealed to parents for any cast-offs or spare lengths of material with which they could devise costumes. Later we were able to hire proper ones. Until we got our own hall, we had to borrow that of the Nelson Haden Secondary Modern Girls' School."

One senses an excitement and an enthusiasm at the Boys' High School in these post-war years that was new.

A Carol Service was held at Holy Trinity Church at Christmas, 1948; clubs and activities were started, particularly for the senior boys, and room was made for them in the school day, during the latter part of Friday afternoons whilst the juniors went on with their ordinary lessons; German was provided as an option in the fourth year; and the science/arts divide, introduced by Leslie Smith in 1937, was done away with in the first three years and replaced by the more usual A/B split, with promotions and demotions possible, at least in theory. (That the system worked in practice as well as theory is evinced by Mr Bucknall's recollection of one boy in the B form who, having gained promotion to the A stream, went on to become School Captain and, later, a don at the University of Aberdeen.) In 1949, school uniform was again made compulsory, ambitious visits were organised – at home, to the Festival of Britain and the opening of Parliament, and abroad, to Paris and Switzerland, for example – and Speech Days, albeit in the girls' school hall, were able to be celebrated more lavishly than had been the case during the war. Mr Bucknall hosted a Head Master from Germany for a month. A number of Polish boys (the first of many) were admitted to the school. And – something that I find interesting but rather sad in the light of their more recent total disappearance from the school calendar – swimming sports were an annual event.

1950 was the year in which the School Certificate and Higher School Certificate examinations gave way to the General Certificate of Education at ordinary, advanced and scholarship level. Under the old examination, the Boys' High School in these post-war years would typically enter between 12 and 18 candidates annually for the HSC, with 8 or 9 or 10 being successful. For School Certificate, between 45 and 50 would be entered, with something like a 70%-80% pass-rate. With the new examinations, success and failure in these rather stark terms was more difficult to assess, candidates at A level being entered for anything from 1 to 4 papers. At O level, however, roughly the same number of pupils as took School Certificate were entered for 3 or more subjects, with the percentages passing in 3 or more papers being similar to the pass-rate in the old examination – 35 out of 45 in 1951, 26 out of 45 in 1952, and 40 out of 53 in 1953 being sample statistics.

The severest effects of war time were now in the the past, but it was felt that the sacrifices made by those who had fallen during the war should not be forgotten. A fund, therefore, was opened for the provision of a memorial to those from the school who had died, it being decided that this would take the form of a bronze plate to be placed in the Library. A service was held on 30 April 1950. It was conducted by Rev Noel Calvin and Rev G J Jenkins, and it was for the dedication of the plaque which today can be found on the wall outside the Headmaster's room. Inscribed on it are the names of those fifty pupils who fell during the war, and the words: Greater Love Hath No Man. On the opposite wall, appropriately, is the memorial to the seventeen boys from the school who died in the 1914-1918 war.

The way in which the Governing Body of the Trowbridge High Schools was constituted had remained largely unchanged for 23 years. Under the terms of the 1944 Education Act, however, a reconstitution took place in January 1950 which reduced the number of Governors from 19 to 14. There were 12 representative Governors – 4 from the Local Education Authority, 3 from Trowbridge UDC, 1 each from Melksham UDC, Warminster UDC, Westbury UDC, Bradford on Avon and Melksham RDC, and Warminster and Westbury RDC – and 2 cooptative Governors. Kenneth Ponting (he of the Preparatory Department of 1920) was one of the latter, but there was no place for Paul Henson as a representative Governor in this slimmed-down Body. Frank Beer retained the Chair initially, but, for the new school year in September, Brigadier V F Browne was elected Chairman, and remained in that office until 1957.

One of the first duties undertaken by the new Governors was to make recommendations to the authority about the future of sex education in the two schools. The lead here had in the past been taken by the Girls' High School, with a Dr Griffith being invited to lecture in 1942 both to pupils and parents on different aspects of the subject. Miss Dawes reported that, prior to this, sex education had been rudimentary, with "certain girls being removed in order to improve the general attitude to the subject". The little that was done was amateurish and unstructured (though it was possibly bold for its time), and the teachers involved were very conscious of their lack of expertise in this field. In 1949, Dr E R Matthews had undertaken a far more comprehensive treatment of sex education at the High Schools, with pupils, staff and parents all involved appropriately, but there was now the suggestion that, rather than lecture to pupils on the subject, Dr Matthews' skills should be devoted to training members of the teaching force to deliver sex education in their own schools. Volunteers from the two staffs were asked for, to work under Dr Matthews' guidance. None was forthcoming from the girls' school and only two from the boys', but as neither of these could be released for the work anyway, the project was dropped for the time being and Dr Matthews continued to lecture and instruct as before.

Girls' High School staff, 1948, standing, left to right: Misses Richards, Haines, Quine, Mrs Smith, Misses Hazell, Sanders, House, Metheringham,; seated: Misses Urquhart, Thomas, Wright, Dawes, Morris, Horton White, Cadwallader.

Between 1947 and 1954 there were, not unusually, many staff changes at the Girls' High School, some of them of great importance, but before looking at them in detail we can enjoy the view of her teachers taken by Millie Bennett who arrived in Trowbridge from the Midlands and joined the third year of the High School at this time.

"Miss Wright's maths lessons were a study in economy of word and gesture. Many people did eventually learn maths. Miss Wright herself was above pettiness and suffered no fools, but her dry brand of humour meted out in small doses at appropriate times brightened what often seemed interminable lessons to me. Miss Trafford's music lessons were as tentative and sensitive as she herself, and I remember enjoying them very much, while I used to marvel at her variety of expressions, from harassed to happy in quick succession. Miss Haines I remember as a cheerful, practical soul, who livened up her lessons with occasional homely details like this one: 'My mother thinks we all had a common ancestor, a sort of cow-like creature', which tickled me....

I was sorry when Miss Thomas left us as her encouragement, mixed at all times with ruthless criticism, was always stimulating. But the pure joy in reading poetry, old or new, was somehow transmitted by her successor, Mr Boulding. His patience and endurance helped matters no end when we did 'The Importance of being Earnest' in the Sixth Form. French with Miss Borries was perhaps, next to English, what I enjoyed doing most....The arrival of Miss Morris heralded reform and a different atmosphere. 'Millie, you look like a South Sea islander. Try to do something about your hair.'"

And, knowing Miss Morris, one presumes that Millie did!

In geography, Miss Metheringham gave way to Miss Rogers and then Miss Montague, who became the first Old Girl to return as a member of the teaching staff; Miss House (art) gave way to Harman and Lord; Cadwallader (Latin) to Sergeant; Sanders (biology) to Perry and Woodruff; Haines (chemistry) to Jefferies and Jones; Richards (junior history) to Jackson, Snow, and Mrs Lowe; and Rudd, who was appointed as an addition in 1950 for English and French, to Pinton. Miss Horton White had joined the school to teach French in 1927; she retired in 1954 after 27 years' service, to be replaced by Miss Soo. And two men were appointed to the staff – Mr Boulding for English in place of Miss Thomas, and Mr Clemence for work with junior forms as replacement for Miss Ward. The appointments of Boulding and Clemence were as a result of a new policy adopted by the Ministry of Education to try to overcome the shortage of women teachers. It became a requirement that "non-mobile" teachers, or men, or those already employed at other schools in the County, should be employed henceforth rather than women, and so the Girls' High School acquired its first two men. Finally, Miss Wright, Senior Mistress and Senior Maths Mistress, retired in the summer of 1951 after 24 years at the school.

At the school Speech Day in February 1951, Miss Dawes paid Miss Wright a handsome tribute, speaking of her "loyal and faithful service" and commending her clarity as a teacher. That she was something of a martinet, perhaps, is hinted at in Miss Dawes' description of her "competent and bracing ways of dealing with the whole school on such occasions as this [the annual Speech Day], or such slackers as come her way from time to time", and her duty of "bracing the slacker" also receives mention. She is certainly remembered by those who knew her as a lady not to be trifled with. Miss Wright's maths teaching was picked up by Miss Hatch and, from 1954, by Mrs Rees, and the post of Senior Mistress went in September 1951 to Miss Morris.

By early 1954, then, Miss Dawes had as her teaching staff: Miss Morris (Senior Mistress), Miss Sergeant, Miss Hazell, Mr Boulding, Miss Urquhart, Mrs Rees, and Miss Borries, all of whom were in receipt of special allowances either for subject or more widely based school responsibilities, and Misses Soo, Trafford, Symmons, Quine, Lord, Montague, Woodruff, Jones, and Pinton, Mrs Lowe, and Mr Clemence. Caretaker Gay had resigned in 1951 and been replaced by Mr Dunn.

However, the most significant, and in some ways the saddest, change to take place was the retirement of Miss Dawes herself and the appointment in her stead of Miss Morris on 28 May 1954. As early as 1951, Miss Wright had had to take on extra responsibilities because of the illness of the Head Mistress, but it was Miss Morris, only recently appointed as Senior Mistress, who really had to shoulder the burden of running the school when Kay Dawes suffered a serious breakdown that forced her absence from school for the whole of 1953 and the first two terms of 1954. Miss Morris officially became Acting Head in March 1953 when it was realised that Miss Dawes "needed complete rest and care for some months", but thereafter there was confusion and uncertainty with, from time to time, rumours of Miss Dawes' possible return or of her needing yet more time for convalescence. The Governors were able initially to grant sick leave, of course, but as time went on difficulties arose about the

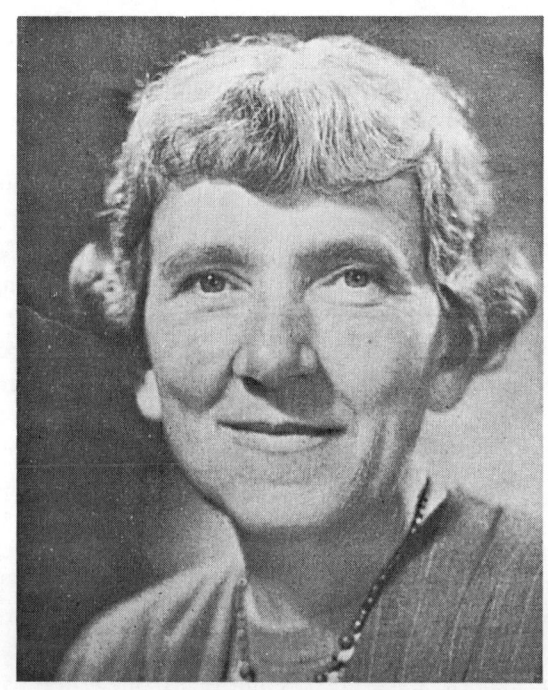

Miss K M S Dawes,
Head Mistress, 1939-1954.

125

payment of salary and about how much leave could actually be taken, and such was the length of the Head's absence that the Governing Body and the Local Authority were in something of a quandary about how to proceed. In the end, Miss Dawes felt that she had no alternative but to resign, and Miss Morris was appointed Head Mistress in her place in the summer term of 1954.

In *That's How It Was*, Maureen Duffy describes the Head Mistress of Wortbridge High School from a young girl's viewpoint.

> "She was a strange woman with short wiry, greying hair. She wore a tweed brown costume and thrust two fingers into the plaquet of her skirt, leaning back from the hips at a curious angle. Her voice grated and purred as she questioned us in her Oxford drawl..... I realised, as if I could see right through her, that she was really terribly shy instead of brusque and awesome as we had all thought."

Miss Dawes, I think, is recognisable. Many remember her as often being seen around Trowbridge pushing a bike (apparently somewhat fearful of the traffic) and with a copy of *Sporting Life* tucked under her arm. She was keen on horse racing and looked upon beating the odds as something of an intellectual challenge. KMD was clearly a lady of great character – not, perhaps, the most organised of people or at her best with administrative detail, but academically very able, keenly interested in the philosophy of education, and essentially kindly and interested in those for whom she had responsibility. After her resignation in 1954, she was, happily, restored to health and able to return to school a few months later to say her goodbyes in a proper fashion. I met her just once, shortly after I came to Trowbridge, at her home in Bradford Road where we had tea and talked about her time as Head of the Girls' High School.

The number of girls on roll had dropped from the 370 of the 1940's to between 340 and 350 in the 1947-1954 period. The High School was, in fact, a two-form entry selective school with a fairly wide range of ability in its first five year groups, and with a small Sixth Form, not all of whom were contemplating higher education. Four or five girls were entered each year for Higher School Certificate, the majority passing and going on to college or university. So, in 1951, there were some 10 girls currently at universities, including both Oxford and Cambridge, and about 12 at training colleges. At School Certificate level, most of the top form were entered for the London examination, with between 70% and 80% passing in an average year, and some of the lower form, together with a few from the top form, were entered for the Oxford examination which was felt to be better suited to their abilities. The pass rate here was much lower. Of these School Certificate results for the last year in which the examination existed, Miss Dawes commented somewhat cryptically: "One of the girls who failed was probably responsible for her friends' successes, since she showed greater ability to teach than to pass examinations herself, and another would certainly have got through had the National Health Service been able to supply her with spectacles more swiftly." There are always human and interesting stories behind the bald statistics.

Extra-curricularly, too, the High School was active during Miss Dawes' headship. The first of a number of large-scale summer entertainments took place on the lawn in 1950 – a Grand Pageant of Local History, in which, amongst other oddities, "the third form enjoyed being pigs in prehistoric Bath". At short intervals, a display of Historical Dances and a Masque of the Seasons were to follow. Tennis, folk dancing, music, and (as with the boys) swimming were all enthusiastically supported. The Sixth Form cooperated with pupils from some of the schools in Bath in promoting discussion groups under the aegis of the Council for Education in World Citizenship. Trips abroad flourished – to Holland and Paris, for example. A Film Society for local teachers was inaugurated, and a reinvigorated PTA became an active and effective backer of school activities.

Miss Urquhart and the country dance team, 1949.

It was at this time that a number of Polish girls were admitted to the school from the Polish Hostel at Keevil and the Settlement at Steeple Ashton – 8 in 1949 and 4 more in 1950; pupils of Polish families still form a recognisable element in the school today. And in 1952 a modest expansion of the buildings was achieved with the erection of two new classrooms (now the single room G 81) adjacent to, and leading on from, the chemistry lab at the western end of the ground floor.

Speech Days continued to be occasions at which the school could show itself off to some advantage. As was traditional, the Chairman would introduce the proceedings, the Head Mistress would report on the work of the school during the past year, there would be music and a distribution of prizes and certificates by a distinguished guest who would then address the pupils and their parents, and the occasion would close with votes of thanks and, probably, more music. At the Girls' High School, the guests of these years included Miss Darbishire, former Principal of Somerville College, Oxford, Professor James from Bristol University, and Professor John Murray from Exeter, but in 1952 it was decided to change the format of the occasion. It was thought that it had become too cumbersome, and so, as an experiment, there were to be a more modest prize giving ceremony and a separate Open Afternoon for parents. It was an experiment, however, that survived for two years only, for in 1954 the traditional Speech Day was restored by Miss Morris with an address and prize distribution by Miss Scott Baker, Deputy Director of Education for Wiltshire.

As with the boys' school, there is a positive feel about these years at Trowbridge Girls' High School, and if the impetus was temporarily halted by uncertainties arising from Miss Dawes' long absence, it was soon to be resumed under the enthusiastic leadership of Bronwen Morris.

Reconstruction:
Trowbridge High School for Boys: 1954-1969

The matter of most immediate moment for the Boys' High School when the new school year began in September 1954 was the impending visit of Her Majesty's Inspectors. It was some sixteen years since the last inspection and, after this most recent visit, those aspects of the school that had found favour with the Inspectors in 1938 were again found to be either satisfactory or better. The ethos of the school, its organisation, leadership, curriculum, and standard of academic attainment all (with minor exceptions) came in for praise. The teaching of maths and physics in particular, and the individual contributions of Mr Gibson (in maths), Mr Newell (in physics), Mr Prosser (in English), Mr Roberts (in biology), Mr Hardy (in geography, "where he has effected a great improvement in what had plainly become a very weak subject"), and Mr Johnston and Mr Belcher (in art) were commended. There was unhappiness, however, at the level of stress imposed upon the teachers by what the Inspectors saw as the inadequate staffing level of the school. All were having to teach too heavy a timetable, and Mr Bucknall's commitment to a half teaching load was felt to be unreasonable. Relief was forthcoming in that the Governors acted speedily to counter this particular criticism by appointing D J Roberts as an addition to the staff in September 1955, for maths, physics, and chemistry, and, at the same time, making Frank Lavery's appointment full-time, principally for music, but also for general subjects with junior forms.

Unfortunately, the main plank of the HMI report, as it had been in 1938, was the total inadequacy of the school buildings as accommodation for a two-form entry boys' grammar school. Virtually nothing had changed in sixteen years other than the building of a dining room, a kitchen, and two classrooms, and what had been criticised then as being inadequate, or too small, or sub-standard, was still the same – only sixteen years older. The school was essentially the building of 1890, the added wing of 1897, an agglomeration of huts at the rear of the building, and the Hut (or part of it) on the girls' school site. The Governing Body grasped the nettle. They used the Inspectors' report to bring pressure to bear on the Local Authority in the years 1955-1958 to effect a virtual reconstruction of the Boys' High School, their task being completed only when the new buildings were opened by Sir John Wolfenden, Vice-Chancellor of Reading University, on 22 February 1961.

Whilst the report was generally critical of the premises, specific concerns were also highlighted. The chemistry and physics laboratories (W 35 and W 33) were too small and, in the case of the chemistry lab, dangerous; and there was no real biology lab, this subject being taught as best he could by Gareth Roberts in the old dining room. The library, cramped and badly stocked, was not effective. Teaching and study accommodation for a Sixth Form of 41 boys was virtually non-existent. There was no real gymnasium, exercise being taken in the makeshift accommodation offered by the Hut. Changing facilities were poor, and the toilets (at the end of the east wing) were squalid in the extreme. And so the litany of inadequacies continued. There was, of course, no school hall, and the workshop was in an old, temporary hut across the back yard. Even the ordinary classrooms came in for criticism; they were adequate in number, but too many of them were hutted, in need of decoration, and lacked sound-proofing. The situation was, indeed, desperate, and the best that the Inspectors could envisage was a whittling away of the deficiencies by piecemeal development and additions to the premises. To their very great credit, the Governors, in collaboration with the County Architect, did better than that.

Throughout 1955 negotiations took place between the Governors and the LEA about how new premises – which it was now agreed were essential – were to be achieved. There was already a commitment to the building of new physics labs in 1955-56 as a minor project, but this could not be added to. The best that could be hoped for was the construction of a new toilet block in 1957-58, and then a major rebuilding project could be scheduled for 1958-59. The Head, the Governing Body, the County Architect, and representatives of the County Education Committee met frequently. Obstacles were encountered and overcome. Hopes were raised – and dashed. Deadlines came and went. The Minister (Sir David Eccles) was consulted and actually came to the school himself to give his view on the situation. And eventually the two smaller projects were completed, the major development plan agreed, work put in hand, and the reconstruction accomplished – this being a combination of completely new accommodation and a gutting and rebuilding of much of the main Wingfield building. The maintaining of an orderly atmosphere of work and academic study and examination achievement during this period of major upheaval must have tested the ingenuity and patience of Mr Bucknall and his staff considerably, but it was done, and after the grand opening of what was in effect a new school in February 1961 only details remained to be tidied up. The report that followed the inspection of 1954 had indeed born fruit.

The new accommodation was all in what today is known as the Lancaster building. The physics labs (L 27 and L 29) and the preparation room (L 37) went up in 1955, built by Parsons and Sons of Westbury for £8301. This was followed by an internal reorganisation within the Wingfield building whereby the old physics lab (W 33) became part fiction library and part chemistry lab preparation room; a new staff room was created in what had been the library (W 6 and

W 8, the two rooms overlooking the main entrance at the front); and the library reference books went into the two small rooms that had been used by the staff. Early in 1958, the Lancaster toilet block was built, and then, late in 1959, work began on the major additions to the Lancaster building (known at the time as the Science Block) – first the two chemistry labs (L 31 and L 33), followed by the two biology laboratories (L 43 and L 45), the lab steward's room (L 41) and the greenhouse. It was at this time, too, that the old toilets dating from 1897, at the end of what is now the Sixth Form common room, were demolished to make way for a road running round the eastern corner of the Wingfield building. Indications of the existence of this former lavatory block are still visible on the outside wall. Then, late in 1959 and throughout 1960, work went ahead on the new rooms that were to form the first floor of the Lancaster building – classrooms L 2, L 4, and L 6, a division room for the Sixth form (L 8), a prefects' room (L 10), and a larger division room (L 12). Finally, there was the technology room, L 14.

Aerial view of Boys' High School, 1958, showing the two huts in the playground, the old ATC hut by the cycle sheds, the physics labs of 1956, and the new toilet block of 1958.

As the new buildings went up, the old was converted, so there was nowhere in the school that was free of noise and dirt and confusion at this time. To the left of the main door at the front was Miss White, the Secretary, with "the meter room" (a small room full of electrical apparatus) behind her. To the right was the Head, with the staff lavatory and shower in the fourth room of this central block. The old schoolroom / woodwork room / classroom / changing room, cloakroom, and lavatory (W 27 and W 27a) remained as it was, a lavatory and cloakroom. The physics lab (W 33) and chemistry lab (W 35) became classrooms, and the short corridor was built that now gives access to them. What today is the Sixth Form common room became the woodwork and metalwork shop, and the old dining room became the MI room, with a complex of changing rooms and lavatories, a drying room, and an apparatus room behind, much as it still is other than that the MI room is now the school's general office. Most importantly, the assembly hall was built, giving a new entrance to the school between it and the main building, and a new boiler house was constructed at the back of the hall, rendering the old, subterranean boiler house obsolete. On the first floor, the partition was removed from what had been the old west dormitory (W 4) to form a new library, and the old external staircase was demolished. The former long dormitory remained much as it was – two classrooms (W 14 and W 18) with a multi-purpose space between, and W 22 was refurbished as an art room with its own art store (W 24) en suite.

This was the new Boys' High School that was officially opened in February 1961. What it provided by way of teaching accommodation was clearly long overdue, but it is equally clear, both from articles in the school magazines of the time and from what former pupils and teachers have said, that great affection had been felt for the old High School, cramped and uncomfortable and inadequate as it was. There are still nostalgic memories today of the disreputable collection of old huts that graced the back yard for so long, though I have heard no regrets over the final vacating of the so-called gymnasium and other facilities afforded by the Hut on the site of the girls' school that at this point was returned to them.

If the Head and his Governors were preoccupied with planning in the mid 1950's, and if the school was massively disrupted by the actual process of construction in the late 50's and early 1960's, teaching still had to go on, the academic and cultural life of the school had to be fostered, and examinations had to be passed. The surprise is that so much was achieved and so little lost in the confusion. Drama, for example, actually flourished in what were very adverse circumstances. Despite the lack of a hall and a stage and female participants, Rhys Prosser put on a performance in the premises of the Nelson Haden Girls' School every year until the new hall was available at the High School in 1961. "King Lear" had been the outstanding production prior to 1954, but in that year there was "The Rivals", followed by "The Tempest", "Le Bourgeois Gentilhomme", "Noah", "The Ugly Duckling" and "Trial By Jury" (in the hall of the Girls' High School), "HMS Pinafore", and, in 1960, "The Importance of Being Earnest". In March 1961, the new hall was used for the first time, and the production was "L'Avare" by Molière. An ambitious undertaking, it was enthusiastically received, but there was disappointment over the suitability of the hall for drama "as it seemed to reduce all voices to grey and sibilant whisperings, without harmonics, overtones or variety. Most school productions have to lean rather heavily on broad - even obvious - strokes of character comedy, and the deadening quality of the hall tended to kill any attempts of this sort stone-dead almost before they had crossed the footlights." (I well remember this peculiarity of the Wingfield Hall. I hated taking morning assembly there; one's words were lost as soon as they were spoken. And this acoustic difficulty was one reason for the hall's being abandoned as anything other than an overflow gym, a storage space, and an examinations hall less than 20 years after its opening.)

In these years, too, there was an expansion of the Sixth Form of the Boys' High School and a corresponding increase of examination success at A level. From a Sixth Form of 9 in 1938, numbers had risen to 41 in 1954 and to almost double that some eight years later. A tradition had been established for the ablest boys to move on logically from school to university; the number of A level applicants rose from 11 in 1954 to 30 in 1960, and the number of scholarships and awards gained also increased markedly. 1957 was a particularly good rather than a typical year. Twenty boys were entered for A level; all passed in at least one paper, ten in three or four, and there were a total of 51 subject passes out of a possible 60. Eight boys were awarded County Scholarships as a result (most in maths and science), one reached the reserve list for a State Scholarship, and earlier in the year five boys had gained entry to Oxford or Cambridge, one with an Open Scholarship in modern languages. It is clear, therefore, that there was an assumption of academic achievement, and an advance on the situation that pertained prior to 1954 about which HMI wrote: "Over the past fifteen years the school has gained Open awards at the rate of one every two years, State Scholarships at the rate of two every three years, and County Scholarships at the rate of rather under two a year."

At O level the picture at this time is both more patchy and less clear. Mr Bucknall often reported "average" or "rather disappointing" results to his Governors. From pupils in their fifth year of secondary education, a typical set of results would be those of 1957 when 51 out of 52 in the age group were entered and 42 gained three or more passes. But behind these figures, as is always the case, are unnoticed and unrecorded triumphs, disasters, hopes realised, and ambitions dashed.

The teaching staff of 1954 lost some of its stalwarts before they could enjoy the benefits of the new buildings. Ted Ralph joined the staff in 1957 for maths and science, taking the place of D J Roberts, F S Harris in chemistry was replaced by Keith Mayell, the Senior Science post passing to Len Newell, W E Kemmery was followed by B J Watkins in English, and E R Webster by Jack Marsh for woodwork in 1958. W E Bingham gave way to John Broome for Latin the following year. However, four very long-serving teachers also left the school during this period – Walter Luckman (after 41 years), Herbert Lambert (37 years), Reggie Beams (40 years), and Tom Powell (40 years). As has been said before, their contribution to the education of generations of Trowbridge boys is incalculable; all who were taught by them will have their own favourite stories of the outrageous deeds and memorable sayings of one or other of them, and together they represent an enormous chunk of the history of the Boys' High School. I met one of them only – once. This was Reggie Beams whom I called upon at his home just before his death in 1989. On the occasion of my visit, he was being sternly reprimanded for having been seen riding his bicycle recklessly in Wingfield Road – at the age of 95! R C Lawrie replaced Luckman in 1955, with Gerald Gibson becoming Second Master and Douglas Bridgeman Head of Modern languages; Frank Bastian replaced Lambert as Head of History in 1958; Rowlands and Deans (who stayed only briefly and was replaced by A P Jarvis) took over from Beams and Powell in 1959 and 1960 respectively. An extra appointment for junior science in 1959 was that of A W Griffiths.

Retirement of Tom Powell, 1960, with, left to right: Messrs Gareth Roberts, Powell, Bucknall, Prosser, Gibson and Wilson.

Not all the personnel matters to concern Geoffrey Bucknall involved the teaching staff, of course. Late in 1957, J H Case was elected Chairman of Governors in succession to Brigadier V F Browne who was ill and whose death occurred shortly afterwards. Brigadier Browne had served the school well as Chairman since 1950 and had been an enthusiastic supporter of all its activities. Four years later, in 1961, the Board also lost the services of Frank Beer who resigned on account of advancing age. He had been Chairman from 1946-1950 and a Governor of the High Schools for over thirty years. His commitment to the schools was total, and his knowledge of them encyclopaedic. The position of Secretary to the Governors, too, changed hands. Mr S Holding resigned after thirty years in the position, being succeeded, briefly, by P W Inglis before the post was taken by L H Davidge in January 1958. (Secretaries to the Education Committee, or, later, the Governing Body, are a long-lived breed, it seems. Two of the first three, Messrs Ledbury and Holding, both served for incredibly long periods. Inglis was in post for less than a year, whilst Davidge was to remain for four, but in the thirty years since 1963 only Mrs Sylvia Garlick and the present Secretary, Mrs Tricia Pike, have held the position.)

It is a truism that in any school the Secretary and the Caretaker are more important and influential than any Governor or Head. More will be heard of the formidable Miss Rene White later, but her status as School Secretary was underlined when, in 1961, she was allowed to make a gate from the garden of the property in Avenue Road where she had lived all her life through into the grounds of the Boys' High School, thus providing her with a convenient short-cut from home to work. There was a proviso that this unorthodox access should be removed when she left the school's employment. Caretaker Lewis had served the school for 23 years; Mr Stevens retired in 1956 after 19. His successor was a Mr Yuille, but after little more than a year he resigned and was replaced by Mr Pickett in 1957, and he remained as Caretaker of the boys' school until amalgamation. Someone who survived amalgamation was Phil Pound. He was appointed as lab assistant in 1955, and in view of his great age at that time he had to have a specially adjusted wage arranged for him. Nevertheless, he stayed until 1980, and after 25 years of loyal service it was a great pleasure to see him at many of our social activities after his official retirement. Phil Pound acquired an assistant in 1960 – Peter Gray – as by that time six laboratories were operating.

So between 1954 and 1961 advances were being made on many fronts in addition to building developments. Societies and clubs were active – art, photographic, radio, natural history, geography, chess, music, cinematographic, and literary and scientific, to name a few – school trips at home and abroad were regularly organised, often, it seems, by Gareth Roberts and John Colin, and the school was able to take a justifiable pride in its achievements in football, rugby, athletics, and cricket, with tennis and swimming of somewhat lesser importance. But a Head Master is never without his worries. The travel arrangements to and from Melksham both for his pupils and for the girls beyond the hedge were the cause of some anxiety; the hedge itself needed watching for gaps unaccountably developed in it and a certain amount of in-filling had to be undertaken from time to time; and, more seriously, there was real concern about what was felt to be a deterioration in both the number of boys applying to join the Boys' High School at the age of eleven in the 1950's, and in the quality of the intake. For these new pupils, the grey flannel suit option was withdrawn in 1958 as it was little used, and there was thereafter an insistence on blue blazers as uniform, with soberly coloured pullovers and shirts.

1st XV rugby action, 1960.

Mr Bucknall's greatest worry, however, must have been over the matter of the Grass Cutter. The Secretary to the Governors reported in 1959: "The Head Master complains that he ordered a Grass Cutter which, on arrival, was found to have no seat. As the distance covered in one cutting of the outfield approximates to 23 miles, and as this cutting might be done two or three times a week...." Groundsmen had to be very fit in the 1950's!

Labour came to power in the general election of October 1964, and it very quickly became clear that the pattern of secondary education in this country was to change. Rightly or wrongly, in selective schools at least the feeling was of things about to be lost rather than of exciting opportunities opening up, so if the early 1960's at the Boys' High School were years of development and expansion springing from the building of virtually new premises, the later years of the decade were a period of retrenchment during which, with some anxiety and a degree of sadness, people were waiting to see what would happen. Despite (or, perhaps, because of) this uncertainty, there were few changes of teaching staff between 1961 and Easter 1969 when the two High Schools became one. Mr Greenaway became Head of Geography in 1965 when H W Hardy left for Zambia, and Andy Shearn also joined the school for geography in 1968 in succession to Rowlands, Ellis, and Eaton. Sidney Wilson, appointed in 1937 for physical education, left after twenty five years and was replaced first by Mr Keay, then by Mr McCarter, and finally in 1966 by Mr Wadey in English. Jones and Llewelyn followed Watkins, also in English; Cornish, Moakes and Bowcock in turn replaced Griffiths in science; G Sutton came as maths teacher in place of Jarvis in 1966; and an extra scientist, T D Martland, appointed in 1963, was replaced by D R Bignell two years later. Geoffrey Bucknall himself, to whom we shall return later, decided to retire at Christmas 1968, just one term earlier than Miss Morris, and for that one term's interregnum Gerald Gibson held the position of Acting Head Master. These changes in personnel over a period of eight years were few indeed when compared with the comings and goings south of the hedge.

By the time of amalgamation, then, the full-time staff of the Boys' High School, in addition to those mentioned above as being appointed in the 1961-1969 period, were: Messrs Gibson (maths), Bridgeman (French), Prosser (English), Bastian (history), Mayell (chemistry), Newell (physics), Roberts (biology), Johnston (art), Broome (Latin), Marsh (technical subjects), Lawrie (French), Colin (PE), Lavery (music), and Ralph (maths).

Roger White who had been appointed as junior laboratory assistant in 1965 was still there, but Rene White had gone – though not willingly. Appointed School Secretary in 1942, Miss White had become almost a part of the fabric of the place; a redoubtable lady, she involved herself in many aspects of school life. She reached retiring age in July 1965, requested that she be allowed to stay until July 1966, was granted an extension until December 1966, and sought yet another stay of retirement after that. The answer finally had to be "No", and Mrs Routledge took her place in January 1967.

The quality of the intake to the boys' school in the 60's was felt generally to be disappointing. Total numbers initially rose, but the 408 of 1963 had slid back to 363 four years later. Where there was no sense of disappointment was in the academic achievements of the Sixth Form. As has been said above, 1957 had been a particularly good year, and by the late 1960's success at A level and in the gaining of university entrance was very firmly established. About a group which at the age of 11 had looked distinctly unpromising, Geoffrey Bucknall was able to report in 1967:

"The A level results were altogether excellent....All told, out of 92 subject entries, there were no fewer than 89 passes....J E L Maslen gained 3 grade

A's and M E Mason a distinction on the Special Paper in mathematics, and between them the boys gained 22 grade A's and 28 grade B's which represents nearly 60% top grades. These were, in fact, by far the best results we have ever had."

The weight of success was in science and maths, with R H Johnston winning a Stapleton Scholarship in mathematics with physics at Exeter College, Oxford. Four boys gained university places that year on their 1966 results, and 20 out of 22 won entry on the 1967 results. High academic success at A level, rather narrowly focused perhaps, was what the Boys' High School strove for; the tradition at the Girls' High School was different, with a broad general education for five years followed by a Sixth Form course offering a wide range of options tending to be the aim.

After 10 years in office, the Chairman of Governors, J H Case, resigned in 1967, a generous tribute to his tireless work for the two High Schools having been paid by Mr Bucknall in his Speech Day address at the end of the previous autumn term. His successor was Mrs M H Melliar-Smith, and it was to her that the task of piloting through the amalgamation of the High Schools fell.

Geoffrey Bucknall himself retired at Christmas 1968. I know him as a witty, scholarly, civilised man, with a keen memory still for the boys and the teachers who passed through the school during his twenty one years' stewardship. Those who served under him speak above all of his "human understanding and warmth of personality". The Boys' High School was fortunate indeed in his leadership during those critical, formative post-war years, and he left the school in good heart for the difficult period that was to follow.

The interregnum between the retirement of Mr Bucknall and the arrival of Mr Suggitt was managed by G E G Gibson, now Acting Head for a term. And it was not an uneventful term. It saw the death of a man who had been a great friend to both High Schools – Dr Matthews – but by 1969 his work in Personal Relationships was being done by Gareth Roberts. In February there was a joint production with the Girls' High School of Benjamin Britten's "Noyes Fludde" in Holy Trinity Church, and what better augury for future cooperation between the two schools could there have been than for the French assistant at the Boys' High School to marry the French assistante at the Girls' High School in the summer of 1969!

A Golden Age:
Trowbridge High School for Girls: 1954-1969

Miss Morris, who had already been in charge of the school in an acting capacity for almost two years, was officially appointed Head of the Girls' High School on 28 May 1954. In the memories of those who taught there, this heralded a period of great stability, happiness, and positive achievement, partly because of the quality of the leadership given to the school, and partly because of the professional togetherness of the staff, who combined mutual professional respect with a social compatibility. There was, too, the contrast of the confidence of this time with the uncertainty and sadness that Miss Dawes' long period of illness had caused. The Girls' High School had a growing belief in itself and a sense of knowing where it was going.

Visible evidence of the school's entering a new period in its history was not hard to find. From September 1955 a dark green pinafore frock was introduced as the uniform for all new girls, and it was Miss Morris's declared aim "in two or three years to have turned the whole school quite green." Another change was the redesigning of the school badge. Miss Moore had chosen the daffodil as its emblem some forty years earlier, and the badge since then had been a rather geometric, six-petalled daffodil head within a circle, and the letters T G S. Now the Rev St John Battersby, who had designed the Trowbridge town crest, created a new and visually more interesting badge – crossed daffodils, with a vertical torch of learning, above a scroll with the school motto – *Vigor et Integritas*.

Between 1954 and 1961 the number of girls at the High School increased significantly. For a long time the roll had stood at about 340 or 350, but in 1960 and 1961 it shot up to 388, almost entirely because of an increase in Sixth Form numbers. But herein lies something of a mystery. Unlike Mr Bucknall at the boys' school, Miss Morris seldom had cause to complain about either the quantity or the quality of girls who opted to join the Girls' High School, but there was some anxiety about the number who still either failed to sit or failed to gain any passes at O level. Even more puzzling was the fact that, though the Sixth Form was immeasurably larger than it had been some twenty five years earlier, it was producing only the same number of girls as then who had both the ability and the desire to go on to university. Careers in nursing or secretarial work, and entry to Training College, were more popular. As is ever the case, however, just as there was the occasional academically disappointing year, so too there were years of distinguished achievement – like 1956. In that year, former pupils Margaret

Viles and Ann Maidment graduated in chemistry and history, Edna Lerwill and Judith Cooke were awarded State Scholarships, Sylvia Ingram a County Scholarship, and Felicja Przybos a Special Polish Scholarship; and Oxford continued to attract the most ambitious. But university was the aim of only a tiny minority of the girls in the school. Results at O level, which from 1955 was that of the Oxford rather than the London Board, tended to be either good or, at worst, satisfactory, but the experiment that was tried in 1959 of entering a set of pupils from the Fourth Year in English Language and Literature was not repeated.

Miss B Morris, Head Mistress, 1954-1969.

In her Speech Day report of 1959, Miss Morris was constrained to say:

"One great problem today besets girls' schools especially, the acquisition of sufficient staff. Gone are the days when many devoted women spent long years in the same school, building up the traditions of the school. The new staff arrive, give us their services for a few years, and depart, to marry, to follow their husbands, to found a family, or just to move, and we adapt ourselves to the changing times".

The theme of the difficulty in staffing a girls' school had been a recurring one in Trowbridge, but never was it more acute than in the years before amalgamation. Bad in the years 1954-1961, it became worse in the period 1961-1969. If Miss Morris were lucky, she had an applicant for a vacancy, but the luxury of being able to choose between competing candidates was virtually unknown. More probably, a number of part-time teachers had to be employed to plug a hole as best they could until a full-time, permanent appointment could be made – and, as Miss Morris said in 1959, "permanent" might mean a few years, or a single year, or one or two terms only.

Of the staff that she inherited in 1954, Miss Hazell and Miss Quine (domestic science), Mr Boulding and Miss Pinton (English), Miss Urquhart (PE), Mrs Rees (science), and Miss Trafford (music) remained in 1961. Miss Sergeant, the Second Mistress (re-titled Deputy Head in 1955) died in February 1958 after a short illness. She had been at the school since 1948 when she was appointed Senior Classics Mistress, but she is remembered by former pupils as much for her work with school dramatic productions and her enthusiasm for using the medium of detective stories as for her teaching of Latin. Her personal books were left to the school as a gift, and the Central Townswomen's Guild presented the school with a silver cup in her memory. She was followed as Deputy Head by Miss Hazell, and the teaching of classics was taken up by an old pupil of the school, Ann Mortimer (later Mrs Thompson). Two other teachers who had given long service to the Girls' High School left during this period – Miss Symmons, who completed 22 years, and Miss Borries, who had taught at the school for 35 years, served under all four of the school's Head Mistresses, and been a formidable presence in the staff room. There, she and Miss Horton White had seemed always to be at odds with each other. Miss Hellmann replaced her as Head of French. Others, too many to mention, came and went, sometimes so quickly as to leave no mark, but often making a significant contribution to the life of the school during a relatively short stay. Mrs Meg Hughes was appointed for maths in 1958 and she was to teach at the Girls' High School and its successor schools in various capacities for over 30 years; Mrs Goldthorpe will be remembered in biology, and Miss Knight (who replaced Miss Lord, later Mrs Mower) in art. There were, too, Mr Whittaker, "little" Mr Pugh, Miss Watkins, Mrs Wheller.... Finally, an important appointment was made in 1956. Mrs Lowe resigned. Miss J A Fletcher was appointed as Head of History, and it was she who was responsible for the exhibition of material illustrating the 50-year history of the Girls' High School mounted in 1962.

Another difficult post to fill was that of laboratory assistant. No solution could be found to the unsatisfactory procession of willing but ill-paid and poorly qualified young women who filled the post until 1966, when it was up-graded from that of an assistant to that of technician. But in its Caretaker and Groundsman the school was fortunate. Mr Dunn and Mr Mogg worked well together, and when the former was ill for some time, Mr Mogg proved to be a reliable and capable substitute. The aggravation that set the tone in the days of Lucas and Symonds was a thing of the past.

Presentation by Miss Dawes and Miss Morris to Miss Borries on her retirement in 1960.

And from the past, late in 1955, came Miss Moore. She sent a telegram one day to say that she would like to visit the school. "So," wrote Bronwen Morris, "at about four o'clock, a taxi drove up and from it emerged the valiant and indomitable little figure of Miss Moore, a small, very old, very lively person, sadly crippled with rheumatism, but alert and vigorous. She sat in my room and received the mistresses who worked with her, and the Head Girl, who presented a bouquet made by the girls from flowers in the garden." It was her last visit. She died on 9 February 1956 and her funeral took place at Holy Trinity Church, Combe Down, four days later.

If these were difficult years from the point of view of staffing, and if the academic ambition of the ablest girls was pitched lower than might have been expected, it was a very healthy and fruitful time in other ways. The pond was cleaned up; the Barnardo's fetes – later to become very much a tradition – were started; and the threat of a major road's being developed across the front of the school, joining Pitman Avenue and Gloucester Road, came to nothing. The list of activities that was available to the girls, the success of the clubs that operated on a regular basis, inter-school games – tennis, rounders, hockey and netball particularly –

and the school's own swimming and athletics competitions, the variety and scope of the trips that were organised both to events in this country and abroad, the tradition of drama that was fostered by Miss Pinton after the death of Miss Sergeant, and the insistence by Miss Morris on high standards of work and behaviour from her pupils and her staff ensured that, when it came to be inspected, the Girls' High School would be seen as a stimulating and positive environment; and that it was so was celebrated annually at Speech Day. This was always in March. It was a genteel occasion, beautifully organised, with the gardens looking their best and the trees full of blossom. The guest was usually some dignitary – the High Sheriff, a titled landowner, a Rear Admiral – but, in 1955, for the first time the presentations were made by a former pupil, Dr Marjorie Reeves, Vice-Principal of St Anne's College, Oxford. Speech Day was an occasion for justifiable self-congratulation; its basis was a previous year of hard work for the quality of which the school was accountable to HMI and the Ministry of Education in London.

Tony Mottram, the British Davis Cup player, giving the girls tennis coaching, 1956.

It was in February 1961, just as the new buildings on the other side of the hedge were being officially opened, that HMI turned their attention again to the Girls' High School. Their report was positive, commendatory, and very well received by the Governing Body. As far as teaching accommodation was concerned, one would not expect them to have had concerns of the same magnitude as those they had felt about the boys' school in 1954. Indeed, they say: "The main building is now almost thirty years old and has stood the test of time well". To that main building two classrooms, which by 1961 were a geography room and a physics lab, had been added in 1952, the Hut had long contained the two needlework rooms and, now, additional accommodation that had just been vacated by the boys' school, and the kitchen had been enlarged on several occasions to cope with the increased number of pupils who stayed at school for lunch. However, in the thirty years of its existence, faults had shown up and deficiencies that required rectification had developed.

The two staircases, one at each end of the building, were felt to be inconvenient, but little could be done about what was really a major design fault. The art room in the attic, too, was clearly inadequate, and it was something of a worry as a fire risk. Though suggestions were made at this time about its replacement, nothing was done. A further fault in the original design of the building was identified in the lay-out of the gymnasium and the adjacent changing room behind the assembly hall. These had always been a disaster. Miss Urquhart remembers the efforts she had to make to keep the girls quiet in the gym because Miss Trafford was teaching music in the hall. The four showers in the changing room had never been used as they were completely open and were more effective in wetting the room than in spraying hot gymnasts, and both rooms – the changing room and the gymnasium itself – were too small and obsolete in concept; but no alterations were forthcoming in this area despite HMI criticism.

Miss Trafford and the Girls' High School choir, competing at the Devizes Music Festival, 1955.

Developments took place elsewhere, as for example in the Hut (known also at this time as the Black Huts). Even before the visit of HMI, the two needlework rooms were beginning to get something of a face-lift with the installation of a new lighting system and the removal of a corridor wall. Now the improvements were extended to comply with the Inspectors' recommendations. The dividing wall between the two rooms was removed, new floor covering was provided, and they were redecorated. So, cut off from the main building though they were, the accommodation provided for needlework was now much more congenial. In 1963, an alteration long contemplated took place. The MI room was moved from its position on the first floor to the corner between G 61 and G 73 on the ground floor, and again a programme of redecoration accompanied the change. The following year, additional and much needed toilet and washing facilities were provided on either side of the assembly hall, beyond the existing rooms that were used by the staff and the Head. The building of these toilets created short, enclosed corridors on both sides of the hall. And later that year the first hard-surfaced tennis courts, the two Jubilee Courts, were laid out end-to-end just beyond the west wing of the main building, and officially opened in May 1965 by the Chairman of the Education Committee. It was in 1965, too, that the lower corridors of the school were finally enclosed, twenty eight years after a similar improvement was effected on the first floor and long after Miss Field had complained of the school's intolerable draughtiness. Finally – in this catalogue of structural alterations – the hutted classrooms that are today known as G 83, G 85, and G 87 were erected during 1966 and opened late in the year as the new geography department. This important and substantial addition to the buildings freed the two classrooms that had been opened some fourteen years earlier and used for geography and physics for conversion to a properly equipped and urgently needed physics laboratory.

If these were the developments in accommodation that flowed over the next five years from the Inspectors' report of 1961, its more important findings lay in its summing up of the state in which they found the Girls' High School.

"The school continues to maintain successfully its well established tradition in all those imponderable social values which are the characteristic excellence of a good girls' school. On the academic side there has been genuine progress since the last report was made and the present staff are well fitted to provide a strenuous intellectual programme for those who are able and willing to profit from it. It is much to be hoped that the unprecedented increase in Sixth Form numbers this year is the beginning of a permanent expansion and that parents in this area will be more alive than heretofore to the very great advantages which a longer school life in a school such as this can bring to their daughters."

Perhaps the few years around 1961 were the golden years of the Girls' High School. In July 1965, Circular 10/65 was to appear, and with it the knowledge that radical change was imminent, not only in the two Trowbridge schools but in secondary schools everywhere.

One might have expected a dip in the fortunes of the school during the 60's when its future as a single-sex selective institution was beginning to be in doubt. But it was not so. The number and quality of girls applying for admission was maintained. From 388 in 1961, the roll rose to 398 in 1963 and 410 in 1964, and thereafter, until the amalgamation of the two High Schools in 1969, it remained at about 400. Examination results, too, seldom proved to be less than satisfactory and in some years were the cause of very great pleasure. In 1964, an average of 6 passes per candidate was achieved by the 69 girls who were entered for O level, and at A level the results were equally distinguished, with 10 girls going on in that year to university and many more entering other forms of higher education. Indeed, from 1964 onwards, 10 or 12 was the usual number entering university from the school annually rather than the 2 or 3 of the years pre-1961. New ground was broken in 1967 when a group of girls entered the CSE examination in German and French; all achieved a grade 1 in German and about half the group in French. There was nothing narrowly traditional about the High School curriculum; German had been introduced some years earlier, as had physics, economic history, Greek, Spanish, statistics, religious knowledge and music; and other idiosyncratic subjects – like Italian – were accommodated from time to time.

If curriculum is at the heart of a Head's concerns, there are other more mundane issues which cannot be ignored. One such was the problem of the stage in the school hall. Should a proper proscenium arch with curtains be built? After much discussion, a temporary structure only was agreed upon, with curtains planned for the front and rear of the stage. And then there was the very long-running concern about the state of the school's hockey pitches and tennis courts; these occupied the same ground, and it was ground that was uneven and often waterlogged. Despite this, the school's record in games was a proud one, with girls frequently representing the Area and the County. Miss Urquhart and Miss Morris agitated over many years for better facilities, and the mention above of new hard-surfaced courts being opened in 1965 gives no indication of the period of time over which pressure was exerted by the school and its Governors for the provision of better tennis courts. The original intention had been that the school would finance the building of a court, and to this end the Jubilee Fund was opened. It stood at £460 in 1963, and the following year at £700, income being derived from fetes and concerts and a great deal of hard work by the Parent Teacher Committee. Eventually, the school obtained two courts, built "on the high ground by the laboratories", one paid for by the Education Committee and one by the Parents'

Association (£679.10) with a contribution from the Education Committee. Another problem that reared its head was the threat of the joining up of Pitman Avenue and Gloucester Road into a main road running across the front of the Girls' High School, but, as in 1955, it disappeared again. And – a problem that had not gone away even in my time – boys were reported to be invading the small wood at the far end of the field ("Miss Woodruff's wood") in the evenings and at weekends, and getting up to mischief there!

> Trowbridge Girls' High School
>
> Dramatic Society
>
> presents
>
> "The Beaux-Stratagem"
>
> by
>
> GEORGE FARQUHAR
>
> LANSDOWNS, PRINTERS, TROWBRIDGE

A matter more central to the academic life of the school was the continuing liveliness of drama. "Everyman" and "The Farce of Pierre Pathelin" were presented in 1962; "The Beaux Stratagem", "The Importance of Being Earnest", "Gammer Gurton's Needle", "The Boy With a Cart", "A Midsummer Night's Dream", and a cycle of Mystery Plays followed, all owing much to Miss Pinton's enthusiasm. Sport was healthy, competition being stimulated by the resurrection of a House system in 1961 – Berkeley, Conway, Ludlow, and Windsor being the names this time round. The BBC "Any Questions?" team visited the school in 1962; the first TV set was acquired in 1965; and Trowbridge Girls' High School won the finals of the Inter Schools Debating Festival for the first time in that year, too, thanks to Carole Davis and Bel Mooney. It was Bel Mooney who wrote the editorial in the new-look school magazine, View, in the summer of 1965, and an excellent, aggressive, and unusual editorial it was. A few years later, however, she was less than kind (and less than accurate) in some of the things she said about "that pleasant but unimaginative little school". A pupil from 1960 to 1966, she wrote:

> "It was an ordinary small-town grammar, separated by a high hedge from the tempting boys' equivalent. Not distinguishupil through Oxbridge entrance, TGHS sent a steady stream to the redbrick universities and teacher training colleges. The rest found jobs easily enough in Wiltshire in those days, and married, and watched a new generation of girls walk to the school in their bottle-green uniforms. Uniform was strict: dark green knickers for gym, and a constant war against the fashionably absurd practice of pinning the green beret vertically and invisibly behind a towering beehive."

Mrs Sue Keefe (formerly Sue Thomas) also remembers the uniform of the Girls' High School in the 1960's.

> "It had seemed strange at first, being a pupil at the 'big school', but you soon found yourself adjusting to the new discipline, the homework, and the wearing of a school uniform. This latter was a bottle-green gymslip, green woolly stockings, and a green and yellow striped tie that I was constantly fiddling with. Oh yes, and the awful beret! This item of clothing was absolutely compulsory and we were given an order mark for not wearing it. Most of us girls had huge, back-combed, beehive hairdos at that time, so all we could manage was to pin it onto our heads in a vertical fashion, secured by dozens of small clips....In summer, we were into our green and white chintzy dresses and Clark's sandals."

Those who attended the school in the 1960's will recognise the picture! And after recalling English under Mr Boulding (with pleasure) and gym and games under Miss Urquhart (without pleasure), Sue Thomas remembers music with Miss Trafford

> "who must be the most ancient teacher of all because she was even there when my mum was a pupil. We do some really strange songs in her class. At the moment we are studying this weird thing called 'The Magic Flute'. (Give me the Beatles any day!)"

By 1963, the annual Speech Day had been split into a Junior Prizegiving for the younger girls and their parents, and a more traditional sort of occasion for the senior school. The last such occasion was in November 1968 when Vera Silcocks gave the address. Miss Silcocks had been a pupil of the school in the early days of Miss Moore, and she had just retired from the headship of Ying Wa Girls' School, Hong Kong, where she had been for 45 years. (Her successor as Headmistress at Ying Wa was Evelyn Jenkins, an Oxford graduate and another former pupil of Trowbridge Girls' High School. And a further link with the colony was the school's financing in Hong Kong of the education of a Chinese refugee girl, Wai Lin.) Mrs Dugmore, the School Secretary, retired in 1963, to be replaced by Mrs Chalk; Groundsman Mogg retired, too, in 1965, Mr Fox taking his place; and the arrival in the same year of the new Laboratory Technician, Mr Huntley, stemmed the flow of young assistants and provided stable support for the teaching staff in science for the first time. Finally, Dr Matthews gave his last lecture on Personal Relationships in 1968, responsibility for this passing to Mrs Mead.

It had been clear for some time that a reorganisation of the Trowbridge secondary schools was to take place when, in 1968, Miss Morris announced her intention of retiring at the end of the spring term, 1969. A sensation of things running down and of an era ending, therefore, was inevitable. As has been said, the appointing of full-time, well qualified staff had become a matter of great difficulty, and one imagines that morale was not high when the new Head, Geoffrey Suggitt, took over the combined High Schools on 14 April 1969. His full-time staff from the Girls' High School were: Messrs Boulding and Johnson (English), Allen (Latin), and Verrinder (RE); Mrs Mead and Mrs Devon (jointly teaching geography), Mrs Perraton and Mrs Melhuish (jointly teaching science), Mrs Rees (science), and Mrs Carter (maths); and Misses Hazell and Quine (domestic science), Urquhart (PE), Parkhouse and Sales (French), Rogers (music), Knight (art), Baker (science), Fletcher (history), and Dawes (maths); and Miss Cooper (French and English) joined the school at this time in place of Miss Brierley.

In her last report on the occasion of Speech Day 1968, Miss Morris was very up-beat and positive about the future. "I have raised no problems, announced no difficulties," she said, but she must have been very conscious of the ending of the Girls' High School's 57 years as a unique institution. During this time, 4,469 girls from 39 towns and villages in West Wiltshire had passed through its classrooms. In her leadership of the school, she had shown "concern without interference and toleration without unawareness", and tributes to her emphasised the sensitivity with which she made the transition from being an assistant teacher to Head Mistress. "She has striven to raise the standard of academic achievement, though she has never made the mistake of over-valuing this, and has recognised, and urged her staff to recognise in the girls they teach, other and at least equally valuable qualities and excellences." Miss Morris had been a good Head, a good teacher, and a good friend to many.

Together Again:
Trowbridge High School: 1969-1974

DES Circular 10/65 of July 1965 led to the creation of The John of Gaunt Comprehensive School in September 1974. But the conversion of two selective schools to a single non-selective school was not straightforward. Initially, the Authority's plan was for two eight-form entry comprehensives – one on the High School and one on the Nelson Haden site – and it was on this basis that discussions took place throughout 1966 and 1967. However, by early 1968, as a result of public pressure, the plan was changed to the establishing of one very large all-through comprehensive, the first three years of which would be on the Nelson Haden site, with Years Four and Five and the Sixth Form at the High School. It was at this time that the Heads of the two High Schools, Miss Morris and Mr Bucknall, indicated their intention to retire during the course of the next school year. The question then was what was to happen to these two schools between the resignation of their Heads and their integration into the huge, sixteen-form entry comprehensive that was now planned for the early or mid 1970's. The answer was that they would be merged to form a mixed selective school under one Head from January 1969. (In the event, Mr Suggitt could not take up his appointment until 14 April, so the new school actually opened at Easter 1969, with Miss Morris remaining in post until then, and the boys' school operating with Gerald Gibson as Acting Head for one term.) Meanwhile, on the national stage, Labour were ejected from office in 1970 and a youthful Mrs Thatcher found herself the Secretary of State for Education and Science in the new Heath government; and she it was who, in 1972, turned down the plan for the large, single comprehensive school "because of the immense problems of administration and coordination" that it would present. The Authority, having had to go back to the drawing board unexpectedly, quickly reverted to its original plan of two eight-form entry comprehensives on the Nelson Haden and the High School sites. The time-span for preparation was now much shorter. Nevertheless, both schools opened in September 1974, The John of Gaunt School under a new Head, Frank St George, as Geoffrey Suggitt's application was rejected.

Such, in outline, was the complex, and not untroubled, transition of the two High Schools of 1969 to the single comprehensive school of 1974.

From 1965, through 1966, 1967, and into 1968, there was discussion and planning about how the two High Schools should be converted into a single, all-through, eight-form entry comprehensive. A Special Sub-Committee of the Education

Committee had been formed to negotiate the change, and during this period it met regularly with Heads, Governors, school staffs, and other interested parties in order to sound out opinions, engage in feasibility studies, and work on such areas of concern as accommodation, pupil numbers, catchment areas, curricula, and staffing implications. The comprehensive school formed from the former High Schools would serve only part of Trowbridge and some of its neighbouring villages. Pupils would cease to come to Trowbridge from Melksham (which would have its own comprehensive school) after September 1968, and Bradford, Westbury, and Warminster would similarly be reorganised for secondary education. But a more limited catchment area was only one change; others were to be a move from single sex intakes to a mixed intake, despite the powerful lobbying of the Heads and teaching staffs for some form of segregation to continue, and, of course, exclusively academically able pupils were to be replaced by an all-ability pupil population. When the reorganised school finally came into being in 1974, very much on the lines of these early plans, it was unique in being the only comprehensive school in the County to be formed exclusively from a grammar school, and the professional shock that this caused to the teaching body cannot be over-emphasised.

Pupil numbers worked out rather neatly. The two High Schools between them took in four forms of entry, but rather less than half the pupils actually came from Trowbridge. This shortfall would be more than made up by the anticipated rise in the size of year groups of the Trowbridge area primary schools from 290 in 1966 to 480 (i.e. sixteen forms of entry) in 1981. So, in the interim period between 1966 and the opening of the proposed comprehensive school, declining numbers entering the High Schools from outside Trowbridge would be balanced by a corresponding increase in numbers from the town and the nearby villages, thus allowing the schools to continue as two-form entry for as long as they remained selective. Whilst this was happening between the Wingfield and Gloucester Roads, on the other side of Frome Road the Nelson Haden Schools would also be reorganised to form a second eight-form entry comprehensive school in the town.

This, then, was the plan as originally formed.

By early 1968, two complications had arisen. The first was that, under pressure from several quarters, the Local Authority had changed its mind and submitted proposals for the setting up of one very large reorganised school on two sites. The second complication was that both Miss Morris and Mr Bucknall announced their intentions of retiring, and it was this issue that was of the more immediate concern. The pros and cons of two new appointments being made were debated; the views of the staffs of the schools were canvassed, but the decision was taken that a single Head for the two High Schools should be appointed as a halfway house towards the eventual amalgamation of the High Schools and the two Nelson Haden Schools into the planned single comprehensive. It was decided that the integration of the High Schools would take place on 1 January 1969, following Geoffrey Bucknall's retirement. A new Head for the combined schools would be in post, and the new school would operate, from that date. However, Miss Morris would be "entirely responsible to the Governors and the Local Education Authority for the conduct of the Girls' School during [the spring] term!" This would have produced a very curious situation indeed, but it was fortunately never tested in practice as the new Head, Geoffrey Suggitt, could not get to Wiltshire until the second week in April, and it was then, at the start of the summer term 1969, that the Trowbridge High School began its short life.

Geoffrey Suggitt was appointed from 59 candidates for the post. A Scholar of Queen's College, Oxford, and a first class honours graduate in Classical Greats, he came to Trowbridge from George Watson's College, Edinburgh, where he had been Head of Classics. His brief was to integrate the two High Schools into a mixed selective school, and then, in the longer term, work on the detailed planning of the future comprehensive school for Trowbridge. His immediate concerns were rather more prosaic. He needed an office and a Secretary. These were provided. A mobile office arrived and was positioned near the bottom of the steps that led up to the playground at the back of the Gloucester building. Further mobile rooms were approved as extra accommodation for the Sixth Form and as a toilet unit for the girls who would have to use the former boys' school building. Mr Gibson and Miss Hazell, the two Deputies, were granted additional allowances for the next four terms for the responsibilities they would have to shoulder, and Mrs Lewis was appointed to give part-time secretarial help to the new Head. So, in summer 1969, Trowbridge High School opened and was ready for business.

Geoffrey Suggitt's intention had been to spend the summer term in getting to know his staff, the pupils, and the problems for integration posed by the school buildings. In the event, much of his time was taken up in appointing new staff, and in resolving, as far as it could be resolved, the question of how to amalgamate two teaching staffs, and two sets of departmental headships, into one without bitterness or acrimony. That he was not entirely successful he himself admitted.

> "My most difficult and most unpalatable task of the term was to choose between the Heads of Department and recommend appointments to the Governors. Whatever I did was bound to cause disappointment in some quarters, but I felt that I should not leave staff in suspense longer than was absolutely necessary. Since I did not see that I could come to any different conclusions if I postponed recommendations to the autumn term, I recommended the appointment of the majority of the Heads of Department from the boys' side of the school. This caused the turmoil that I expected on the girls' side, but I simply had to ride the storm. I thought it better to start a new year with all this settled."

It was a matter about which Miss Hazell, on behalf of the former Girls' High School staff, wrote to the Governors.

Mr Wadey and Mr Llewelyn (English) and Miss Sales and Mr Bridgeman (modern languages) left in the summer of 1969, the latter after teaching at the boys' school for 27 years, to be replaced in September by Mr Collier and Mrs Powell in English, and Mrs Cable in modern languages. This left a vacancy, the first of many at this time, which had to be filled by temporary and part-time appointments. So the full-time staff of the High School as it started its first full year in September 1970 (with Heads of Department marked *) was:

Head	Mr Suggitt	**Latin**	Mr Allen *
Art	Mr Johnston *	**Mod. Langs.**	Miss Parkhouse *
	Miss Knight		Mrs Cable
			Mr Lawrie
Biology	Mr Roberts *		Mrs Potter
	Miss Baker		
		Maths	Miss Dawes *
Chemistry	Mr Mayell *		Mrs Carter
	Mr Bignell		Mr Gibson
			Mr Ralph
English	Mr Prosser *		Mr Sutton
	Mr Boulding		
	Mr Collier	**P.E.**	Mr Colin *
	Mr Johnson		Miss Urquhart *
	Mrs Powell		
Geography	Mr Greenaway *	**Physics**	Mr Newell *
	Mr Shearn		Mr Bowcock
			Mrs Rees
History	Miss Fletcher *		
	Mr Bastian	**R.E.**	Mr Verrinder *
	Mr Broome		
		Tech. Studs.	Mr Marsh *
Home Econ.	Miss Quine *		
	Miss Hazell		

Additionally, there were many part-time teachers, the number of whom Mr Suggitt set about reducing – Mr Belcher (art), Mrs Mead and Mrs Devon (geography), Mr Francis and Mrs Shearn (physics), Mrs Perraton and Mrs Melhuish (science), Mrs Hughes (maths)....Mrs Rees and Miss Baker resigned at Christmas 1969, and Mrs Potter the following term. Mrs Shearn replaced Mrs Rees, but "as

Mr Shearn was teaching at the school, Mrs Shearn could only be appointed as a temporary teacher"; and another wry note is struck by the Clerk to the Governors about the difficulty in filling vacancies when she writes: "three candidates were offered modern languages posts, none of whom accepted." Applicants for posts at the school could see some of the problems that already loomed.

Caretaker Pickett retired in July, to be replaced on the boys side by Mr Clothier. Mr Stephens followed Mr Fox as Groundsman, and one of the boys' school's great servants, Mrs Lyddieth, School Cook for 27 years, retired in October.

Committees had been set up to discuss and pave the way for the implementation of many issues that integration threw up – an overall policy-making committee, and separate groups for uniform, games, social activities, reports and records, library and magazines, and class and timetable arrangements. A threefold, horizontal division of the school into lower, middle, and upper was intended by Mr Suggitt, but in these early days he only went so far as to appoint Miss Urquhart as Head of Lower School and charge her with responsibility for the first mixed intake in September 1970. The entry of 1969, although not admitted as a mixed cohort, showed how the catchment area had changed; of the 125 offered places, 91 were from Trowbridge, 21 from Westbury, 11 from Warminster, 1 from Melksham, and 1 from Bradford.

By the end of the 1969/70 school year, Mrs Cable and Mrs Potter had gone, but more new staff had been appointed – Mr Hayward in chemistry, Mr Francis in physics, and Miss Crouch in biology, Mrs Allen, Mr Bennett, Miss Henderson and Miss Allpress in modern languages, Mr Lycett in English, Mr Duffield in maths, and Miss Hyde in PE. A five-form entry was expected in September. "She Stoops to Conquer" had been a success, and a musical, "Oliver", was planned for Christmas. So far, the Local Authority had been unable to promise any new buildings for the school, or for the intended comprehensive school, but by the summer of 1970 modest plans had been agreed for more mobile classrooms, a mobile mixed staffroom, with a lounge, toilets, and a kitchenette, and the removal of the projection room from the centre of the balcony in the Gloucester hall. (Miss Field had tried to have this small room removed in 1938, but had been thwarted by lack of funds. Now it was done, its removal explaining the pointless central door that remains in the balcony today.) A School Council was established with a pupil representative from each form, and six members of staff; the implementation of one of its first recommendations resulted in the establishing of four new Houses named after Wiltshire rivers – Avon, Bourne, Kennet, and Wylye. Money was sought with which to equip a school orchestra; the usual summer activities of swimming, cricket, athletics, and a Barnardo's fete continued as before; and, importantly, a standing committee was formed to ensure a sensible and rational programme of studies available both to the Sixth Formers at the school and the students at the FE college. This latter innovation was to stand the test of time and it resulted in a significant curricular opportunity for senior students into the 1990's.

1970 saw the resignation of Mrs Melliar-Smith and her replacement by P R Sylvester as Chairman of Governors. And the deaths occurred of F S Harris and E R Webster, former science and woodwork teachers at the boys' school, and of Weg Griffiths after a road accident. Mr Dunn, Caretaker of the Gloucester Road building, retired after 19 years and 1 day. Mr A E G Pearce succeeded him, and was given responsibility for the whole site, with Mr Clothier and Mr Williams as his assistants. By now, there were 876 pupils on roll, and a number of improvements to the facilities had been effected. A concrete path had been laid between the Gloucester and the Wingfield buildings, more mobiles had arrived and been connected to the necessary services, a new classroom (G 14) had been created next to the library, chain-link fencing had been provided for one of the Gloucester playgrounds, and part of the dividing hedge between the two former schools had been removed. On the other hand, the new mixed staffroom, although in place, was not ready for use.

G Suggitt, Head of Trowbridge High School, 1969-1974.

Mr Suggitt remembers this as an exciting time, but one that is now for him imbued with an almost dreamlike quality. The school was moving forward positively on many fronts. There was a substantial fund of goodwill for the new ways of doing things and the compromises that had to be made from many of those involved day-by-day in the life of the school. Undeniably, however, there were some who did not welcome change, who were set in their ways, and who were resentful at having to adapt to altered circumstances, so, sadly but probably inevitably, an undercurrent of disaffection persisted which inhibited total acceptance of the new order and that grew as the impact of the more dramatic changes inherent in moving to comprehensive education began to be felt.

By October 1971, Geoffrey Suggitt was able to claim that the integration of the High School was almost complete and that the focus should shift to comprehensive reorganisation. This, nevertheless, was still three years away. The roll rose from 876 to 930 in 1974 and a number, though not an inordinate number, of staff changes took place before the High School ceased to be. Messrs Bowcock, Hayward, Bastian, Bennett, Bignell, Duffield and Perkins left, as did Miss Henderson, Miss Allpress, Miss Knight, Mrs Allen, Mrs Hayward and Mrs Carter. Mrs Mackie (art) and Mrs Ludlow (maths) came and went. A significant departure was that of Miss Fletcher, Head of History, who had been at the school since 1956. She retired at the end of the summer term 1973. And, very tragically, Miss Hazell died after a lengthy illness in October 1973. Involved in many aspects of education both within and without the school, she had borne much of the burden of the integration of the High Schools and had been a tremendous support to the new Head. In her place, Dorrie Urquhart became temporary Second Mistress pending a permanent appointment to the post in the new comprehensive school. During the same period, Mrs Mead and Mr Belcher became full-time members of staff, and Mr Angus (maths) and Mr Stacey (English) joined the school, initially in a supernumerary capacity, from the Adcroft School which closed. New arrivals, too, were Mrs Haxell (maths), Messrs Snow, Sherwell, and Shepherd, and Miss Drane (modern languages), J A Wright (geology and chemistry), Mr Collyer (biology), Mr Malcolm Roberts (technical), Mr Foster (chemistry), Mr Williams (PE), Mrs Newman (biology), and Mrs Daly and Mrs Behan (history), Mrs Behan replacing Miss Fletcher as Head of Department. For a large school in a state of reorganisational uncertainty, these changes were not unduly numerous in a period of over three years. One other matter of significance as far as teaching staff are concerned should be mentioned here: Miss Urquhart, Mr Gareth Roberts, and Mr Greenaway were made Senior Teachers in 1973 in recognition of their responsibilities as Heads of Lower, Middle, and Upper Schools respectively. This freed Mr Gibson and Miss Hazell from much day-to-day administration and allowed them to concentrate more on the general oversight and development of the school. (Technically, Mr Gibson was Deputy Head and Miss Hazell Second Mistress, but in practice the two were accorded equal status.)

Ancillary staff were appointed in increasing numbers, but some, of course, retired: Mrs Chalk (Secretary), Groundsman Wright, and Mrs A Morris who had worked as a cleaner at the school for almost 40 years. Bert Eldridge arrived as technical assistant, Mrs Johnson from Adcroft to share the secretarial duties briefly with Janice Lewis, Mrs Todd as library assistant, and others.....

By the start of the school year in 1971 all year groups were mixed. The plan now was for there to be 1,400 lower school places on the Nelson Haden site, with 960 upper school and 300 Sixth Form places at the High School. This implied new buildings, but so far little had happened other than the provision of mobile accommodation, the latest addition to which had been the mobile science lab – G 89/91. With the closure of the Adcroft School, its playing field along the Wingfield Road had been formally transferred to the High School by the Building Sub-Committee of the Education Committee, but everything – including the appointment of the Head of the new comprehensive school – now hung on the approval by the Secretary of State of the scheme that had been submitted. And about this there was some doubt. The Governors had already debated the opinion that was live in the area of the proposed school's being too big to be manageable, and throughout the planning process there had been a fall-back position which allowed for the creation of two schools rather than one. So when notice was received early in March 1972 that the large, sixteen-form entry school had failed to gain ministerial approval, there was concern but no great surprise or feeling of devastation. Indeed, the Local Authority was able very easily to go back to its earlier plans so that a Revised Draft Plan for Consultation was circulating within a couple of weeks of the Secretary of State's refusal being received. County Council approval for this Revised Plan was given in May 1972 and ministerial approval in January 1973.

The change in plans meant fewer alterations than might have been imagined. Instead of about 1,300 pupils aged 14-18 there would be 1,400 aged 11-18 on the High School site. More practical spaces and classrooms would be needed, but fewer labs. Arrangements for staff accommodation would be unaltered, and the hope still was that a Sports Hall, subsidised by the Town Council, would be provided. All the recently installed mobiles were moved during the Easter holidays of 1972 to positions out of the way of the building operations that were imminent, access and services were put in, two new mobiles for Sixth Form use arrived, and work began on four hard tennis courts beyond the mobiles. From late summer 1972, much of the campus took on the appearance of, and, in fact, was, a building site, but interference with the work and life of the school was minimal.

The initial phase of building resulted in what today are known as the Hertford and Chiltern blocks – essentially laboratories in the first and practical rooms in the second, with the Chiltern kitchen and boiler house being brought into use early so that the heating in Gloucester could be provided by the new installation. This was to be followed by phases 7 and 8, for 270 and 150 places respectively, and they included the provision of a shell for a Sports Hall, gymnasium and changing rooms (with heating, lighting and floor covering to be provided when funds allowed, as the hoped-for subsidy had not been forthcoming), a teaching block (Dunston), a staff suite, and some adaptations to existing buildings. There were plans, too, for the playing fields, with the provision of a large all-weather games area being among the improvements intended. The work on Hertford and Chiltern went on throughout 1973, and in March Geoffrey Suggitt wrote:

"It is planned to start the road from Old Wingfield to the Black Huts, including the car parking area, in June 1973. I have insisted that this work must be complete by the end of August. The contractors have agreed not to demolish the Black Huts before the practical block is ready for use."

So the end was at last in sight for the Hut, or the Black Huts, of 1921.

The Hertford building was completed and the Dunston block begun late in 1973, and Chiltern was finished early in 1974. The staff accommodation and Sports Hall followed somewhat later, in 1974/75. In addition to this major building work, during late 1973 and early 1974 some important adaptations were made to existing buildings. The Wingfield heating system was replaced and the boys' changing rooms extended; a girls' cloakroom and toilets were also provided in that building; the woodwork room was converted to a Sixth Form common room (and it remains so today); the adjacent pottery room became a snack bar; upstairs, the art room was given over to geography; the Gloucester kitchen and part of the dining room were converted to a packed-lunch area; part of the Gloucester dining room was converted to a girls' changing and showering area; and the domestic science room became the base for music. By mid-summer 1973, after four years of planning and contriving and putting up with shifting and less than satisfactory situations, Geoffrey Suggitt could at last see an end to improvisation. The physical basis for the comprehensive school was in place; much still had to be done by way of staff training, but the future was clearer than it had been for many years. And it was at this point that he learnt that he was not to be the new school's Head.

Once the plans for reorganisation had been accepted by the Department in London, a Governing Body for the new school, running in parallel with the Governing Body of the High School, had been appointed. Whilst not being exactly the same, there was a substantial similarity in the composition of the two bodies, but it was the Governors of the new school – for the moment rejoicing in the name of Trowbridge North Comprehensive School – who decided, despite a contrary wish by the Local Authority, that the headship of the school should be advertised for open competition. This was done, and short-listed candidates were interviewed during the summer term of 1973. Disappointed at having to apply for what he and the staff of the school saw as being his own job, Mr Suggitt was both angry and amazed when the announcement was made, after what he felt had been a hostile interview, of an outside appointment's having been made. It was this public demonstration of their lack of faith in him, unsupported by any prior criticism at Governors' meetings of his performance as Head of the High School, that he felt so bitterly. Whatever the reason for what happened, its effect

Opposite: Trowbridge High School, 4th Year 1972, with, from left to right: Vic Belcher, John Colin, Agnes Routledge, Gareth Roberts, Geoffrey Suggitt, Ted Ralph, Jan Shearn, Rex Bignell, Andy Shearn.

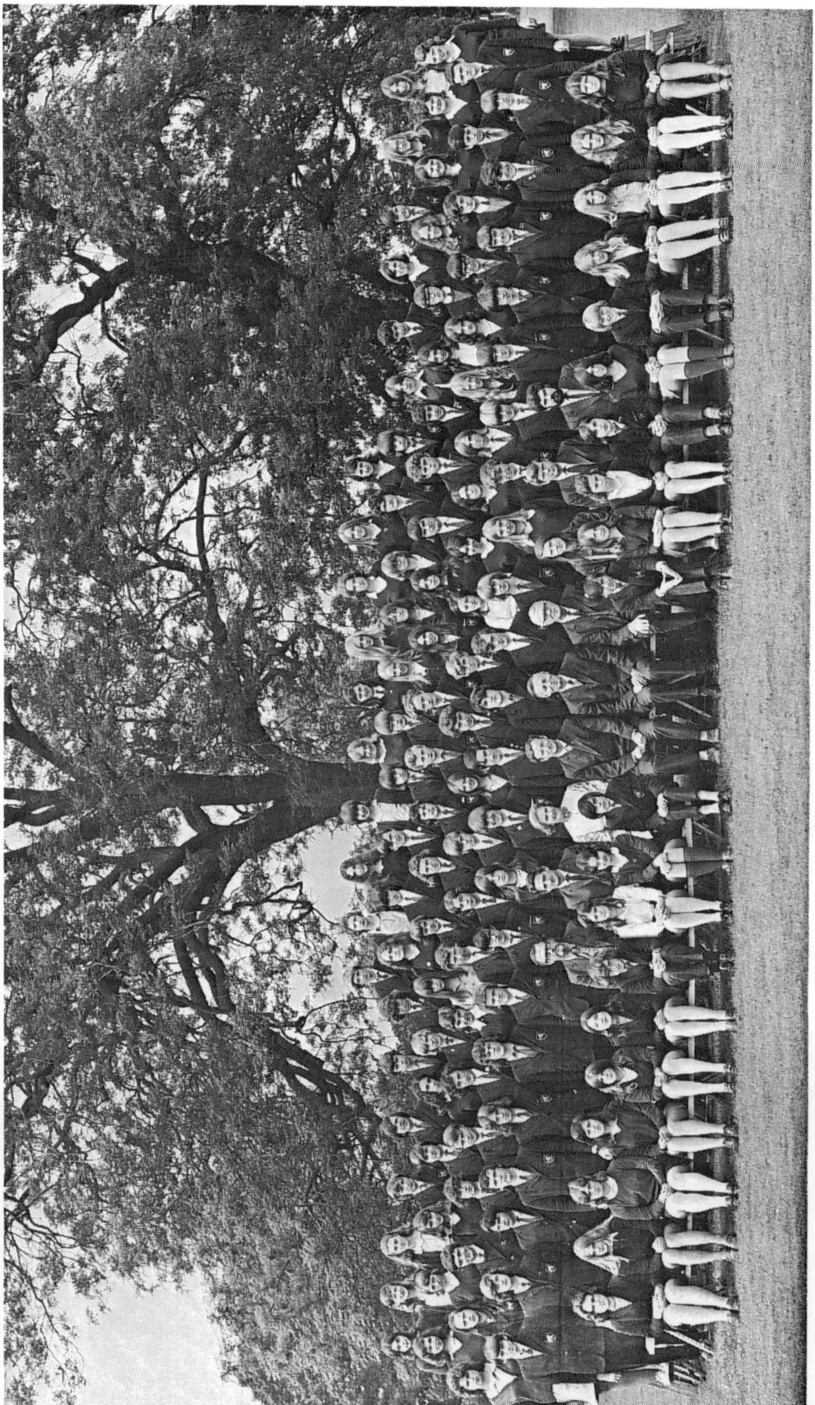

upon the teaching staff of the school was unfortunate in the extreme. The two senior members of staff wrote to the Governing Bodies of both the High School and the Trowbridge North Comprehensive School about how what had been done was viewed by the school, and the High School Parents' Association was also constrained to write. These were difficult times indeed, and as if the problem of moving from being a totally selective school to having an all-ability intake were not sufficiently traumatic, there was now, rightly or wrongly, a deep feeling of resentment about the way in which the matter of the headship of the comprehensive school had been managed.

Life, however, had to go on, and for the pupils of the High School it was an academically rewarding life. "The Good Person of Szechwan" had been successfully presented in April 1973; there was a richness about the quality and diversity of extra-curricular activities and clubs available in a five-form entry selective school that had not been possible in the smaller High Schools, the Friday Club, organised by the Parents' Association and the School Council being a case in point; the O level pass-rate hovered around the 75% mark during the early 1970's, and for A level it was usually over 80%, with around 30 pupils annually going on to university, many with distinguished examination performances to their credit. A good working relationship had been built up with the new Parents' Association, leading to many pleasant social occasions and an extremely successful Sponsored Walk. It was this latter that made possible the purchase of a minibus for the school, outdoor pursuits equipment, and orchestral instruments. And the Governors agreed on the abolition of compulsory school uniform for the Sixth Form. On the negative side, it was not felt appropriate to go ahead with the normal Speech Day arrangements in 1973, so extended assemblies in the lower school and evening social functions for older students, to which parents were invited, were held instead. Additionally, a commemorative evening to mark the passing of the High School was organised, with exhibitions, presentations, and dancing – a bitter sweet occasion that was attended by many who had been connected with the High Schools over a long period.

Early in 1974 Geoffrey Suggitt announced his resignation as from Easter. He had obtained the headship of the Stratton School, Biggleswade, and in that post he continued until his retirement many years later. His achievement in Trowbridge had been a significant one. With patience and persistence he had tackled the problems inherent in joining together two schools with widely divergent traditions and ways of working, dissipating the inevitable wariness with which they viewed each other, so that by the time of his leaving, Trowbridge High School was a unified school in much more than name. Regret was felt in many quarters that he could not remain to complete the job that he had begun. For the third time in his career, Gerald Gibson became Acting Head. The first time had been during an illness suffered by Mr Bucknall, the second for the term prior to the arrival of Mr Suggitt, and now, for the summer term of 1974, he held the position

The Wing.

in alagro alacritas.

Price 6d.　　　　Summer Term, 1920.

SUMMER 1941.

Fiat Lux

The Wing

BOYS HIGH SCHOOL

· TROWBRIDGE ·

again before retiring at the point when Trowbridge High School became The John of Gaunt School. He had been at the school for 20 years, first as Head of Maths in succession to Tubby Downing, and latterly as Deputy Head at the boys' and then the mixed school. A sportsman (he represented Selwyn College in five major sports and won a county cap for hockey) and a Cornishman, he nevertheless served Wiltshire and academia well.

As a postscript to the story of selective education in Trowbridge, there needs to be a final word about the school magazines. Each of the High Schools began a regularly published magazine in 1920, as has already been said – "TGHS Magazine" in the one case, "The Wing" in the other. They tended to be annuals, with short periods of over-enthusiasm when termly publication was attempted. "TGHS Magazine" was clad in sober dark green from 1920 to 1947 when it suddenly blossomed into a light buff, patterned with the silhouettes of girls reading and dancing. In 1954, this frivolity was put aside for a return to the plain dark green cover of earlier years which bore the newly created girls' school badge. The magazine became "View", and took on a new look, in 1965 under the editorship of Bel Mooney, and such it remained for the life of the Girls' High School. "The Wing" was so named from the start. It originally had a reddy-brown cover bearing the design of a wing shielding a field, and beneath it the alliterative mock-Latin motto IN ALAGRO ALACRITAS. ("Alacritas" is "brisk-ness" or "keenness". "Ala", a wing, and "ager", a field, were put together to complete the rather forced pun – "briskness in wing-field"!) In 1932 O'Flaherty redesigned the cover in blue and yellow with a rearing white horse, the rising sun, and Stonehenge, and the more conventional motto, "FIAT LUX". This continued until 1956 after which "a wallpaper style magazine" was tried, with a final change to a larger format publication in yellow, incorporating a small rising sun motif, from 1959 to the end of the boys' school's existence as a separate entity. With the opening of the mixed High School, "The Falcon" was born. It combined the creativity of "View" with the more solid reporting of "The Wing" and it gave an attractive impression of the liveliness and fullness of life at Trowbridge High School. Sadly, it petered out after reorganisation, a final edition appearing in 1979 after an absence of several years.

Trauma:
The John of Gaunt School: 1974-1979

The John of Gaunt School opened at the beginning of the autumn term 1974 – on 28 August, after a staff meeting and the return of most of the Sixth Form on the previous day – but there had been activity directly related to the school's opening for over a year prior to that date. A Governing Body had been appointed early in 1973, and its first task was the choosing of a Head for the comprehensive school. Mr F H St George, Head of a 1,000 strong school in Peterborough that had become comprehensive from grammar, was their choice. His appointment was to date from 1 January 1974, so there were some fourteen months for him either as Head or Head Elect in which to plan and consult and make himself familiar with the situation in Trowbridge. Another early task of the Governing Body was to choose a name for the new school which, for convenience, was known for the moment as the Trowbridge North Comprehensive School. They themselves suggested that name, and other possibilities were the Selwood School, the Old High School, the Wingfield School, the Bradley School, the Falcon School, the Gaunt School, and the Pitman School. The opinions of the pupils of the High School were canvassed, and it was decided that, if one of their suggestions were adopted, a modest prize should be awarded to the pupil who had made it. So consideration was then given to the Tyning School, the John of Gaunt School, the J H Bradley School, the Henson School....Two boys, Stephen Kyte and Patrick Gover, were responsible for suggesting the name that was eventually chosen, and each was sent a book token for £2 as a reward. A conscious decision was taken not to include "Comprehensive" in the school's name, and some research had to be done to decide which of the two versions, "John of Gaunt" or "John O'Gaunt", was the more respectable historically!

Other, more substantial, decisions had to be made. Mr St George's room, when the buildings were complete, would be in Dunston, with his Secretary's office adjacent (D 23 and D25), but until then he would operate from temporary accommodation in a small room off the Library in Chiltern. Whether Mrs Routledge, Mrs Lewis, or Mrs Johnson would act as his personal Secretary remained unresolved at this stage. Teaching in Year One would be in entirely mixed ability classes, but thereafter setting would be possible in some subjects; and for the moment there would be no change to the school uniform. The most important decisions of all, however, were about the staffing of the new school and the status to be accorded to individual members of that staff. None of the teaching staff had security of tenure (though salaries were safeguarded) and many meetings took place to thrash out a structure before the delicate process of fitting individuals into the agreed structure was undertaken. By January this had been done, and before the end of that spring term the staffing of the John of Gaunt School (apart from a few appointments that still had to be made) had been agreed. Miss Drane resigned before the new school came into being; Miss Ashton (Head of Biology), Mr Bramley (Head of Basic Studies), Miss Heath and Miss J M Jones (modern languages), Mrs Wagstaff (English), Mrs Cooper (art), and Miss Hodder and Miss Rosie Jones (maths) were appointed. So the full-time teachers at the school when it opened in late August 1974, with Heads of Department listed first, were:

physics:	Mr Newell, Mr Francis, Mrs Shearn;
chemistry:	Mr Mayell, Mr Wright, Mr Foster;
biology:	Miss Ashton, Mr G Roberts, Mrs Newman;
combined science:	Mr Collyer;
mathematics:	Miss Dawes, Mr Ralph, Mr Sutton, Mrs Haxell, Mr Angus, Miss Hodder, Miss R Jones;
English:	Mr Prosser, Mr Collier, Mr Johnson, Mrs Powell, Mrs Wagstaff, Mr Stacey, Mr Lycett, Mr Boulding;
modern languages:	Miss Parkhouse (Head of French), Mr Lawrie, Mr Snow, Mr Sherwell, Mr Shepherd, Miss Heath, Miss J M Jones, Mrs Hourizi, Mr Regan;
classics:	Mr Allen;
history:	Mrs Behan, Mr Broome, Mrs Daly;
religious education:	Mr Verrinder;
geography:	Mr Shearn, Mr Greenaway, Mrs Mead, Mrs Sharples;
technical studies:	Mr Marsh, Mr M Roberts;
art:	Mr Johnston, Mr Belcher, Mrs Cooper;
basic studies:	Mr Bramley;
home economics:	Miss Quine;
music:	Mr Lavery, Miss Rogers;
PE and games:	Miss Hyde and Mr Williams, Miss Urquhart, Mr Colin.

Additionally, there were a number of part-time teachers, some of whom served the school for many years and who were often willing to come in at very short notice to help out in an emergency; Mrs Bradford, Mrs Perraton, Mrs Meg Hughes, Mrs Farmer, and Mrs Janet Jones, for example, though part-time, were an invaluable asset to the school over a long period of time.

This departmental structure was underpinned by a new pastoral system which is essentially that still operating today. There was a division into upper, middle, and lower schools, under Mr Greenaway, Mr Roberts, and Miss Urquhart, with Year Heads and Assistant Year Heads for Second, Third, and Fourth Years. Bryan

Francis was Assistant Head of Sixth Form, and Gareth Roberts and Dorrie Urquhart were permanently in charge of Years Five and One respectively, with the other appointees advancing annually with their year groups.

Dunston building nearing completion, with Head's temporary office in the foreground, July 1974.

Despite the clarity of this organisational plan, and the inevitable excitement attendant on a new beginning, the atmosphere in which the comprehensive school opened was a disquieting one. There had been some in-service training to prepare the staff for an all-ability intake, but for the majority there were unanticipated problems in the classroom when boys and girls of average ability, not to mention those with learning difficulties, were encountered for the first time. As has been said, no other school in the county had been reorganised from a purely selective base. There was, too, the residual awkwardness arising from the amalgamation of two independently minded small schools into a larger institution some five years earlier, with a reluctance on the part of some of the staff to accept the change gracefully. And of more recent date there was the very real anger about what many saw as the injustice and unwisdom shown in the appointment of the new Head.

All of this unrest was intensified when the two new Deputies for the John of Gaunt School were also appointed from external candidates for the posts. Two senior members of the High School staff had applied; neither was interviewed as it was felt that previous comprehensive school experience was necessary, so Tony Regan (Deputy Head) and Sue Hourizi (Second Mistress) were appointed from outside. Mr Regan came from the same school in Peterborough of which Mr St George had been Head, and Mrs Hourizi from a comprehensive school in Oxford. It has to be admitted, therefore, that Frank St George laboured from the start under a burden of difficulties that were not of his making; but, if the prospects for the new school were unpropritious in 1974, they were to go downhill rapidly from that point, so that the next five years were to become increasingly turbulent, destructive and unhappy for the fledgling comprehensive school.

Paul Sylvester was the first Chairman of Governors of the John of Gaunt School, combining this with the Chairmanship of the High School until its demise in August 1974. Also on the Governing Body for the first time was a parent representative. Prior to the opening of the school, one piece of business that the Governors attempted was the purchase of Talbot House and Westfield House on the periphery of the campus with the idea of using them either as centres for environmental and rural studies or as houses for a Caretaker or Groundsman. To defray the cost of purchase, it was suggested that that part of the Lambrok field west of the public footpath across it could be sold. The County Council, however, were not interested and the scheme was eventually abandoned. The old art room in the attic of the Gloucester building had been earmarked for remedial classes, but the Governors indicated that mobile accommodation should be retained for this purpose as well as for an ESN class should it be decided in the future to establish such a class at the school. Mr Hopkins was appointed Groundsman. A meteorological station was set up on the roof of the Lancaster kitchen. And the new school opened.

However the story of the John of Gaunt School in its first five years is told – whether one wishes to be generous or to apportion blame, and with whichever faction one sides – what remained at the end was a battlefield littered with casualties. It is a period remembered by many today with distaste and a degree of incredulity. The pupils of the school must have suffered to some extent from the all-pervasive discord of the time, but the results of public examinations continued to be reasonably satisfactory as a grammar school curriculum was maintained for all pupils who had been admitted to the school in its selective form. It was in ways which are not so easily quantifiable that they were let down – in lack of continuity of teaching, for example, (as during these five years there were some 98 movements, resignations and new appointments, of permanent full-time members of the teaching staff), and in a lack of positive and relevant pupil-centred initiatives brought about by the preoccupations of their teachers. Despite a public display of personal animosities, which increased as the decade drew to a close, and which affected everyone connected with the school, there were also strands of normality which can be teased out, and these are worth recording.

Two recurrent themes at Governors' meetings were the need for a Caretaker's house on the site and the unsatisfactoriness of there being no swimming facility for the school. On neither issue did the Governors win. Proof was sought that the lack of a resident Caretaker had already led to an increase in vandalism, but what evidence was forthcoming turned out at best to be equivocal. There could be no doubting that vandalism was rife (£3,000 worth in the first nine months of 1978, for example, with over £300 spent on replacing windows during the summer holidays of that year), but the Local Authority was simply not willing to build a house on, or purchase a house near, the campus for a Caretaker, no matter what pressure the Governing Body brought to bear. Equally unfruitful were attempts to have the site more securely fenced, and gated at the Wingfield Road end. Over the matter of swimming, Clarendon School also were intransigent. They had a pool; John of Gaunt did not. This was because the swimming pool for the single, large comprehensive school, the plans for which had eventually been discontinued, was on the Frome Road site, and when two schools, rather than one, came into being, that is where the pool remained, with no parallel facility provided for the High School site. All appeals for a shared use of the pool failed (including a suggestion for some sort of reciprocal arrangement whereby the pupils from Clarendon could use the John of Gaunt buildings), and swimming was lost to the school's programme of extra-curricular activities. Both these deficiencies – there being no Caretaker on site and no swimming pool – remain as major problems today.

1st rugby XV, 1974-75 with, back row, left to right: Mr Williams, Jock Durham, Ian Hunter, Geoff Thomas, Ian Lock, 'Muddy' Waters, Mr Shearn; centre: Pete Bull, Mike Rutter, 'Bug' Wrightson, Chris Irwin, Stuart Miller, Pete McGrath; front: Dave Crucifix, Ivor Mitchelmore, Mark Howarth, Andy Stewart (capt.), Simon Pizzey, Paul Riddiford, and Kevin Adlam.

It was partly the lack of a house to go with the job that led to Pearce's resignation as Caretaker soon after the comprehensive school opened. Mr Pearce's assistant, Mr Clothier, took his place until his death a couple of years later, when the

Assistant Caretaker again succeeded to the senior post. This was Rob Rose who was assisted in turn by Mr Knight (for a year), Mr Band (for eighteen months), and finally Fred Saxby, who joined him in May 1979.

There were other important changes among the non-teaching staff in the years 1974-1977. Peggy Parsons joined the new school as reprographics assistant. And in 1977, Roger Emerson from County Library Headquarters was appointed Bursar when Mrs Routledge retired; Audrey McAlister and Ann White came as clerical assistants; Eve Buckley took up the post of welfare helper to the ESN unit, which by then consisted of 27 pupils in two classes; and Pam Kaile joined the school as Headmaster's Secretary, replacing Janice Moore (formerly Janice Lewis). In the same year, David Tucker was appointed Groundsman. Some of these members of the non-teaching staff were to serve for a considerable time, and as the school grew, so did the importance of the parts they played in its everyday life.

The number of pupils on roll rose rapidly, to 1,147 in 1975, 1,247 in 1946, 1,354 in 1977, and to the all-time high of 1,422 in September 1978. Thereafter, it stayed just below that mark for a year or two before dropping back in the mid 1980's. Even with the completion of all the scheduled buildings for the comprehensive school and the retention of some of the mobiles, with this number of pupils accommodation was extremely tight. The Dunston building was nearing completion as the new school opened, and it became operational early in 1975; the Staff Common Room, too, was taken over at about the same time; and Mr Lavery agitated for music practice rooms to be constructed in the Gloucester washroom and cloakroom next to his music base. The Sports Hall, however, lingered on until the end of the year, and it was early in 1976 before the Governors were willing to make it available for outside lettings. On the credit side, when finished it was complete with heating, floor coverings, and lighting – a degree of sophistication that had at one time seemed unlikely.

The relationship between school and parents has always been good, but in the early years of the John of Gaunt School the formal Parents' Association achieved a degree of effectiveness that it has not had in more recent years. It held a sponsored walk on 28 September 1978 that raised £2,447.52 for school funds; it (quite forcibly) expressed its concern at what parents saw as a failure of the school's policy on homework; and it suggested that the Parents' Association should become a Parent Teacher Association. The Governing Body liked this idea, and were disappointed at its luke-warm reception by the teaching staff. But it happened anyway. A constitution for the PSA (Parent Staff Association) was drawn up; valuable parental help was given in manning the MI room and in administering first aid, in continuing to push for swimming to be made available to the pupils, and in providing a second minibus for the school. Another matter about which parents had a voice was that of uniform. Green was settled on as the school colour; the falcon badge was (rather unhappily) redesigned; and both Wilkins and Darkin of Trowbridge and Pople's of Bristol became the official school outfitters. In 1977, Mrs Tilt replaced Mr Cunningham as the parent representative on the Governing Body.

The very many changes of teaching staff between 1974 and 1979, some of which were undoubtedly due to the atmosphere of hostility and the general unpleasantness that prevailed in the Staff Common Room at the time, have already been mentioned. In detail, they are relegated to Appendix C. Some departures and arrivals, however, merit particular attention. Len Newell, an outstanding teacher and physicist, retired in 1976, as did Mr Lavery's long-time colleague in music, Miss Rogers. George Johnston, Head of Art, retired the following year, and Alice Quine, Head of Home Economics, in 1978. The Deputy Head, Tony Regan, gained the headship of Market Bosworth High School near Leicester, and he also left John of Gaunt in 1978. Keith Mayell, Bill Wright, Margaret Behan, Ted Ralph, Tessa Daly...and "Bert" Boulding.

Formerly Head of English at the Girls' High School, Denis Boulding took early retirement in 1975. Bel Mooney paints a vivid and affectionate picture of him – "A Sweet Shambolic Man" – in *People,* an anthology compiled by Susan Hill. "When you first went to the school you were taught English by a firm, brisk lady called Miss Pinton, with dark hair and upswept spectacles. Mr Boulding taught the fifteen-year-olds upwards, and we greeted the information that we were to graduate to him with ribald anticipation." Nevertheless, Denis Boulding was to be a lasting influence upon Miss Mooney, as he was upon many others. Deaf, reliant upon a hearing-aid, eccentric, vulnerable, passionate about his subject, "for me he was The Teacher, the only teacher," she admits. "He told me what to read and showed me how to read, and articulated the truth I had already guessed: that through literature you may 'suffer dully all the wrongs of man' – but overcome them too." Denis Boulding had been passed over when it came to making the appointment of Head of English for the combined High School; he was an unusual man and a remarkable teacher. Sadly, Graham Angus died in office in 1979. So these, and others, were lost to the school in the first five years of its life. To balance them, teachers were appointed who were to make a very significant contribution to the school's later success – Roger Powley, Andy Slade, Georgina Blackshaw, Myra Link, John Treble, Bryn Parfitt, Peter Eyles, Keith Wright, Annita Hyde, Jean Weedon....But success, as I have said, came later.

In 1977, there was an Evaluation (a Local Authority as distinct from a DES inspection) of the John of Gaunt School, but if this was to highlight the difficulties that the school was experiencing, there were clear signs that all was not well long before that date. Governors visited the school with a degree of anxiety about its health; there were parental complaints about some of the teaching; as a result of reports made to Governors that there was staff unrest, "the Head said he had not wished to cause friction by over-exerting his authority, but he would be taking a harder line knowing that he had the Board's support"; curricular difficulties rose to the surface; and – in retrospect, the spark that lit the fire - there was criticism from the Governing Body about the public examination results of one particular department in the summer of 1976. All these were rather more than straws in the wind. Their effect was heightened by general staff unrest following a formal visit by three Governors that was designed to assess what was happening, by a number of serious disciplinary problems among the pupils, and by concern about the performance of two or three members of the teaching staff. So it was a very hot potato indeed that was handed to Peter Riddiford – Vice Captain of the rugby XV in 1946 – when he succeeded to the chairmanship of the Governing Body in 1976.

One supposes that on the surface much appeared normal. Prizegivings continued, though without the pomp and ceremony that accompanied them in the former selective schools. There were careers conferences for the Lower Sixth in the Civic Hall and activities weeks for Year Four at the end of summer terms. Early in the life of the comprehensive school, special furniture for the careers room had been accepted as a memorial to Miss Hazell; "All the King's Men" was presented on three evenings in May 1975; Christmas concerts became an annual feature; and Mr Roberts' Wombles from Year Five collected £304, and a lot of litter, in 1977. A year earlier the successor to the old, long-gone, external staircase at the side of the Wingfield building appeared – a fire escape that led from the upstairs door, over flat roofs, down to the rear of the building. In my time, happily, it was never used – other than illicitly.

The report of the Evaluation of 1977 makes disturbing reading. It was moderate and balanced in what it said, but there was no way in which it could be other than gloomy about much of what had been seen. Whilst acknowledging that some of the difficulties experienced by the new comprehensive school could only have been avoided with the wisdom of hindsight, it nevertheless was heavily critical about almost every aspect of school life, from the litter, damage, and graffiti that were evident in many of the buildings, to the quality of the leadership offered to those who taught and learned there. It would be a painful and unprofitable exercise to analyse the findings of that report in detail. Its flavour can be gained from just one sentence: "The evaluators are not aware of any other secondary school in Wiltshire in which there are such tensions amongst the teachers or from which there emanates such a volume of bitter complaint". The hope, doubtless, was that the findings of the Evaluation could be used to work constructively and positively in settling the school on a more even keel, but, if this were so, events overtook that hope.

It was seven months after the event, in June 1978, that the report on the Evaluation was presented to the Governors, but during those seven months the situation deteriorated further. One manifestation of this worsening of the atmosphere was a letter sent to the Governors by some 36 members of the teaching staff about concerns over the curriculum and what they felt was the failure of anyone in authority to listen to their views. But the situation now had an impetus of its own. Centred on one department and pushed on self-destructively by one particular member of the teaching staff, issues became personalised; reasoned, albeit bitter, argument gave way to abuse and vilification. Warfare was open. The Head and the Chairman received letter after letter, the tone of which was immoderate and hostile, questioning their competence and integrity and raising the dispute well beyond the level of a formal professional grievance.

As has been said, the comprehensive school opened with a number of serious difficulties to be overcome, but in the few years following the opening they were compounded rather than resolved. Too many of the staff failed to grasp the enormous shift in curriculum, classroom control, and teaching methods that comprehensivisation implied. Perhaps their needs in this respect had not been fully grasped and provided for by the LEA. On the other hand, they felt left out of the processes of consultation, and where they looked for strong direction they found a relaxed (or, as they saw it, a complacent) leadership that might have worked in an established school that was confident about where it was going, but that was out of place in view of the classroom crises and the organisational isolation that they felt they faced. There was deep dissatisfaction about the curriculum in general, and about individual teaching timetables; and it was the failure (as many teachers saw it) of the Head and the Governors to tackle these problems with sympathy and understanding and personal concern that led to the final, damaging confrontation.

Inevitably, casualties abounded. The Head, Mr St George, announced his move to an inspectorial/advisory post in Coventry and tendered his resignation as from the end of the 1978/79 academic year. One teacher, against whom it was intended that disciplinary action should be taken, left the school on medical grounds after a lengthy absence. Another was dismissed in a glare of publicity. And there were one or two others who were permanently damaged by what had happened. The majority of the teaching staff, who desperately wanted professional fulfilment and the knowledge that they were valued members of a respected institution, felt battered and demoralised by the dispute that raged round them. The Local Authority itself was not unaffected by events, but of those who were not actually members of the school, it is probable that the Chairman of Governors, Peter Riddiford, felt most keenly the sadness of his old school's situation. In September 1979, the Rev Stephen Venner was elected Chairman, and the minutes of the Governors' meeting of that month record, baldly and inadequately, what was felt. "The Chairman expressed his appreciation of Mr Riddiford's years in the Chair during what was probably the most difficult period that the school would ever experience." Fortunately, Peter Riddiford remained a Governor and was able to share in the happier times that lay ahead.

A Brighter Future:
The John of Gaunt School: 1979-1991

As Head of the John of Gaunt School from 1979 to 1991, I find it impossible to be objective about what happened in those years. They are too near in time, and I was too closely involved to view them with any degree of detachment. I shall not attempt, therefore, any rounded or chronological history of the period. I shall simply trace a few of the lines of development that occurred between 1979 and 1991 without attempting an evaluation (except in one instance), and record one or two events, the details of which may not be generally known. Anything more comprehensive will be for someone else at another time.

I believe that the one situation in which a value judgement is permissible is in assessing the overall health and morale of the school from 1979 onwards. It recovered remarkably quickly from the traumas of the 1970's, so much so that it was very soon thought of by those who taught there as a good school to work in; visitors felt it to be a friendly and civilised place; pupils of all shades of ability were respected and encouraged to achieve the best of which they were capable; the buildings were clean, welcoming and soon became vandal-free; examination results were regularly either very good or, at worst, satisfactory; and a pride in what was being achieved was evident in everyone connected with the school. So how was this position reached, and so comparatively quickly, from the bitterness and self-destruction that came to a head in 1979?

I came to John of Gaunt from the headship of the Tom Hood Senior High School in Leytonstone, East London, and it was my good fortune to inherit a number of senior members of staff who had struggled hard to keep the school on an even keel during years of great difficulty. In particular, Dorrie Urquhart, Gareth Roberts, and John Greenaway were enormously supportive to me in my new post, and I was keenly aware of their determination to make the school one of which its pupils, parents, and teachers could be proud. It was wholehearted commitment at this level more than anything else that made possible the remarkable transformation in the school's fortunes from 1979. (Miss Urquhart taught at John of Gaunt and its predecessors for 36 years, became Acting Deputy Head in 1980, and has been a Governor since her retirement in 1983. Mr Roberts, after his retirement, became a County Councillor and Chairman of the Education Committee. And Mr Greenaway maintained a remarkable resilience and cheerfulness in his position as Head of Upper School throughout the period of my headship.) So, at this crucial level of management there was a positive working towards better things by teachers in key positions; and there were others who had been at the school for many years who had also been wearied by the strife of the immediate past and who were anxious to create a healthier teaching environment.

It was my good fortune, too, to recruit a senior management team of outstanding ability at a relatively early date – Stephen Gee in 1983 and "Flic" Hart the following year as Deputy Heads – with John Croft coming from Warminster as a third Deputy in 1988. Through them, the school was given direction in positive and forward-looking ways to a quite unusual extent. And a third strand of teaching strength lay in the deliberate appointment throughout the period of young, optimistic staff who liked children and who put a great deal of thought and hard work into their guidance. Some of these were Faculty or Departmental Heads; others joined us in their first teaching posts. It was in large part due to their enthusiasm and idealism that the cynicism of the 1970's was finally relegated to the pages of history, and the whole atmosphere changed from one in which the school's preoccupation was an apportioning of blame to one in which excitement and expectation prevailed.

Another characteristic of these years was the greatly increased level of support afforded both in and out of the classroom by non-teaching staff. George Dowd became Caretaker in 1985. An ex-army Warrant Officer, he tended in moments of forgetfulness to refer to the school as "the barracks", the playground as "the square", and the dining hall as "the mess". He brought a new sense of discipline to the care of the site. But there had long been a Caretaker, a Groundsman, and a Secretary; what was new was the proliferation of ancillary helpers – welfare assistants who operated with individual pupils in the classroom; technicians, not only for laboratories but for audio-visual work, for the workshops and in home economics, for work in TVEI, in humanities, and for reprographics; a bursar, a librarian, a finance officer, a medical room supervisor, word processor operators, a receptionist, and clerical assistants. There were, too, my personal Secretaries. Pam Kaile stayed until 1983. She was replaced by Thérèse Underwood who was with me for nearly seven years, and Jenny Barnes succeeded to the post in 1990. A Head's Secretary has a complex and vital role to play in the effective management of a school. Pam, Thérèse, and Jenny did far more than could reasonably have been expected of them, and each, in her own way, was important in the day-by-day running of the school as well as in her secretarial expertise.

If I was fortunate in my Secretaries, so I was too in my Chairmen. Both Fr Stephen Venner (at the time Vicar of St John's, Upper Studley, now Bishop of Middleton in Lancashire), and, from 1982, John Elliott were unfailingly supportive; and, perhaps unusually, the various Governing Bodies of John of Gaunt between 1979 and 1991 never allowed either personal or political considerations to deflect them from making decisions based purely on the best interests of the school and its pupils.

From the teaching staff, Rhys Prosser and Frank Lavery had retired in 1980 and 1982 respectively, each having taught at the school for 30 years or more and having contributed enormously to the development of drama and music in Trowbridge. Rugby football, too, owed much to Rhys Prosser. Dorrie Urquhart (after 36 years) and Gareth Roberts (after 33) went in 1983. John Colin retired in 1984, Jack Marsh in 1985, John Broome in 1986, and Evelyn Mead in 1989. The last four had taught in the old High Schools, and their combined length of service was well over one hundred years. So, whilst a much younger staff was in process of being brought together, and one with no burden of historical prejudices to carry, the steadiness and reliability and expertise learned over many years of teachers like these was an undeniable loss to the school. All were skilled in their own specialisms, all were immensely experienced teachers, and without exception they were involved in the life of the school beyond the bounds of their academic departments. So, if there were losses as well as gains in the building of a different sort of teaching force, it was the temper and calibre of the staff overall that was the principal difference between the John of Gaunt School of 1979 and that of (say) 1989.

Another change was that from Avon, Bourne, Kennet, and Wylye to Beaumont, Charlton, Foster and Wade, but this had no significance except on Sports Days. (These House names still exist, but how many of today's pupils know who Beaumont, Charlton, Foster and Wade were?) Far more important was the change in curriculum for all pupils that took place between 1979 and 1991. This was in part due to imaginative developments that were driven forward by some of the Faculty and Departmental Heads, and in part to the ideas generated by Stephen Gee. It meant that when National Curriculum requirements were introduced for all schools by the Education Reform Act of 1988, John of Gaunt was already well down the road of curriculum innovation and found the compulsory requirements either of little concern or, in some ways, inhibiting rather than helpful. The secondary curriculum in the 1980's and 1990's, however, is an on-going story that is now bedevilled by ill-informed political interference. Opportunities for trail-blazing are fewer today than they were for most of the years of my headship.

    A parallel development was that of the pastoral system of the school under the guidance of Mrs Hart. In 1979, the Head of Year was the teacher called upon to discipline a pupil when all else (bar the intervention of the Head) had failed. He dealt in punishment, and indeed, in one case that worried me considerably, could become demoralised by the negative nature of his role. By 1991, whilst discipline within the year group was still one of the Head of Year's responsibilities, he/she had a more wide-ranging and positive role, and was much more directly in control of everything that affected the education of the pupils in the age-group. A good example of how this worked in practice was in the changed atmosphere of morning assemblies. When I arrived at the school in 1979, they were events to be endured, trouble-free if one were lucky, policed by teachers but not exactly uplifting to the spirits of either pupils or staff. In later years, they came to have much more of a family atmosphere about them, with a sense of everyone's sharing in an enjoyable and friendly meeting of interests. The changed relationship of the Year Head with his pupils, as well as his changed status within the school, was the reason.

From 1404 pupils on roll in September 1979, numbers fell steadily (as they did in secondary schools nationally) to a low of 1058 in 1990; thereafter, a rise was predicted which was to be significantly affected, either beneficially or adversely in individual schools, by the policy of open enrollment that was another element in the Education Reform Act of 1988. At John of Gaunt, fewer numbers meant that the remaining mobile classrooms could be disposed of, and that some teaching spaces, as and when money allowed, could be adapted to other purposes, such as the creation of computer suites, private study accommodation, offices, AVA facilities, and seminar rooms. Parents supplied labour and materials for some of these alterations, and a great deal of help was had at various times from groups of government trainees – young men and women on YOP and Community Service schemes. They tended to progress rather slowly, but, under supervision, their work was good, and their very presence around the site proved to be exciting for some of the pupils. The old gymnasium of the former Girls' High School at the back of the assembly hall had been transformed into a drama studio in 1978. It had never been a success as a gym, but it performed a very useful function in its new guise. And finding myself both isolated from visitors and inconveniently cut off from the rest of the school's administration, I moved my office from Dunston to Wingfield, into what had been Mrs Hourizi's room, in the spring term of 1980. (Earlier, of course, it had been Mrs Routledge's room, and its original function was betrayed by my discovering a nice Victorian fireplace long hidden behind a plywood panel.) It remains the Head's room today. Mrs Kaile moved into "Mavis's Room", the small office by the rear entrance to Wingfield. Other positive achievements were the creation of suites of rooms for the different Faculties and the complete re-roofing of the Chiltern and Dunston buildings in 1985 after years of leaks and consequent damage. Two events, however, overshadowed all others in the matter of school buildings during the 1979-1991 period, both of them extremely serious and very expensive to put right. These were the two major incidents of arson in 1984 and the storm damage to the school roofs of 1990.

On the night of 9/10 February 1984, the Wingfield building was extensively damaged by fire. I was called by the Caretaker at about 2.00 a.m., by which time the building was well alight. Six brigades attended – two from Trowbridge, and one each from Warminster, Westbury, Bradford on Avon, and Melksham – and it was a fine cooked breakfast from the fire brigades' mobile canteen on the playing field that I enjoyed at about 6.00 a.m. on a freezing morning prior to broadcasting about the disaster on local radio and television. The fire had been started deliberately in the late evening by a former pupil of the school who had broken in through the back door by Mrs Underwood's office in search of money. Failing in his search, he climbed the stairs to the attic rooms. There, close to the top of the stairs, he lit a small fire on a wooden table simply to entertain himself. The result was an extremely damaging conflagration that would have been much worse had it not been spotted in the early hours by a passing motorist. The attic rooms were almost completely burnt out and there was extensive damage to the whole of the roof of the building; on the floor below, the centrally situated rooms were destroyed, and there was some damage even on the ground floor where Thérèse Underwood's room, directly below the seat of the fire, was worst affected. Furniture, school records, a quantity of equipment, and many text books that had been stored in the attic were also lost. The total cost of the damage was just short of £100,000.

Fire damage to the Wingfield building, 1984.

Reconstruction, begun in June 1984, was not completed until November, and for much of that time the roof of the Wingfield building was sheathed in a plastic tent that became a dominating feature of West Trowbridge. John Greenaway lost items of personal value, but, inconvenience apart, the ultimate effect that the fire had on the school was minimal. Indeed, there were benefits. Old text books were replaced by new, and in place of the warren of old attic rooms we acquired a large and useful Conference Room.

Unfortunately, the staff common room, too, fell victim to the arsonist. Again I was called out at 2.00 a.m., this time on Saturday, 17 March. The building had been broken into, a number of fires had been lit, but the one that caused significant damage was in the vestibule where a bank of pigeon-holes was burnt out, with extensive damage also to the floor, the ceiling, and to fitments many yards away from the seat of the fire. More inconvenience was caused, but in this case the cost of repair was something under £5,000.

Intensive police surveillance, involving 30 extra officers being called in from other parts of the county, resulted in the culprit's being caught on 29 March 1984. He then admitted to almost a score of fire-raising incidents in the Trowbridge area, committed by him as a result of the rising excitement he felt from hearing about his offences in the press and on television. At his trial, he was sentenced to four years imprisonment for the Wingfield fire and lesser periods, to be served concurrently, for various other offences.

The damage of 1990 occurred on 25 January and 26 February. On those two days very violent storms struck the area, leading to the closure of the school for all pupils on 30 January, and 27 and 28 February. For some hours at the height of the storms, conditions in the school were dangerous, with doors being ripped from their hinges, tiles torn from roofs, and debris generally being flung around in the high winds. The roofs of the Gloucester and Wingfield buildings in particular were badly damaged, their repair being both expensive and long drawn-out. The Wingfield re-roofing took until Christmas to complete (and not to our satisfaction even then); Gloucester was finished by November. And there were two rather bizarre consequences of this repair work.

One was a small "topping-out" ceremony that I arranged to celebrate the completion of the work on the Gloucester building. The foreman builder and his mate, an officer from County Hall, Mr Gee, and I donned safety helmets and, on a flat part of the roof, toasted the success of the repair operation with champagne. Microphones had been rigged up for my speech, carefully crafted for the occasion. Unfortunately, Mrs Hart had forgotten to assemble the audience that we had planned for, and so the rather surprised witnesses to the ceremony, and the recipients of the speech, were one boy who had been sent out of class, two girls on their way to the toilet, a visiting plumber, and a dog. The occasion was not a success. The one rather strange consequence of the work on Wingfield was the incorrect re-carving of the date of construction of the building on the stone block above the central front door. Over a century of attack by weather and pollution had eroded the original inscription, and the repair work that was taking place gave us an opportunity for restoration. Our research at the time was inadequate, with the consequence that the correct date (1890) was replaced by a foolishly incorrect 1889. And so it remains today – an inadvertent rewriting of history that, embarrassingly, is plain for all to see.

A rewriting of history, 1990.

Ambitious musical productions that aimed at the involvement of as many pupils as possible, either on stage, in the orchestra, or in technical roles, became a feature of the period: "The Messiah" and Vivaldi's "Gloria" on the one hand, "Oh What a Lovely War", Horovitz's "Horrortorio", "Oklahoma", "The Pirates of Penzance", and "Guys and Dolls" on the other. Frank Lavery and, later, Philip Springate were exceptional music teachers, and Roger Powley's sets were memorable. Dance, too, came to be celebrated with an annual production. Teacher exchanges flourished, with Marion Gibbs going for a year to Australia, Peter Harris to South Dakota, Kate Rees to New Zealand (whence she failed to return), and John Treble to Idaho; in the other direction came Stephen Bouvet, Peggy Tomscha, Grant Saul, and Dr Ken Wright. And a pupil exchange at Sixth

Form level was inaugurated in 1988, with reciprocal visits on an annual basis to and from Laguna Blanca High School in Santa Barbara, California. Rather different was the Academic Year Programme which, under the aegis of the British Council, brought a number of Spanish boys and girls, aged between 11 and 14, to John of Gaunt for the whole of one academic year. In 1990, we welcomed Amaya, Juan Jose, Asier, David, Javier and Jaume, with a further eight Spanish pupils the following year. As, by this time, German had been dropped from the curriculum, with Spanish and French having parity of status as the two modern languages that the school offered, for these Spanish pupils to be with us was mutually beneficial.

Laurey and Curly, alias Jane Greenaway and Grant Slade, in 'Oklahoma', 1984.

Mention has been made above of Faculties and Faculty Heads. When I came to John of Gaunt in 1979, an academic structure of 25 virtually autonomous Departments, each with its own Head, was a matter of concern. So, within the first year, I moved to a Faculty structure which made possible more cooperation and the adoption of common policies between Departments that should have been working closely together. Faculty Heads were appointed, and some of these teachers made, and continue to make, an outstanding contribution to the life of the school. Another change was the reintroduction of staff meetings. These had had to be abandoned prior to 1979 because of the tensions that they created, and their reinstatement was another aspect of a reversion to more normal professional practices. Unfortunately, these and other meetings of teachers, the running of clubs and societies, the taking of games out of school hours, parents meetings, and the supervision of pupils at lunch time all fell victim to the prolonged industrial action that started early in 1985. Lasting in some form or other for almost eighteen months, it cast a blight over schools and had long-term effects that are still felt today.

I say above that, after 1979, our buildings were "soon vandal-free". "Soon", of course, is relative. For a number of years we were plagued by burglaries and motiveless vandalism, particularly at night and at the weekends, the openness of the site initially making prevention of these morale-sapping activities almost impossible. By the late 1980's, however, they were a thing of the past. Internal vandalism was negligible; what little graffiti appeared was removed immediately; the smashing of windows at weekends ceased; and break-ins became extremely rare. One reason for this was undoubtedly the feeling of ownership of the buildings and the equipment that pupils by this time were feeling; it was their school, their classroom, their computer, their work – and they took a pride in it. Another reason was the LEA's being persuaded to install sophisticated alarm systems in the more vulnerable areas of the school. And a third reason may have been the publicity given to the fate that befell a group of vandals in November 1985. The external walls of the school were found to have been plastered with unpleasant graffiti from aerosol cans during the course of a weekend. On the assumption that there would be a repetition of this activity, late on the Saturday evening of the following week, Mr Dowd (the Caretaker), Mr Gee (Deputy Head), and I sat for several hours (consoling ourselves with several bottles of a good red wine) in an unlit classroom that provided us with a clear view of the site. We were rewarded by the return of the gang with more aerosol cans which they used for a further defacing of the walls. On this occasion, however, to their bewilderment and fright, the three of us sprang out and apprehended them. The following day, the four teenagers concerned, together with their parents, and under the far from benevolent eye of the Caretaker, cleaned up the mess they had created. Police prosecutions followed. Thereafter, the incidence of vandalism of all kinds declined markedly.

Storms, arson, and vandalism make for gloomy reading, even when there are beneficial spin-offs. I want to end on a happier and more positive note. From the welter of half-baked initiatives that affected secondary education in the second half of the 1980's, by the law of averages some had to be useful. One such was the devolving to schools of responsibility for their own financial affairs, and at

Tree planting by Steve Cram and pupils, 1990.

John of Gaunt the liberating effect of this was quickly felt. Only now, however, some four or five years later, with a learnt expertise and a carefully created financial cushion to fall back on, are the benefits being fully exploited. Local management of finance was introduced during the period of my headship; the realisation of its possibilities came later. Another initiative that gathered momentum after 1991 but that was launched during my time at the school was the involvement of all pupils in active work on improving the environment. Peter Eyles was the teacher responsible. He began by holding a mass tree-plant on the banks of the canal in Trowbridge. From there, he moved to the grounds of the school itself, and the project really came alive in November 1990 when 105 native trees and shrubs were planted by pupils, members of the local community, and national celebrities, under the aegis of the Tree Council. Athlete Steve Cram flew in by helicopter to open the event; Jeremy Guscott, the Bath and British Lions rugby player, planted a tree, as did John Leslie of "Blue Peter", BBC's Chris Vacher, and many others. This was the first stage of a larger scheme for tree planting, the creation of a tree nursery, the growing of wild flowers, and a programme of after-care. A wild-life area was also created, incorporating a pond, hedges, walls, and an orchard.

And this was the beginning of a much larger programme, not least of the benefits of which was the fostering of a feeling in the pupils of the school that it was theirs, a place in which they had a stake and which they physically had helped to create.

In this history of the Trowbridge High Schools and the John of Gaunt School I have from time to time mentioned examination results. They are important, but not all-important. It is both impossible and undesirable to compare the examination results that the pupils achieve today with those gained when the schools had a selective intake. The pupil population is different in character, drawn from a different geographical area, different in size, and, at Sixth Form level, studying in many cases with a different purpose. Nevertheless, some indication of how the school fared academically in the 1979-1991 period should be given. As ever, there were merely reasonable years and there were good years, both at "A" level and for "O"/CSE/GCSE. A good year at "A" level was 1989. In that year, 95 pupils gained a total of 239 subject passes out of 273 entries, with a pass-rate of 87.5%. There were many among them who went on to higher education, 5 to Oxford or Cambridge, and other years produced comparable results. John of Gaunt, however, is a comprehensive school, and with this in mind I think it worth quoting, in conclusion, a comment that I made to the Governors on the examination results of 1983: "In spite of these distinguished achievements," I wrote, "the teaching staff derived almost the greatest pleasure from Robert's single CSE grade 2 English pass. This, for him, was as great a triumph of determination and application as results that, for others, have led to university."

Keith Berry and Stephen Gee, retiring from, and appointed to, the headship of the John of Gaunt School, December, 1991.

Postscript

The Trowbridge schools whose history this is have served not only the town of Trowbridge but much of West Wiltshire for the best part of 100 years. Their pupils are to be found in every walk of life, most of them not particularly well known except to their colleagues and their class-mates of years ago. A few, however, have achieved eminence either locally or nationally.

John Atyeo played for England at football, winning 6 international caps between 1955 and 1957; Sir William Cook directed the H-bomb tests on Christmas Island, was a member of the Atomic Energy Authority, and in 1964 was appointed Deputy Chief Scientific Adviser in the Ministry of Defence; Maureen Duffy is a well known writer to whose book, *That's How It Was*, first published in 1962, I am indebted; John Garrett became Headmaster of Bristol Grammar School; Kenneth Harris, historian, TV interviewer, and author, as well as being Director and Associate Editor of the *Observer*, wrote a fine tribute to Reggie Beams " who started me on the road which led to my writing 'Attlee'"; Dr Joan Hussey became Professor of Byzantine History at the University of London; Dr A M Lane, author of *Nuclear Theory*, was appointed Head of Research into Theoretical Nuclear Physics at Harwell; Bel Mooney (Mrs Jonathan Dimbleby), journalist and broadcaster, contributed, amongst her other writings, a retrospective article on the "Class of '65" to the *Listener* some twenty years later; Dr J H P Pafford was Goldsmiths' Librarian of the University of London; Dr Marjorie Reeves, a distinguished mediaevalist, became Vice-Principal of St Anne's College, Oxford; Miss Vera Silcocks was a missionary who spent 45 years at the Ting Wa Girls' School, Hong Kong, becoming its Headmistress; and Dr S P Wiltshire was Director of the Commonwealth Institute of Mycology.

To this dozen former pupils could be added many more who have achieved distinction in science, politics, and the arts; and waiting in the wings are others, boys and girls from the John of Gaunt School who will make their mark in the future either locally or, in some cases, nationally.

This history takes us from 1897 to my retirement in December 1991. There are gaps in the story which need to be filled; undoubtedly there are errors to be corrected. And already the date at which my narrative ends is some years in the past, so further chapters will soon be needed. I look forward to reading them, but, more than that, I look forward to the huge party that will undoubtedly be organised for Saturday, 27 September, 1997, when the true centenary of the John of Gaunt School, through the Trowbridge High School, the Boys' and Girls' High Schools, the Boys' and Girls' Secondary Schools, the County Day School, and the Trowbridge and District Secondary School, will be celebrated.

Appendix A

Trowbridge Education Committee: Chairmen

J Poynton Haden	1903-1915
E Fear Hill	1915-1920
W Walker	1920-1924
W Nelson Haden	1924-1927

Trowbridge High Schools: Chairmen of Governors

W Nelson Haden	1927-1946
F Beer	1946-1950
Brig. V F Browne	1950-1957
J H Case	1957-1967
Mrs M H Melliar-Smith	1967-1970
P R Sylvester	1970-1974

The John of Gaunt School, Trowbridge: Chairmen of Governors

P R Sylvester	1974-1976
P D J Riddiford	1976-1979
Rev. S Venner	1979-1982
J M Elliott	1982-1992
I B Coates	1992-1993
D A Roy	1993-

Clerks to the Committee/Governors

H Ledbury	1897-1901
A Randall	1901-1909
H Ledbury	1909-1927
S Holding	1927-1957
P W Inglis	1957
L H Davidge	1958-1963
Mrs A S Garlick	1963-1983
Mrs P A Pike	1983-

Appendix B

HEAD TEACHERS

Trowbridge and District Secondary School
(County Day School)

J W Henson, BA 1897-1912

Trowbridge Secondary School for Girls	Trowbridge Secondary School for Boys
Miss E M Moore, MA 1912-1914	J W Henson, BA 1912-1914

Trowbridge High School for Girls	Trowbridge High School for Boys
Miss E M Moore, MA 1914-1932	J W Henson, BA 1914-1937
Miss J I Field, BA, BSc 1932-1938	L G Smith, MA, BSc 1937-1947
Miss K M S Dawes, BA 1939-1954	G V S Bucknall, MA 1947-1968
Miss B Morris, BA 1954-1969	

Trowbridge High School

G Suggitt, MA 1969-1974

The John of Gaunt School, Trowbridge

F H St George, BA 1974-1979
K D Berry, JP, BA, FRSA 1979-1991
S C Gee, BEd 1992-

Appendix C

**The John of Gaunt School:
permanent, full-time teaching staff to 1979**

Headmaster: F St George (1974-1979);

Deputy Heads: Mrs S Hourizi (74-), P Jenner (78-), A Regan (74-78);

science: Miss M Ashton (74-), J Ball (74-79), J Collyer (72-),
P Eyles (76-), C Foster (72-78), B Francis (70-),
K Mayell (58-79), L Newell (47-76), Mrs J Newman (74-),
G Roberts (50-), Mrs J Shearn (68-), C Taylor (76-79),
J Treble (74-), J Wright (71-79);

mathematics: G Angus (71-79), R Case (75-78), Mrs M Cormack (76-77),
Miss D Dawes (62-), B Donnan (77-78), Mrs T Grice (Miss Gladman) (78-), Mrs S Haxell (74-75), Miss J Hodder (74-75),
A Johnston (76-), Miss R Jones (74-), B Parfitt (78-),
E Ralph (57-78), Mrs K Rees (78-), G Sutton (66-);

English: D Boulding (48-75), Miss H Brown (77-79), P Collier (69-),
P Gwilliam (75-79), P Harris (78-), Mrs A Hyde (76-),
S Icke (78-), A Johnson (68-78), S Lycett (70-75),
Mrs D Powell (69-), R Prosser (50-), F Stacey (71-),
Mrs J Wagstaff (74-75), K Wright (75-);

modern
languages: Mrs L Elstob (77-78), Mrs G Forsyth (Miss Heath) (74-77),
Mrs S Halvorsen (Miss Parkhouse) (65-), Miss A Hudson (76),
Miss J Jones (74-78), R Lawrie (55-75), Mrs G Lindsay (78),
P Morgan (76-78), J Shepherd (73-79), D Sherwell (72-),
J Snow (71-79);

classics: C Allen (64-);

history: F Bastian (58-78), Mrs M Behan (73-78), J Broome (60-),
Mrs T Daly (72-78), D Gadian (78-), Mrs J Hatcher (78-),
N Proudfoot (78-);

geography: M Broom (77-), J Greenaway (65-), Mrs E Mead (67-),
Mrs C Sharples (72-79), A Shearn (68-77);

R.E.: E Hulme (76-), D Mosley (77-), W Verrinder (64-76);

art: V Belcher (50-76), Mrs J Charlton (76-), Miss M Gibbs (77-), G Johnston (53-77), Mrs S Phillips (Miss Pullin) (76-), R Powley (77-), Mrs J Wright (Mrs Cooper) (74-79);

music: R Bates (76-77), F Lavery (51-), Miss H Roberts (77-78), Miss E Rogers (63-76), Miss C Schafer (78-79);

technical studies: J Chancellor (76-), D Gardner (75-), J Marsh (58-), M Roberts (72-), B Willmott (78-);

home economics: Mrs G Blackshaw (78-), Mrs M Link (76-), Mrs E McMenemy (75-78), Miss A Quine (47-78);

P.E.: J Colin (51-), M Davison (76-), Mrs B Easterbrook (78-), Miss S Elworthy (77-), Miss G Hyde (70-75), Miss M Jones (75-79), A Slade ((78-), Miss D Urquhart (47), J Williams (74-77);

basic studies: P Ainley (77-), W Bramley (74-76), Mrs L Chilcott (75-), R Osborne (78-79), P Wallis (76-79), Mrs J Weedon (75-).

Appendix D

**The John of Gaunt School:
permanent, full-time teaching staff, 1979-1991**

Headmaster: K Berry (1979-1991)

Deputy Heads: J Croft (88-), S Gee (83-), Mrs F Hart (84-91),
                 Mrs S Hourizi (74-83), P Jenner (78-83), R Mason (91-);

science and   R Alexander (79-85), Miss M Ashton (74-88),
technology: J Collyer (72-81), Mrs C Deans (91-), Mrs S Denning (80-86),
                 Miss S Eisaks (80-88), P Eyles (76-), B Francis (70-),
                 Miss H Garner (81-), B Hewett (79-90),
                 Mrs B Johnston (79-80), C Keay (79-), P Keen (85-),
                 Mrs J Newman (74-), G Roberts (50-83), Mrs J Shearn (68-85),
                 J Treble (74-), N Wadley (88-), Mrs J Whalley (86-),
                 J Wilkes (88-);

mathematics: Mrs C Ashford (91), Mrs A Cleary (82-),
                 Mrs E Coe (Miss Ball) (80-84), K Coleman (83-84),
                 A Cook (86-), Miss D Dawes (62-), Mrs T Grice (78-79),
                 C James (81-83), K Jennings (80-86), A Johnston (76-81),
                 Miss R Jones (74-82), Miss Z Kondrat (82-85),
                 Miss C Lee (91-), B Parfitt (78-), S Peplow (86-),
                 Mrs K Rees (78-90), D Ross (88-), G Sutton (66-),
                 A Taylor (80-85), S Wilson (85-88);

English and   R Basley (89-), J Bishop (88-), Miss A Blofeld (91-),
drama: Mrs H Bourns (79-83), Mrs V Bradley (80-82),
                 Miss S Busby (89-), P Collier (69-), Miss S Davies (82-),
                 Miss L Hanrahan (79-80), P Harris (78-85), G Hill (86-89),
                 Miss S Hill (89-), Mrs D Howells (Miss Barber) (84-89),
                 W Howells (81-), Mrs A Hyde (76-87), S Icke (78-80),
                 Miss A Johnson (80-82), D Johnson (88-), Mrs R King (82-),
                 Mrs S Moore (88-90), Mrs D Powell (69-81),
                 R Prosser (50-80), G Rich (81-87), F Stacey (71-81),
                 K Wright (75-87);

modern   Miss S Ariaratnam (90-91), P Atkinson (84-), R Ball (79-83),
languages: Mrs M England (Miss O'Kelly) (88-91), Miss H Grainger (85),
                 Mrs A Green (Miss Pilling) (79-81 and 84),

                Mrs S Halvorsen (65-82), S Harris (85-),
                Mrs J Henderson (90-), Miss P Lloret (82-),
                Miss S Lomax (91-), Miss V Lopez (91-),
                Mrs C McCombe (Miss Heneghan) (81-89), D Sherwell (72-83),
                J Taylor (81-85), Miss H Thompson (81-82),
                Mrs W Vaughan (Miss Higgins) (85-88);

classics: C Allen (64-81);

history: J Broome (60-86), I Clarke (79-88),
                Miss C Cornock-Taylor (82-83), W Dewar (80-85),
                D Gadian (78-80), Mrs J Hatcher (78-82),
                Mrs K Hemmett (Miss Harries) (87-), Miss R Hucker (88-),
                M Lyons (86-89), M Pardoe (81-87), N Proudfoot (78-80),
                Mrs A Rackham (Miss Caisley) (88-), Miss J Reed (83-86),
                Miss J Roberts (86-88);

geography: N Andrews (79-86), M Broom (77-89), J Greenaway (65-),
                Mrs E Mead (67-89), C Montacute (89-), M Stevens (88-);

R.E.:   E Hulme (76-79), Mrs S Hughes (80-84),
                Mrs J Mathews (Miss Bright) (85-), D Mosley (77-),
                Mrs G Roots (85-87);

art: Mrs V Andriopoulou (88-), Mrs H Brain (Miss Yaldren) (89-),
                Mrs J Charlton (76-80), Miss C Cushion (79-),
                P Matthews (80-88), Miss A Parkinson (80),
                Mrs A Partridge (Miss Casey) (80-90),
                Mrs S Phillips (76-80), R Powley (77-),
                Miss J Williams (83-84);

music: Miss H Bilkey (90-), P Clark (79-84), Miss A Foster (84-87),
                Miss J Fry (87-90), F Lavery (51-82), P Springate (82-);

technical   A Carson (87-89), J Chancellor (76-), S Clarkson (88-),
  studies: M Fotheringham (86-87), D Gardner (75-88), R Kilby (89-),
                J Marsh (58-85), W Mossop (85-89), A Pocock (81-),
                M Roberts (72-81), B Willmott (78-86);

home   Mrs G Blackshaw (78-), Mrs G Button (Miss Sellars) (79-85),
  economics: Mrs M Link (76-), Mrs J Thurman (84-);

P.E.:	Mrs Z Banks (Miss Young) (84-), J Colin (51-84), Mrs S Cooper (80-82), M Davison (76-), Miss A Drinkwater (83-84), Mrs B Easterbrook (78-80), Miss R Gollop (89-), Mrs S Hawkins (Miss Elworthy) (77-88), Mrs B Hodsman (82-83), Mrs G Oliver (Miss Hall) (81-84), Miss M Shaw (85-86), A Slade (78-), Mrs D Taylor (Miss Chambers) (86-89), Miss D Urquhart (47-83);
remedial and Unit:	P Ainley (77-84), Mrs L Chilcott (75-80), Mrs S Hopkins (80-86), Mrs E Howe (79-80), Mrs J Saunders (81-), D Skene (80-), A Trinder (91-), Mrs J Weedon (75-89), Mrs J Young (80-81).